# The Spiritual Dimension of Ageing

*of related interest*

## Spirituality and Ageing
*Edited by Albert Jewell*
ISBN 1 85302 631 X

## Care Services for Later Life
**Transformations and Critiques**
*Edited by Tony Warnes, Lorna Warren and Mike Nolan*
ISBN 1 85302 852 5

## Hearing the Voice of People with Dementia
**Opportunities and Obstacles**
*Malcolm Goldsmith*
ISBN 1 85302 406 6

## Spirituality in Health Care Contexts
*Edited by Helen Orchard*
*Foreword by Julia Neuberger*
ISBN 1 85302 969 6

## Spirituality and Mental Health Care
**Rediscovering a 'Forgotten' Dimension**
*John Swinton*
ISBN 1 85302 804 5

## Including the Person with Dementia in Designing and Delivering Care
**'I Need to Be Me!'**
*Elizabeth Barnett*
*Foreword by Mary Marshall*
ISBN 1 85302 740 5

## Spirituality and Art Therapy
**Living the Connection**
*Edited by Mimi Farrelly-Hansen*
*Foreword by Deborah Bowman*
ISBN 1 85302 952 X

## Faith, Stories and the Experience of Black Elders
**Singing the Lord's Song in a Strange Land**
*Anthony G. Reddie*
ISBN 1 85302 993 9

## Wholeness in Later Life
*Ruth Bright*
ISBN 1 85302 447 3

# The Spiritual Dimension of Ageing

*Elizabeth MacKinlay*

Jessica Kingsley Publishers
London and Philadelphia

## Acknowledgments

*I wish to acknowledge the valuable assistance of a number of people in the process of my doctoral studies, on which this book is based. First, my thanks to Dr Paul Rule for his valuable guidance as supervisor, thanks also to Dr Victor Minichiello for his supervision, to Dr David De Vaus for statistical advice, to Rev'd Canon Keith Stephens for reading and sharing of his pastoral experience with older people, and to my nursing colleagues, particularly Zilla Wooster and Margaret Proctor for willingness to listen to ideas and to offer valuable criticism.*

*I also acknowledge the generosity and willingness of the elderly participants in the study who shared so much of their life journeys with me. Without them, there would be no study, and this book is dedicated to them.*

*Finally, but not least, my thanks to Karen and Robert, whose patience and support has been most valuable throughout the process.*

---

First published in the United Kingdom in 2001 by
Jessica Kingsley Publishers Ltd
116 Pentonville Road
London N1 9JB, England
and
325 Chestnut Street,
Philadelphia, PA19106, USA

*www.jkp.com*

**Library of Congress Cataloging in Publication Data**
A CIP catalog record for this book is available from the Library of Congress

**British Library Cataloguing in Publication Data**
A CIP catalogue record for this book is available from the British Library

ISBN 1 84310 008 8

Printed and Bound in Great Britain by
Athenaeum Press, Gateshead, Tyne and Wear

# Contents

# Figures and Tables

## Tables

## Figures

# *Preface*

Spirituality has been a component of nursing in some way for me since, in the late 1960s, I first felt drawn to this dimension of care. At that time I was a nurse; however, spirituality was not perceived to be part of nursing. Years later when I was ordained as a priest in the Anglican Church I did not stop being a nurse, but rather took on an extra aspect to my life, with a whole new outlook on the spiritual dimension and health.

What I am suggesting is that the spiritual dimension constitutes a large part of what nursing is; that is, the core of caring. I am also suggesting that nurses, whatever their religious outlook, can be a part of giving spiritual care in nursing. This dimension should be just as much a part of nursing as physical or psychosocial care. And yet the need to understand more of what is happening in the spiritual dimension as people grow older is evident and important for other workers, as well as nurses – for clergy, for social workers, activity officers and pastoral carers.

A project during my final year of theological study, on the spiritual needs of frail elderly people, has grown and continued since then. This area of study has exciting implications for both gerontological nursing practice and clinical preparation of clergy for ministry with elderly people.

## Background of the researcher

My background in nursing and specialty in gerontological nursing have informed much of my focus on ageing and spirituality. My preparation for ministry has given me a wider perspective on the spiritual and on the possibilities and challenges of ageing. Being both nurse and priest give me both advantages and disadvantages for this project. I already had an understanding of the ageing process, and the physical and psychosocial needs, and common disease conditions, of older adults. I realised that there was a gap in knowledge of the spiritual dimension in ageing, and a need to develop knowledge in this area by research, to inform nursing as well as pastoral care and clergy practice. This extended with a realisation that there is a spiritual component in other health practice disciplines, importantly including social work. There was also a need to acknowledge my own belief system, while endeavouring to investigate the spiritual dimension, not only in a Christian context but also within a secular context. At the same time, I was aware that there are possibilities to develop the spiritual area of care into one that will be enriching for patients and residents, and for staff, no matter what their religious beliefs.

## Purpose

In my doctoral studies I attempted to map the spiritual dimension of a number of independently living older adults, and to design an assessment tool for measurement of spiritual needs of older people. My thesis was that spiritual development continues across the lifespan and healthy ageing is dependent on spiritual health as well as physical and psychosocial health. It is my contention that spiritual health in ageing can be enhanced by sensitising older people to their own spiritual journeys, by assessing the spiritual needs of frail older people and by assisting older people effectively to meet their spiritual needs.

## Limitations of the study

As a researcher I had an obvious interest in the area of investigation, and I may be biased towards the development of interventions for spiritual well-being. The sample was composed of volunteers. Owing to the sensitive nature of the material, a number of people may not have wanted to be involved. It is therefore not possible to generalise to others in the community who may not recognise they have spiritual needs. The sample consisted only of Christians and people of no religious affiliation; other faith groups were not included in this study. In fact all informants were of Anglo-Celtic origin. This was a result of the method of recruiting informants, where only these people volunteered for the in-depth interviews.

It is also acknowledged that there may be a miscomprehension within society of the scope of spirituality, with different people interpreting the term differently, yet no more appropriate term was found for use in this study. This was borne out by a worthwhile response to a second letter that was written to attract informants with no religious affiliation. The study was a cross-sectional study of the spirituality of older adults and as such it only samples a 'one-off' view of the spiritual dimension. Others, such as Fowler (1981) have studied faith development across the lifespan, (but still in cross-sectional studies). More data is required in the area of ageing.

This sample is a specific group of older adults with characteristics of the current cohort of people aged 65 years and over, living independently in the community, and as such may be like no other group, either before or after them. While this is only a small sample, and there are difficulties in attempting to generalise the findings, it is pointed out that it is an important starting place for examining the spirituality of older adults. It is highly desirable that this study be the first part of a larger study that will examine the spiritual needs of frail older adults, and it is a necessary preliminary study.

Method of recruitment had to consider the following characteristics of informants. First, the area for research, being of a sensitive nature, made it impossible to use anything but a convenience sample. Therefore, only those people who have an interest in spirituality and are willing to discuss it are likely to be included in the sample. As the purpose is to map the spiritual dimension in elderly people this approach is seen as legitimate.

Participants had to be interested in talking about their spiritual dimension. This had to be carefully defined, as not all people approached had a similar definition or understanding of what 'spiritual' meant. Later letters requesting participation in the project used the word 'meaning' in life rather than 'spiritual' to tap into a broader sample. Participants also needed to have sufficient energy to be able to talk and not tire in an interview that could last up to two hours. They had to be cognitively intact. A good test for this was both their need to respond to my letter inviting them to participate, and being able successfully to take the spiritual health inventory for elderly people (SHIE) before the in-depth interview. And finally, participants needed to speak English well enough to take part in an extended interview.

Pseudonyms have been used to preserve anonymity of informants.

CHAPTER 1

# *An ageing society and the spiritual dimension*

## Ageing and spirituality

Now, in the early years of the twenty-first century, Western society is facing an ageing population of never before experienced proportions. At the same time, greater numbers of these older people are looking forward to years of prosperity and enjoyment. Almost half a lifetime of retirement is available to many. How will these people spend these years? How enjoyable and fulfilling will they be? When they have taken the big trip, gone on extended holidays, indulged in various hobbies, what then?

What is left of life when all that is done? Will these later years be a time of reflection and satisfaction with life, for a life well lived? Will these years have meaning? Or will more opt to finish their lives in suicide, when there is nothing left?

Simone de Beauvoir, writing in 1970, said that there was then a 'conspiracy of silence' on ageing. Older people themselves, she observed, did not wish to acknowledge that they were old. In some respects little has changed since she wrote. There is still an obvious attempt to keep the focus on youth: initiation rites that have traditionally marked the move from adolescence to adulthood still remain important; perhaps the graduation from university; the first job; and, of course, gaining a driving licence, being able to vote and drink legally.

The Christian Church too marks adult membership in various ways. These events clearly demonstrate the young person's acceptance into adult society. On the other hand, there is no affirming ritual that welcomes an older adult into another life stage – that of later life. At best, any rituals are closures, such as retirement parties and dinners, perhaps having to give up a driving licence due to failing sight or other disabilities. Events such as fiftieth wedding anniversaries and birthdays are held to recognise the years gone by rather than to mark new beginnings.

The latter part of the lifespan is a time when roles important in mid life are lost and *being* becomes more central to living than *doing.* This is particularly so for the frail older adult. The importance of environmental factors in influencing continuing independence or a move into dependence in older adults has been observed by Baltes and Baltes (1990). There is also an increasing interaction between the physical, psychosocial and spiritual dimensions, with a tendency for well-being in ageing to be related to the ability to transcend physical disabilities and chronic disease states.

While there may be decline in physiological function in ageing, there remains potential for continued growth in the psychosocial and spiritual dimensions. However, a lack of depth to the spiritual dimension, or an underdeveloped spiritual dimension, may impair the individual's ability to find affirmation in what appears to be a shift to greater interiority in a number of older people.

Some elderly people are deeply in touch with themselves and have an obvious sense of satisfaction with life, even in the face of marked disability, loss and isolation. This could only be described as the person having a sense of integrity (Erikson *et al.* 1986). Other elderly people, however, clearly show signs of despair as they grow older. It is possible that this latter group could benefit from interventions of a spiritual nature. But there remain gaps in the knowledge of spirituality in ageing, so that there is not a sound basis for practice in the health professions or pastoral care.

However, even with knowledge of the spiritual dimension in ageing, nurses, social workers and other health and social care professionals may unconsciously exhibit attitudes of ageism towards the older people in their care, attitudes that can undermine the self-confidence and sense of identity that an older person has. Vulnerability is often close to the surface among older adults. Ageism can be demeaning to the older person and can cut to the core of the individual's being, to their spiritual sense of meaning and being as humans. This is the power of ageism.

## Ageism

This is one of the biggest problems facing our ageing societies. Ageism is subtle and we may all find ourselves indulging in it, almost unconsciously. If, for example, an older person is doing a job, we may question if they are up to it. Older people are often the first to be laid off work. There is a perception that their efficiency falls off after a certain age, and that age seems to be getting lower all the time.

Ageism affirms all that is negative about ageing. It seeks to confine older people to stereotyped potentials, mostly of dependency in ageing. Ageism may even restrain the possibilities for spiritual growth and development in ageing. Ageism flourishes in a climate of myths of ageing and it is important to examine spirituality in ageing to discover what the experiences of spirituality of some older people are in present society.

It is necessary first to define ageing. What is old?

## Chronological versus functional age

### How old is 'old'?

Old age has been defined differently at different times. The general starting point of old age in many Western countries has been arbitrarily set at 65 years, a time defined as appropriate for the start of the old age pension. This age was set by Bismark during the nineteenth century, when few people could expect to live long past that age. But is that definition relevant now?

One framework for ageing has been a three-way classification of young–old, 65–74 years; old–old, 75–84 years; and oldest–old, 85 years plus. This became a useful way of defining ageing in the 1990s, as it fitted with the lifespan of the majority of people. It recognises that there are different periods in ageing; that ageing is not one homogenous period. This classification is also useful in that health of older people can be somewhat loosely related to this age framework; for example, the young–old are usually well and live a lifestyle similar to that of middle-aged people. The oldest–old are definitely greater users of health care services and more of that age group are widowed and more are in long-term care than the young–old and the old–old.

Yet, using chronological age as a predictor of well-being in ageing has limitations: some people are 'old' while still in their fifties, while others are still young in their eighties. A classification being used more recently has been third age and fourth age. Third agers seem to be defined as those who are older and living independently, while fourth agers are those who are older and frail, being unable to live independently. This classification is based on function rather than chronological age; functional capacity does become more important than medical diagnosis in the later stages of the lifespan. 'Old' may continually need to be redefined as society ages, to avoid boxing people into outmoded roles and expectations of ageing. It is possible that 'old' by 2100 may be anyone over 100 years of age.

## How to define age?

The way in which age is defined within a society will have major impact on the way people will age in that society. What are appropriate roles for older people? When should they retire? How should health needs be provided for in a particular society? In fact, what are the opportunities and challenges open to older people in a given society?

It is contended that ageing is defined differently in different cultures and at different periods of history within a particular culture. However, possibilities and opportunities for older people within society may be limited, not by the potential of years available, but by society's definition of what is appropriate. In Western society with the current shift to an ageing society, the possibilities in ageing are changing rapidly, and structures and attitudes do not always reflect these changes. We find that, increasingly, older people are healthier but retiring at earlier ages. There is still a perception that 55 or 60/5 years of age is time to finish work and enjoy life. Yet many now can at 55 expect to experience thirty or more years of life yet to come.

## Is there meaning left in ageing?

Where does meaning in ageing come from, if not from work? Is the coming ageing generation to be a cohort of lost people, stripped of their roles in life, living only for the leisure life? Meaning in life is very much at the heart of what it is to be human. Meaning is closely tied to hope and hope is essential for continued human existence.

## A search for meaning

There is currently an increasing search by many for meaning and for what lies at the centre of life. The term spirituality is being heard more frequently. The term 'spirituality' needs careful definition, and its use in this study is described in Chapter 2.

Humanism advocates the individual being able to completely self-care. In this view the spiritual is seen as being in touch with oneself; Maslow's (1970) self-actualisation is the goal of being. In this view it is believed that we are in charge of our own destinies, our success or failure is completely up to us. On the other hand, the major world religions advocate the importance of human relationship with God, according to the understanding of the particular faith.

Ultimate meaning in life, the spiritual dimension, is derived from both the person's sense of self-worth and relationship with others. For many, God, or a source outside themselves, is an important component in meaning; others find this meaning within themselves, or from within their environments. The value of social supports in ageing is well documented (Gardner *et al.* 1998; Kendig and McCallum 1990). Interpersonal relationships are probably as important for older people as for the young in maintaining spiritual health. For the frail elderly, however, the available range of social supports tends to diminish, and social isolation becomes more likely. Social skills may diminish in the older person living alone, and where sight or hearing deficits are not attended, the older person may suffer from sensory deprivation as well. A lack of social interaction may lead in turn to spiritual isolation, that is, a lack of intimate contact or diminished ability to make connections in relationship with others.

It is often in a crisis that a human being first reaches outside of themselves in a desperate search for meaning and something greater than themselves. The increasing acceptance of psychology to provide the answers to all our problems in life is resulting in more and more people turning to psychologists to help fix relationships and to provide what is missing in their lives. Yet meaning seems to involve a continuing life search, a search that often reaches beyond the individual. This search for meaning may be for many a search for transcendent relationship, a sense of 'otherness' missing from their own lives. In a multifaith and multicultural society transcendence may be searched for in many different ways. Many in Western societies still search for transcendence, not being sure what they search for.

For a large proportion of older adults, practice of religion has been one way of responding to their spiritual needs and a way of relating to the transcendent. Yet it is often the younger members of this pluralist society (Newbigin 1989)[1] who must provide care for the frail older adults. It would seem that the life experiences of these two groups are very different and may make it hard for the younger group to understand the kinds of spiritual needs that the older people may have.

## Religious experience and frail older people

In past generations people turned to God in their times of crisis; the way is no longer known to many. In the current generation of elderly people, religion has been an important part for a high proportion. For the frail elderly, the five per cent or so who live in nursing homes, their experience of

God in their lives is likely to be quite different from that of their carers. This is so for a number of reasons. First, the religious experience of the present cohort of elderly people is different from that of the coming generation. Second, the present group of elderly people by their very maturity will probably be at a different stage of faith development than those younger. Yet often health care providers have made the choices of what *they* thought best for older people, even in regard to recognition and provision for spiritual or religious needs.

The frail older people in nursing homes and hostels are most commonly cared for by younger people. How can the spiritual and religious experiences of these older people be understood by the younger carers? How can these carers identify and address the spiritual needs of the elderly people in their care? Nurses, social workers and other health professionals, as well as clergy, may simply fail to understand what the spiritual needs of the elderly are. In some cases the elderly people themselves may not be able to articulate adequately their spiritual needs, to even ask for assistance. For many, living in a nursing home is waiting for death, and the most difficult part of this is that no one wants to talk about death. It is cleverly covered, even if unintentionally, by the many activities which go on in the nursing home.

Often the spiritual needs of frail elderly residents of nursing homes have not been acknowledged (MacKinlay 1992, 1993) even in the newer well-organised nursing homes, where a pleasant environment and good physical care is provided, and many activities are encouraged for the residents. It seems that even in these environments, for these frail elderly people, there still pervades, for some at least, a sense of hopelessness, and fear of the process of dying, along with all the other indignities, such as incontinence and being dependent on others for all of one's physical needs.

How can we re-establish meaning for these people, or a sense of integrity? Or even a sense of satisfaction in life? What has *being* got to do with ageing? What is the experience of living for these people? What are their wishes, desires? What are the unfinished things of life? How can we help them to gain, or regain, a sense of integrity and control over their lives?

How can a society which sets standards criteria for funding in nursing homes base these purely on physical tasks to be performed for the residents? How can nurses, social workers, clergy or anybody else care for the other needs of the elderly? In fact these other needs, the psychosocial and the spiritual, are what characterises the human being as different from other animal species. These critical aspects are not addressed at all. There is no time, and often no recognition of the existence of these needs. It is vital that we, as a society, do recognise what makes us human. If we fail to do this, and more particularly so at this stage in history, then we fail as humans, and the future is indeed bleak for the human race.

Tournier (1972) spoke of the need of older people, as well as the young, for love. In a society which emphasises the merits of being young, there is often little love reserved for elderly and frail people. Tournier criticised the provision of efficient social services by professionals who neglected the person, who failed to reach out in love to the people for whom they cared. If anything, this has become more evident in practice in our society today.

HACC (Home and Community Care, Australian Government) services provide for many of the needs of frail elderly people, and help to keep them living independently at home. However, major problems seem to be emerging for many of these long-term isolated people. They have no meaningful and intimate connections or communications with any human beings. The time allowed for visits, meals on wheels, shopping delivery, assisting with showers and so forth is the minimum to complete the physical tasks effectively. The spirit of the elderly person who lives alone and is unable to leave the home may be starved of love and meaningful relationship with others.

## The spiritual dimension

### Recognition

How can one even acknowledge the existence of a dimension such as spirituality? Mystery surrounds the spiritual. It has resisted human attempts to analyse and to control. There are probably a number of reasons why the spiritual dimension is so poorly recognised. First, it is difficult to quantify and to measure. Second, it seems to be so subjective and does not appear to fit easily within the scientific model. Even behavioural science had difficulties being accepted as legitimate science. The spiritual domain is even more suspect. Yet study of the spiritual dimension will enable this vital human dimension to be put on the agenda for open discussion. It is hoped that care will improve as a result. Many professional carers may learn to increase their skills in identifying and meeting the spiritual needs of those in spiritual distress. Before that is possible, more needs to be known of this dimension.

*What are the possibilities for putting the spiritual dimension into practice?*

Recent research in the field of spirituality (Highfield 1989, 1992, in oncology; Carson 1989; Carson and Arnold 1996, in nursing and mental health; and in ageing, MacKinlay 1992), has done more to identify the parameters of spirituality in nursing. Highfield's work highlighted the confusion of nurses in distinguishing between spiritual and psychosocial needs. Another study (MacKinlay forthcoming 2001) consisted of staff of nursing homes identifying from a list of spiritual behaviours which were psychosocial or spiritual.

Registered nurses involved in a study (MacKinlay 1992) reported that they benefited greatly from the experience, one saying, 'what an important area this is for registered nurses...we do not properly address this area'. They were often surprised at how ready the frail elderly residents were to share their concerns, and that for a number of residents it was the first time they had felt free to talk about the deeper things of life. These nurses learnt a lot about the people they had cared for sometimes for months, or even years. These were things that led them to see nursing in a new way and to change the way they were giving care.

Teaching and working with nurses in aged care has revealed a lack of nurse understanding of the spiritual dimension of the human being, and the particular needs for spiritual care among frail elderly people.

Based on discussions with registered nurses working in gerontological nursing, I realised that a proportion of staff working in nursing homes do not have a high awareness of their own spirituality. These registered nurses would probably find it hard to assess effectively the spiritual needs of others. An important first move in this area was to increase the spiritual awareness of staff.

It was as a response to nurses' requests for knowledge and strategies to address this component of holistic care that a programme in continuing education was designed. If it had not been for this group of students, registered nurses who were upgrading their qualifications, I would never have achieved the access I had to so many residents in the nursing homes. These students, who had been a part of a continuing education programme in gerontological nursing, were a most enthusiastic support for my work. They helped me by inviting, and strongly encouraging, staff to attend my education sessions, and in following up post survey forms. Above all, they were vitally interested in the whole project.

## The ethic of caring

The ethic of caring (Gilligan 1993) has emerged as an important focus of study in recent decades. This approach to ethics and care has emphasised the importance of relationship, and is at the very heart of nursing and pastoral care. Any consideration of the spiritual dimension must acknowledge this view of caring.

The spiritual domain is one of intimate relationship with others. In the nursing home it is the nurse who largely fulfils this role. Yet so often the nurse feels very inadequate in this respect. This was found in a study of nurses' understanding of the spiritual dimension (MacKinlay forthcoming 2001).

Intervention in the spiritual domain may be seen as belonging to a clergy role, a role for which the nurse, social worker and other health professionals are ill prepared. However, the earliest Christian Church recognised this role of caring as integral to the healing role of the church. It is a role that has been largely lost with all of the sophistication and high technology currently available to health professionals today. It seems that this ability to relate to each other in love and care, to facilitate spiritual growth and to give appropriate spiritual support to those we care for in pastoral relationships, needs to be further recognised and developed. It is contended that there are caring roles for clergy, nurses and other categories of pastoral carers working with older people.

A part of being a health professional has been seen as maintaining a suitable distance from the client or patient. This professional ethos has resulted in a loss of the very essence of the caring relationships for many, both the receivers of care and the givers. Burn-out is one symptom of this.

An abundance of recent literature in the field of caring has begun to recognise this dimension, but often from the perspective of the psychosocial domain rather than the spiritual. Failure to recognise the spiritual means that interventions are planned to meet the psychosocial, not the spiritual, and thus vital and deep issues for people are denied existence. One recent study, not surprisingly from the field of mental health nursing, examined the spiritual interventions provided by mental health nurses; this specialty group of nurses was among the earliest to recognise the spiritual dimension (Tuck *et al.* 1997). This study found that the participating nurses recognised spiritual interventions as part of care, but reported few instances of intervening.

It seems that little study has been done of the need for spiritual care of frail elderly people. For example, research is needed into the effect on the frail elderly person in relation to meaning and hope in life, when admitted to a nursing home. One elderly woman told me, 'If I have to go to live in a nursing home I will die'. This woman struggled to maintain her independence in very precarious conditions indeed. She hoped never to go to a nursing home, and indeed she died having remained at home until about a week prior to her death.

## The case for assessment of spiritual needs of older adults

Assessment of spiritual health is relevant as a health promotion activity as well as for health maintenance and restoration. It is vital that those providing care for frail older people are able to identify effectively the spiritual needs of the older people in their care. Without effective assessment of needs, it is likely that the care may not be directed to the individual's needs. But how to assess spiritual health is a complex task. In this study, where assessing of spiritual health is specific to elderly people, an attempt is made to link knowledge of the ageing process to spirituality in ageing.

While the focus of this study is on spirituality in well elderly people, theory development of the spiritual dimension in older adults necessarily includes the whole of the third and fourth ages. Part of the need for this study was to improve ways of providing spiritual care for frail elderly people. Care of frail elderly people currently focuses on addressing their physical needs and, to some extent, their psychosocial needs. Yet to address the physical and the psychosocial only omits a major component of the human, that is the spiritual, dimension.

In Highfield's (1981) work with nurses who work with patients who have cancer, she found that nurses often confused the psychosocial and spiritual dimensions. While there seems to be some overlap between the two dimensions, strategies used to address them differ. Thus, by only recognising the more studied and widely recognised psychosocial dimension, spiritual needs will not be identified.

It is contended in this study that spiritual needs underlie the psychosocial needs, and that by identifying and addressing psychosocial needs alone, the spiritual, or what I would like to call core needs, of the human being are not addressed.

A more comprehensive knowledge of the spiritual dimension in ageing will assist in making more relevant assessments of spiritual needs of frail older people. This is particularly important in the case of frail older people who have communication deficits, such as aphasia or hearing difficulties, or for those who have dementia. Thus the development of effective methods of spiritual assessment for frail older people is a high priority to really being able to provide holistic health care for these people.

## Being and doing

Tournier (1972) wrote of the need for older people to move from human doers to human beings. The fact that residents of nursing homes are no longer teachers, business men/women, or professionals, is often only too obvious in the way they see themselves and the way others relate to them. They have to a large extent lost their identities. These days they are mostly Fred, Joe, Mary or Wendy. They bring nothing of their previous existence into the nursing home.

How can these people find meaning in their lives now? Is it really necessary? Our society is not interested in people who are not doers or contributors to society. Thus, in a sense, there is no meaning in life for these frail older people, living in nursing homes, waiting to die, in the back room of a death-denying society.

If people are not affirmed because of what they do, how can they be affirmed? For the frail elderly a new framework for meaning is needed. This may need to come, at least in part, from outside the person, in the affirmation of the older person. There is a need to explore ways of affirmation and acceptance of the person, simply because they are created in the image of God, not because of what they can contribute to society or even to their neighbour. Part of this affirmation arises from the recognition of spiritual needs of the individual.

## The need to know more of spirituality and ageing

It is evident that more needs to be known of the spiritual dimension in ageing adults, to enable more effective nurturing of this dimension, both by older adults and by the carers of frail older adults. How do elderly people perceive value and meaning in their lives?

Storytelling as therapy is becoming increasingly recognised in health-related fields (Gustafson 1994). Story is an important aspect for many ageing people. It is probable that in the past, older people were given more opportunities to reminisce, as this was a way of passing knowledge and wisdom from one generation to another. Gutmann 1987 (in Bornat 1994) argues that Western societies have lost a sense of culture. Now, at the start of the twenty-first century, older people's stories are no longer seen as so important, and until recent decades probably few people have been able or willing to give time to listen to an older person's story. It seems we have largely lost this oral tradition from our society.

Reminiscence has been identified as both a valuable and often naturally occurring phenomena of ageing. A number of studies during the past two decades have focused on reminiscence from a life review perspective, as individual therapy, and probably more frequently, as group work (Bornat 1994). Reminiscence or life review has been studied mostly from a psychological perspective. It seems less has been done from a spiritual perspective.

Reminiscence may be a critical part of ageing, connected with Erikson *et al.* (1986) final stage of psychosocial ageing: integrity versus despair. More work has been done in this area during the last decade. Coleman (1994) studied naturally occurring reminiscence.

It seems this final stage of ageing is important, not only as a stage of psychosocial development but also for spiritual integrity. Reminiscence may be regarded as a developmental task of ageing. Perhaps this is more properly identified as a naturally occurring spiritual task of ageing.

## Aims and brief description of the study

The study that forms the basis of this book consisted of two parts, aimed to increase the knowledge of spirituality in ageing as an important basis for improving spiritual well-being and hence improving the care of older adults. Stage 1 mapped the dimensions of spiritual health of a group of elderly people, using a spiritual health inventory for elderly people (SHIE). Stage 2, using in-depth interviewing, explored the dimension of spirituality in ageing in a selected sub-sample of these elderly people.

The study was confined to older adults living independently in the community. The decision to confine the study was made, first, because little is known of the spiritual dimension of older adults, therefore it was necessary to begin to map out the dimension by exploring the area with independent older people to obtain a general picture of the dimension. Second, frail older adults are less able to cope with the rigours of in-depth interviewing, and it was thought better practice to return to that group having acquired a more thorough understanding of the spiritual dimension in ageing.

The study examined how elderly people living independently in the community perceive their spirituality or meaning in life. It provides information through reminiscence, which can be used to facilitate spiritual well-being through the healing of past grief and hurts. The study considered the relationship between reminiscence and spiritual integrity in the older adult. The individual older person's concept of God, meaning in life and perception of what it means to be growing older and the relationships between these were examined.

My hope is that this study adds to the knowledge of spirituality in ageing. By beginning with independent older adults (third age), a picture of the spirituality for well older adults has been produced. Second, this picture, with its data from questionnaires and in-depth interviews, forms the framework and basis for understanding both the spirituality of the third age and its relationship to well-being in ageing. Further, this information forms the basis for understanding spirituality in the next developmental stage of ageing, that of the fourth age. It is anticipated that spiritual assessment instruments may be constructed, using the data collected from well older adults, and refined in further studies. An enhanced knowledge of spirituality in ageing will enable more effective assessment of spiritual needs of older people and thus facilitate meeting these needs.

It is anticipated, however, that it will be important to return to conduct research with frail older adults into the spiritual dimension, armed with knowledge of well older adults' spirituality. The need to do this rests on the already acknowledged great needs for spiritual care among frail older residents of nursing homes, outlined in earlier studies of frail older adults (MacKinlay 1992).

## Starting point of the study

Before beginning this study a number of assumptions were made. First, that all informants in the study acknowledge having a spiritual dimension, or a sense of meaning in life. Second, that the spiritual dimension is universal in the human condition. Third, that there is an interaction between physical, psychosocial and spiritual dimensions of human beings. Further, that the spiritual dimension of older adults can be mapped by using in-depth interviews, following a life review process. It was assumed that selection of informants who are living independently in the community chooses a homogenous group of older people, defined by their ability for functional independence. Finally, it was assumed that all informants would be able to communicate readily and have good verbal ability in English.

### Summary

*In an ageing society the needs for holistic care of frail older adults cannot be neglected. Increasing recognition of the importance of the spiritual dimension in ageing has led to the development of this study. There is a growing awareness of the spiritual needs of frail older adults, and of the need for those who care for frail older adults to be well prepared to first identify these needs and then to be able to facilitate the meeting of these needs.*

## Note

1   Newbigin (1989) writes that in a pluralist society there is no one way of believing; what were once taught as 'facts' to schoolchildren are now a matter of opinion and individual belief (p.15). There is therefore a dichotomy between the beliefs of the younger members of society and the current cohort of elderly people.

CHAPTER 2

# Examining spirituality and ageing

'You're touching the deep stuff now.' (Ben, an informant in the study)

How can these questions be asked?

The study of the spiritual dimension of ageing presented some problems, not least in the selection of an appropriate method of study. One of the aims of this study was to design and test a spiritual health inventory which would identify relevant spiritual needs and at the same time not exhaust the frail elderly person. It was also recognised that the nature of the dimension being studied may in itself present certain difficulties in constructing an appropriate assessment instrument. For instance, a number of nurses I have spoken to, at least initially, see the spiritual dimension as something too personal and private even to enquire about with patient or resident. Further, often they do not feel comfortable about asking such questions and have told me that they believe it is not a nursing area. Other nurses, however, do see the possibilities for including the spiritual within their role, but many acknowledge that they do not have the necessary knowledge of the dimension or the skills for intervening in this area. Social workers may also not acknowledge the possibilities of including the spiritual within their role.

Clergy, on the other hand, have often not had any specialist education in the field of ageing. They may see their role with older people as simply providing the sacraments, without realising the particular needs for the older person learning to live with an ageing body and dealing with grief, guilt, confession, forgiveness and reconciliation, as well as the need to grow spiritually.

## Finding a theoretical framework for the study

This study, an exploration of spirituality in older adults, is examining an area little studied until recently. The nature of the material sought is intimate and sensitive, and required finding a way that would produce a view of the spirituality of, in this instance, well older adults, living independently in the community. The context of enquiry lent itself to a method that would not foreclose on possibilities until all relevant material had been gathered; a method that would allow the older people to be the informers and to feel free to contribute to the collection of knowledge. This study, because of the scarcity of material in the area, was exploratory, and only began to provide a framework for future study in the field.

As spirituality in ageing has attracted little research as yet, grounded theory was the approach chosen to explore and illuminate knowledge in the area. Glaser and Strauss (1967, p.5) remark that one canon for judging the usefulness of a (sociological) theory is how it was generated; a theory inductively developed from social research is likely to be a better theory. Glaser and Strauss believe other canons are also significantly dependent on how the theory was generated. Those necessary for assessing a theory include logical consistency, clarity, parsimony, density, scope, integration, as well as its fit and its ability to work. They also stress the desired emphasis on generating a theory through a *process* of research rather than applying an existing theoretical framework at the end of the study.

This approach seems most appropriate for a study of this kind, where a mapping out of the dimension being investigated is necessary before being able to generate theory.

### Listening to the life experiences

Listening to the people whose life experiences are being considered is a vital starting place; too often, health care professionals have made decisions regarding health care planning based on their own expertise, disregarding the real needs and desires of the recipients of care. Glaser and Strauss (1968) used grounded theory as they studied dying as a social process. In this study they talk of the 'experiential careers' of patients, families and staff that are seen as 'highly relevant to the action around dying patients' checking familiarity with diseases, symptoms, previous experience.[1] This concept of an experiential career appears relevant in a study of ageing, as the spiritual journey into ageing will include all of life experiences and learning. In the spiritual journey there are many aspects to consider, even the individual's acceptance/non-acceptance of ageing and the onset of the final stage of life.

Glaser and Strauss (1968) found that even in dying, a patient's social value may influence the decision making in priorities of treatments (p.106). Factors they found important were age, education, social class, race, marital status, parenthood and occupation, as well as physical condition. All of these factors may be related to the identification of spiritual needs of older adults.

As well, ageism is often part of the decision-making process in assessing health care needs of older adults, although it may be unrecognised and therefore unacknowledged, although remaining as an underlying value in care. This study also sought to expose those aspects of ageism that may adversely affect the opportunities for older adults to fulfil their spiritual needs.

## Using grounded theory

Grounded theory is classically based on the work of symbolic interactionism and had its foundation in the work of Glaser and Strauss (1967). Emphasis in grounded theory is on allowing the data to inform the development of theory. It is most useful in the study of phenomena in the domain of the psychosocial that little is known about. Its greatest value is probably in preventing foreclosure on theory development. The detailed searching for major themes and categories arising from data is a major characteristic of this methodology. Glaser and Strauss (1967) note that:

> Grounded theory is based on the systematic generating of theory from data, that itself is systematically obtained from social research. Thus the grounded theory offers a rigorous, orderly guide to theory development that at each stage is closely integrated with a methodology of social research. (p.2)

Thus it is apparent that generating theory and doing social research are two parts of the same process.

### Recent critiques of grounded theory

Recent critique has included a review of grounded theory's applicability to research in the light of postmodernism. Annells (1996, p.391) draws attention to the current shift in philosophical direction of grounded theory, using the term 'classic' grounded theory to describe that of Glaser and Strauss of 1967, saying that it is in the postpositivist enquiry paradigm, while current movements, particularly of Strauss and Corbin (1990) fit more into the constructivist paradigm of enquiry. Further, Annells (1996) writes: 'Elements of postmodern thought are evident in evolutionary movements regarding grounded theory method and the next decade should sort out relationship of grounded theory method to postmodernism' (p.391). Annells rightly encourages researchers planning to use grounded theory to consider philosophical and paradigmatic aspects of the theory prior to selecting it for use.

## The process of using grounded theory

### THEORETICAL SAMPLING

Glaser and Stauss (1967) suggest a wide range of groups be sampled for developing properties of categories.

> Such a range, necessary for the categories' fullest possible development, is achieved by comparing any groups, irrespective of differences or similarities, as long as the data apply to a similar category or property… It is theoretically important to note to what degree the properties of categories are varied by diverse conditions… The principal point to keep clear is the purpose of the research, so that rules of evidence will not hinder discovery of theory. (p.51)

Glaser and Strauss (1967) write that the researcher must:

> be clear on the basic types of groups he wishes to compare in order to control their effect on generality of both scope of population and conceptual level of his theory. The simplest comparisons are, of course, made among different groups of exactly the same substantive type;… These comparisons lead to a substantive theory that is applicable to this one type of group. (p.52)

They say this can be further extended by comparing more than one group of the same, for example in different settings, then to regional and national levels as relevant.

In this study it was decided to gain maximisation of both the differences and similarities of data (Glaser and Strauss 1967) that are relevant to the categories by choosing informants from a wide variety of backgrounds. None of those who responded was from outside the Christian faith, except for a few who had read widely in the area of Buddhism. These were interesting informants, as they had taken on aspects of Buddhism along with their earlier Christian belief systems. Agnostics were also included in the range of informants. It was not possible to obtain an exact match between practising Christians and agnostics because a limited number of people volunteered to be interviewed from the latter group.

Glaser and Strauss (1967) noted that it is valuable to minimise differences among comparison groups to increase the likelihood of collecting much similar data on a given category, while at the same time noting important differences not detected in earlier data collection (p.55). This is important so that similarities in data on a category can help verify its existence by verifying the data behind it. The number of in-depth interviews (24) conducted in this study were based on this concept of theoretical saturation.

THEORETICAL SATURATION

Glaser and Strauss (1967) note an important aspect of data collection in grounded theory, that of 'saturation'.

> Saturation means that no additional data are being found whereby the sociologist can develop properties of the category. As he sees instances over and over again, the researcher becomes empirically confident that a category is saturated. He goes out of his way to look for groups that stretch diversity of data as far as possible, just to make certain that saturation is based on the widest possible range of data on the category. (p.61)

Both the maximising and minimising of similarities and differences in the data are important, and need to be demonstrated before the data can be said to be 'saturated'.

THE CONSTANT COMPARATIVE METHOD

Glaser and Strauss (1967) note four stages in the constant comparative method of data collection and analysis (p.105). The first is comparing incidents applicable to each category. This part of the work consists of taking the data apart and coding specific incidents and comparing these with others in the data collection. The second is integrating categories and their properties. For instance, Glaser and Strauss found age was the most important characteristic used by staff in calculating social loss. In this study of spirituality in ageing, meaning in life was the crucial characteristic in the informants' reports. The third is delimiting the theory. In this the list of categories becomes more focused. This happens as the categories become saturated, and further material adds no further incidents to the data in the category. The fourth and final stage of data collection and analysis is writing the theory. These stages of data collection have been followed in this study.

## How the study was conducted

Demographic data were collected from all participants, including a self-report of their overall perception of health, and faith.

## Use of multiple research methods

The use of multiple research methods is recommended by a number of authors. Minichiello *et al.* (1995, p.223) notes that multiple methods, or triangulation, are 'regarded as a means of enhancing validity and decreasing possible bias'. He points out that care must be taken not to use triangulation to 'adjudicate'. In this study the questionnaire (Spiritual Health Inventory) used had been developed by a panel of experts before being modified for use with a population of elderly people. It was important not only to administer this questionnaire, but also to examine the findings against the themes obtained from in-depth interviewing, that is, allowing the informants themselves freedom to express their sense of spirituality.

## The process of data collection and analysis

First, a spiritual health inventory for elderly people (SHIE) and in-depth interviews were administered. Then in-depth data were examined for themes and categories arising from the data. Further in-depth interviews from other informants were obtained, to obtain a wider sampling of spirituality in ageing until saturation of categories/themes was obtained. Results of SHIE factor analysis for the sample and individual SHIE forms were compared with the themes arising from each participant's in-depth interviewing. Then a model of spirituality in ageing was constructed from the themes. This led to the construction of a model of spiritual tasks of ageing to use as a framework for clinical practice. This model can be applied to work in ministry, nursing, social work and to the work of other health care professionals.

## Assessing the spiritual needs of older people

THE SPIRITUAL HEALTH INVENTORY FOR ELDERLY PEOPLE (SHIE)

The aim of using a spiritual health inventory in this study was to determine whether a valid and reliable form of assessment for the spiritual dimension could be designed. Assessment of spiritual health and identifying the spiritual needs of frail elderly people may greatly assist in dealing with spiritual distress and bring meaning to life for these people. To date, no satisfactory assessment instrument has been available for this purpose in clinical practice, and certainly not for older adults.

A literature search prior to the 1992 (MacKinlay) study failed to identify any useful instruments previously employed in assessing the spiritual needs of older adults. However, a related area of study revealed the existence of an instrument which could be readily used in the field of gerontology. The instrument was developed by Martha Highfield in her work with oncology patients.

The questions in Highfield's spiritual health inventory (SHI) were judged for appropriateness of definitions and for the list of questions. A panel was asked to identify the spiritual need represented by each of the behaviours/ conditions (Highfield 1981). The panel consisted of: a professor of psychology and assistant director of a counselling centre on a religiously affiliated university campus; an assistant professor of Bible at the same institution with particular interest in needs of the dying person. The third member was a minister, completing a Masters degree in religion.

The instrument (SHI), Patient Survey, was used with permission of the author. The inventory consists of 31 questions and is a Likert-style five-scale format. The respondents were asked to rank each of the items from 1 for never, to 5 for all of the time. The questions were stated either as positive or negative indicators of spiritual health. Scoring of the questionnaires accounted for the negative scores by reversing these to obtain the total spiritual health score.

In the study (MacKinlay 1992, 1993) a sample of 172 nursing home residents was interviewed, using the SHI, by registered nurses taking a certificate course of continuing education in gerontological nursing. Factor analysis was performed on the data from that study and a new SHI(E) (elderly) constructed for use with an elderly population.

DESIGN OF A SPIRITUAL HEALTH INVENTORY FOR USE WITH OLDER ADULTS

A new SHI(E) was designed, based on the results of factor analysis of a previous SHI (Highfield 1981, 1989).

Highfield's SHI was used originally with the sample of older people (MacKinlay 1992) because it was assumed that an elderly population may have some factors in common with her sample of people with cancer. While many older people live very satisfying and independent lives, the chances are that as they grow older they are more likely to experience increasing frailty, and maybe 5 per cent, face admission to a nursing home. Admission to a nursing home in itself may be a life crisis factor, as is a diagnosis of cancer. The diagnosis of a terminal illness and/or being admitted to a nursing home may raise spiritual awareness for these people. Indeed, admission to a nursing home may be a time of heightened spiritual needs, or even spiritual crisis.

Highfield's SHI of 31 items was considered too long for use with frail elderly people. Energy levels in these people are often low and they may be easily exhausted (any questionnaire should be sensitive to this). As well, cognitive changes among nursing home residents may make answering a long questionnaire difficult.

The new SHIE, for use with an elderly population, was designed to be used for the first time in this study. It includes all four factors, derived from factor analysis, loaded in proportion to the importance of these in the previous study. These factors are: factor 1, hope; factor 2, anxiety and anger; factor 3, acceptance by God and others; factor 4, involvement in life. A total of 15 items (reduced from 31 in the original SHI) were constructed, with modification of the wording of some items to remove ambiguities identified in the earlier study. One of these 15 items, relating to importance of family, was not in the original scale. This item was included as family forms an important part of social support for older adults (McCallum 1986). It was felt this new SHIE was a more manageable length and contained all the factors relevant for this population of elderly people. The new SHIE was trialed with five registered nurses, a member of clergy and several older adults for readability, content and ease of administration.

The complexity of the spiritual dimension is acknowledged, and hence the difficulty of constructing a valid and reliable assessment instrument. The use of in-depth interviews with all informants who have taken the SHIE prior to interview forms an important critique of the Likert instrument and its ability to effectively tap into the critical features of spiritual needs of older adults.

RATIONALE FOR ORDER OF ADMINISTRATION OF THE SHIE

How useful will the SHIE be?

It can be argued that the information obtained through use of the SHIE could just as well be gathered from in-depth interviews alone. However, if a valid questionnaire can be designed, this would be invaluable for use with frail older adults to allow effective assessment of their spiritual needs. The SHIE was administered first for each informant to set a standard for the collection of data, as the same process and the same interviewer were used for each informant. This initial visit was also a means of establishing rapport with the informant prior to the in-depth interview. Administering the SHIE first would prevent any effect from the interview on responses to the SHIE. On the other hand, the questions in the SHIE may sensitise the respondents to the spiritual dimension, which may make the interview more fruitful. This may be both useful and a potential disadvantage – useful in raising the individual's awareness of the spiritual dimension, but it may lead the individual towards particular features of spirituality, thereby giving a false impression of the place of the spiritual in the person's life.

### Source and characteristics of participants in the study

Why third-age and not fourth-age informants?

Informants were third age, that is, well elderly people, 65 years and older.[2] With one exception, a woman about to turn 65, all were living independently in the community. It is important not to attach chronological ages to informants, although these are recorded at the original interviews in the collection of demographic data. It is important to distinguish older people on the basis of wellness rather than chronological age, as such marked variation exists between people of the same age. Differences seem apparent whether in physical, mental and/or spiritual well-being. Defining membership of the groups of informants for this study by accommodation seeks to include only older adults who are functioning sufficiently well to be living independently in the community.

These people were residents in private homes, home units or retirement villages. They were recruited from members of University of the Third Age (U3A), some by word of mouth (snowball effect), and from several groups of older people: two day care or contact centres, an older women's network and a group of older people who attend a monthly 'live-alones' lunch.

Third-age informants must be distinguished from fourth-age people in that they are seen mainly to draw meaning in life from doing, some in second careers, some in volunteer functions, some in hobbies which have grown into meaningful occupations in later life. Travel and leisure activities are often expected to take a lot of the third ager's time. Third agers are more likely than fourth agers to be busy 'doing' than 'being'. That is, often, the well older person still has energy and enthusiasm for living, life is more easily engaged, there are often still goals to achieve. The fourth-age person, on the other hand, often has multiple chronic illnesses and lacks energy to engage more actively with life.

It is possible that greater spiritual needs, or at least a greater spiritual awareness, will be identified within a fourth-age group of informants.

An early problem was that almost all those who returned consent forms at first were church attenders, and mostly Anglican, perhaps reflecting my background as an Anglican priest and the use of the word 'spirituality' in the letter. It was desirable to include in the study participants with no religious background to broaden the study of spirituality in ageing. Following consultation with my supervisors, I reworded my letters for informants, requesting participation from people who had no church affiliation. I received a number of responses to this letter, but as more people were interviewed it became apparent that a simple dichotomous response to the question of faith provides misleading results. The people I had expected to say they had no faith answered that they had a faith.

I also wanted to include more older people in my sample, and the second letter asked: 'I also want to interview people 85 years and over, whether they have a faith or not.' Few older people responded.

### Number of participants in the study

The number of participants required for the SHIE (Hair et al. 1995) to enable a valid factor analysis to be performed was a ratio of 5:1 – five questionnaires to each item on the questionnaire. This required a total of 75 informants for the SHIE. The number of informants required for the in-depth interviews was drawn from the SHIE population and informants were interviewed until no new themes were being found in the data. This resulted in a total of 24 in-depth interviews.

### The in-depth interviews

A sub-sample of those who completed the SHIE was interviewed, using in-depth interviewing techniques. Life review and reminiscence, focusing on meaning in life, concept or image of God, (if any) and the relationship between these and growing older formed the main part of the interviews. The purpose of these interviews was to discover common themes of spirituality/meaning in life within this ageing group.

### Characteristic of members of the University of the Third Age

U3A are a broad group. By belonging to U3A it is acknowledged that members have at least one point of social contact on a continuing basis. Members are involved in their community, often taking part in further learning, active and independent living. It could be assumed, although not assessed in this study, that the membership of U3A would be drawn from mainly middle-class and well-educated older people.

### The use of laughter and humour as demonstrated by informants in interviews

A feature of a large proportion of the interviews was the use of laughter when speaking of embarrassing, difficult or sad situations. It had not been planned to examine the use of humour or laughter in this study; however, it appears connected with the spiritual within a large proportion of the interviews. This may be an important aspect of the process of life review and has therefore been addressed in the relevant sections.

## The findings of the study

In this study I attempted to map the spiritual dimension of a number of independently living older adults and to test an assessment tool for measurement of spiritual needs of older people. My thesis is that spiritual development continues across the lifespan and healthy ageing is dependent on spiritual health as well as physical and psychosocial wellness. It is my contention that spiritual health in ageing can be enhanced by sensitising older people to their own spiritual journeys, by assessing the spiritual needs of frail older people, and by assisting older people to meet their spiritual needs effectively.

## The sample for the spiritual health inventories

### The history of the participants

The participants' backgrounds include: the Depression; the impact of the Second World War; doing without – one older woman told how she experienced hunger when she was a child. Lack of career opportunities was spoken of by a number of those who were interviewed in-depth. This was particularly the experience for women in the study. The background of informants is important because it may influence the spiritual journey of these people. But as is seen in other parts of this study, environmental influences are only part of the story. More important is how the informants responded to the choices available to them.

## Who were these people?

The sample was made up of 75 people living independently in the community, over the age of 65 years; mean age 75.3, oldest 90.

### Table 2.1 Religious denomination

| Denomination | Number | Per cent | Per cent population* |
|---|---|---|---|
| Roman Catholic | 12 | 16.0 | 27.3 |
| Anglican | 30 | 40.0 | 23.9 |
| Uniting Church | 14 | 18.7 | 12.6 |
| Pentecostal | 1 | 1.3 | 0.9 |
| Other Protestant | 3 | 4.0 | ** |
| No religion | 15 | 20.0 | *** |
| Total | 75 | 100.0 | |

\*      Source: Australian Census 1991 (Hughes 1993)
\*\*      No exact match with census breakdown
\*\*\*      Difficult to determine from census data because of optional question. 10.2% 'no stated religion'

RELIGIOUS DENOMINATION

Table 2.1 shows the religious denominations of the sample. Note the difference in percentage of Anglicans in the sample and population; there are more Anglicans in the sample than would be expected. There are also fewer Catholics than would be expected. This effect is only slightly less marked in the in-depth group where 33.3 per cent of the sample are Anglicans and 16.6 per cent are Catholics. UCA members are also over-represented in this sample. It is also noted that response to the census question 'What is your religion?' can be misleading as it can mean different things to different people, and as Hughes (1993, p.3) remarked, 'The census data tells us one thing: the religion or denomination with which people identify.'

It is noted that 2.6 per cent of the Australian population are members of Judaism, Islam, Buddhism or other religions. None of these religious groups were included in this sample.

## Table 2.2 Practice of faith

|  | Number | Per cent |
|---|---|---|
| Those who say they have a faith | 69 | 92.0 |
| Those who practice that faith now | 64 | 85.3 |

### Practice of faith

The question on faith, setting up a dichotomy (Would you say you have a faith? Yes/No) has presented a number of problems. First, the content of the concept of faith is too complex to reduce to a yes/no response. Second, faith is interpreted differently by different people.

As I prepared to conduct this study, it seemed that the sample may be more likely to define faith along denominational lines, and the initial aim was to include adherents of Christian denominations in one group and to house a second group with no denominational affiliation. For reasons discussed below this was not fruitful, and there are not two clear-cut groups of informants.

Although 20 per cent of the sample reported having no religion at all, 92 per cent of the total sample said they had a faith and 85.3 per cent say they practise that faith now (that obviously includes some of those who registered as having 'no religion'). (See Table 2.2.) This raises important questions about the meaning of the word 'faith'.

### How is the word 'faith' understood by the participants in this study?

Faith has been defined very differently by various of the informants. To some it is the profession and practice of the Christian faith, while for others it is faith 'in humanity' or even faith 'in myself'. These people seemed very reluctant to disclaim faith. Even where their faith did not include a belief in God, they mostly seemed to acknowledge some deep sense of meaning and a sense of something that made them reluctant to say they had no faith at all. A number of informants asked me what I thought about their practice of faith. It seemed they wanted affirmation or an evaluation from me, as researcher, or perhaps to be seen by a priest to be doing the right thing.

These responses are in line with Fowler's (1981) work on faith development. The high proportion of respondents who say they have a faith (92 per cent) has particular implications for the provision of spiritual and pastoral care to all older adults. It would suggest that those in need of pastoral care are definitely not only those who claim a religious denomination, or even those who attend church; but that pastoral care should be available to all older people.

| Table 2.3 Gender | | |
| --- | --- | --- |
| | Number | Per cent |
| Male | 15 | 20 |
| Female | 60 | 80 |

## Background of the respondents

The findings were examined in relation to developmental stages and faith development, with the emphasis on individuation and gender role. The high proportion of women in the sample (Table 2.3) should give some feeling to the weighting on relationship in meaning in life as opposed to individuation in ageing.

| Table 2.4 Marital status | | |
| --- | --- | --- |
| | Number | Per cent |
| Married | 23 | 30.67 |
| Widowed | 35 | 46.67 |
| Never married | 9 | 12.0 |
| Separated | 3 | 4.0 |
| Divorced | 5 | 6.67 |
| Total | 75 | 100.0 |

Table 2.4 indicates a high proportion of 'Never married' in the sample when compared with the larger community. It is possible simply that more unmarried people responded to the invitation to participate in this study. Could this be because 'Never married' people may be more willing to

contact people outside their immediate family? It is difficult to know why this happened.

On the other hand, in the sample widowhood becomes the norm as people grow older. Of the females 78 years and over (25), 18 (72 per cent) were widowed, one married, three divorced and three had never married.

Three informants were divorced, a lower number than would be expected in a younger cohort, possibly reflecting the social expectations of their earlier years as well as the greater difficulty of divorcing when this group was younger.

## Table 2.5 Accommodation

|                    | Number | Per cent |
|--------------------|--------|----------|
| House              | 45     | 60.0     |
| Unit               | 16     | 21.3     |
| Retirement village | 14     | 18.7     |

All informants resided in independent living situations, the majority in their own homes (see Table 2.5). It was hoped to obtain a relatively homogenous group based on the criterion of independent living.

It was not at first thought to be important to obtain education levels of informants; however, when the in-depth interviews were completed, it was considered that this was a very articulate and perhaps well-educated group of older adults (see Table 2.6). Further contact was made with all those who were interviewed in-depth, except for one who could not be contacted. The levels of formal education of informants were probably higher than would be expected of this cohort of older people.

A number of the informants grew up in depression days and their parents could not afford to send them on to further education. Some of the women mentioned that the boys in their families were given first choice for further study. One of the women who had a degree studied as a mature student and graduated at age 60. When she was ready to go to university as a young woman, men were returning from the war and were given first preference for tertiary study.

The informants were very articulate and most were well read. They had continued to learn throughout life by self-education, mainly by reading and attending short courses. A number are still students; one at 75 years, did a short course in computing because she 'didn't want to be computer illiterate'.

### Table 2.6 Education levels of informants (available for the in-depth interviews only)

| Level | Number |
|---|---|
| Graduate, includes one who graduated at 60 years | 7 |
| Secondary completed, nursing | 1 |
| Secondary completed, plus teaching certificate | 1 |
| Secondary completed | 3 |
| Part secondary (four years) | 2 |
| Intermediate certificate (three years high school) | 8 |
| Merit certificate (2 years high school) | 1 |
| Completed primary school | 1 |
| | |
| Total | 24 |

Is education related to spiritual development? It is uncertain, and data from this study would not provide evidence for or against. For this group of older people it seems that the critical thing for most of them is a life-long curiosity and thirst for learning. This quest may also be related to their spiritual growth, simply because they are survivors and most seem to engage readily with life as a life-long characteristic.

## The SHIE: factor analysis

Seventy-five spiritual health inventories, elderly (SHIE) were completed, enough to do factor analysis on the basis of a ratio of 5:1 inventories to items. Twenty-four in-depth interviews were done, drawn from the 75 SHIE.

The 75 SHIEs were analysed using SPSS statistical package. Factor analysis was used to determine whether a smaller number of factors underlies the pattern of correlations in a larger number of variables (de Vaus

1995). This is a valuable means of examining this type of questionnaire; it is most important that any assessment instrument designed to measure a dimension of such sensitivity as spiritual needs is both measuring what it purports to measure and is also simple to use in a clinical setting. The KMO value was 0.659 indicating that the correlations for the sample were in the low range of suitability for factor analysis, according to de Vaus (1995, p.259), KMO values above 0.7 are sufficiently high to make factor analysis suitable, while more care should be taken when values are between 0.5 and 0.69. Only those factors having eigenvalues of more than 1 have been used. On this basis only 2 factors were extracted: factor 1, with an eigenvalue of 2.69 which accounted for 17.9 per cent of the variance, and factor 2, eigenvalue of 1.83, accounting for 12.2 per cent of the variance, making a cumulative percentage of variance accounted for by the two factors of 30.1 per cent, too low to be a worthwhile outcome. A result of almost 70 per cent unexplained variance is too low to accept.

It is suggested that if the questionnaire was testing for one concept, as may be the case in the dimension of the spiritual, then it would be reasonable to expect that one factor would be found. On the other hand, when the findings of the in-depth interviews in this study are examined, the finding of six themes leads to the suggestion that it would be reasonable to assume that a valid questionnaire would load on six factors, should the questions produce clear discrimination between themes. However, this is uncertain as there is likely to be some overlap between themes.

## Themes identified from the interviews

All 24 interviews were summarised into themes of meaning in life, concept of God, growing older, the connections between faith, meaning in life and growing older, and finally the theme of changes in faith over the life journey. Examination of data then resulted in the construction of six overall themes (Figure 2.1).

During the interviews six major themes in spirituality and ageing emerged. These were, first, the deepest-held meaning for each person, that which lay at the core of one's being. The second theme, and closely related to the first, was the individual's response to what is ultimate in their lives. The other themes identified were hope/fear; relationship/isolation; wisdom/final meanings; and self-sufficiency/vulnerability. There is necessarily an overlap and interaction between the themes. Each of these can be envisaged as a continuum, noting, however, that the category

**Spiritual themes of ageing**

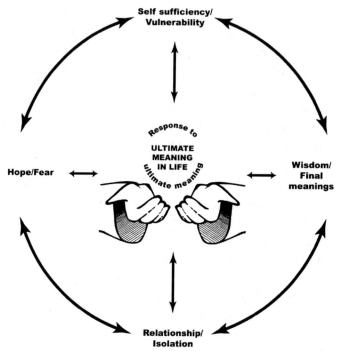

Figure 2.1 Spirituality in ageing: themes from the data

wisdom/final meanings rather than presenting as a continuum, has a range of responses. Final meanings are more possibly tied to the person's perceived nearness to the end of their lifespan.

### Major themes and categories of each

The first major theme was *ultimate meaning* (for each person) including relationship with God (including image of God held by person), sense of other, or absence of religious belief, or other centres of ultimate meaning. The second was *response to the ultimate*, which includes worship, prayer, reading Scripture, symbols of meaning, meditation, experience of 'otherness'.

The following themes seemed to develop according to centres of meaning and the effectiveness of the two major themes listed above. The first listed (not in any specific order) of these was *vulnerability/self-sufficiency*. This is a continuum and includes disabilities and effects of physical ageing. Vulnerability is perceived and/or real, and seems to be associated with the development of transcendence to overcome vulnerabilities. Another theme identified was *wisdom/final meanings*. Wisdom includes discernment, the move towards final meanings, increased ability to tolerate ambiguity and an increased sense of interiority. The theme of *relationship/isolation* includes relationship with others, satisfied/not satisfied and isolation, satisfied/not satisfied. The last theme named was *hope/fear/despair* and includes spiritual integrity, contentment, peace, joy, searching, despair and meaninglessness.

## Comparison of the data collected from SHIE and in-depth interviewing

Even though the factor analysis on the SHIE accounted for only 30.1 per cent of the total variance, it was worth comparing the data collected from both sources.

Individual SHIE items were examined where the item had either a very high (5) or very low (2 or 1) loading. These items were examined for wording and also compared with the in-depth interview data for the same informant.

The following comments can be made of individual SHIE items. First, the items with the word 'God' in them were a problem for informants who did not believe in God and/or did not have an affiliation with any religious denomination. Item 11 was ambiguous as it could either be asking if the person felt the need for forgiveness from God, or from other people. Further, SHIE scores did not reflect the level of spirituality of informants, or even spiritual health: low scores were sometimes obtained by informants who on in-depth interview obviously had a highly developed spiritual dimension. There did not seem to be any pattern with the scores. Moreover, the SHIE did not reflect the complexity of spirituality as expressed through the interviews. The SHIE questionnaire was not sufficiently specific to tap into concerns of the informants. Further, items such as #5: 'The doctors and nurses agree with my comments about my health' and #12 'I actively participate in decisions concerning my health care' would seem to be tapping into the concept of locus of control rather than spirituality. It is noted that item 10 did tap into vulnerability for one informant, Flora, but missed the vulnerability of Carol, as it failed to identify Carol's ability to transcend her difficulties (lack of specificity of the instrument). Finally, items 1, 2, 3 and 9 related to hope, but failed to pick up on this concept as it was expressed by many of the informants in the in-depth material.

## The themes and SHIE

The SHIE did not connect with the themes of ultimate meaning, response to ultimate meaning, transcendence, relationship or final meanings. In a clinical situation these are all important aspects to be considered. Neither did the SHIE connect with the themes identified from the in-depth interviews. There was one question on the SHIE relating to family, and that was too broad to be of value. The in-depth material revealed a wealth of material on the importance of relationships for these informants, both with God and with others; there was no way that this could be reflected in the questionnaire.

### Summary

*The in-depth interviews used in this study provide a rich window on the spiritual journeys of these older people. It would appear from this study that this is a valuable means of tapping into the spiritual dimension of older adults, and a way to enable mapping of this dimension. It would be valuable to use this method again, with frail older adults, to enlarge the profile of spirituality in ageing. The use of in-depth interviewing allows the inform-ants to express their own views on spirituality in ageing without the researcher foreclosing on possibilities. It therefore provides a better basis for constructing assessment instruments than using a panel of experts, who do not include the informants themselves.*

*On the other hand, the SHIE did not compare well either on factor analysis or with the data obtained from in-depth interviewing. Even so assessment of spiritual needs may still be an important direction to pursue, using a different questionnaire, based on the findings of this study.*

## Notes

1   The term 'experiential careers' is used by Glaser and Strauss (1968) to describe the life experience of the patients, families and staff in the particular setting.

2   It is noted that there is no chronological age set for the 'third age'. To do so would detract from its meaning, as it is the very diversity of ageing that is being considered. Use of chronological age as a descriptor confines older people to stereotypic expectations according to age.

# CHAPTER 3

# Religion, faith and spirituality

The term 'spirituality' has gained a popular appeal in recent years and its meaning may be somewhat unclear. Indeed, it may be made to mean almost whatever the user wants. It was thus important at the outset of this study to clarify meaning of the words 'spirituality', 'faith' and 'religion' as used in this book.

First, religion is considered in relation to the spiritual dimension. A number of issues raised by both Greeley (1973) and Bellah *et al.* (1985) are examined, among them: what is religion?; how are older people practising their religion?; what is the content of religion for them?; where and how do they find meaning in ageing and the relationship of this to religion?

## A definition of religion: is that possible?

Lewis (1965) suggests that the task of defining religion is overwhelming, remarking that in one list there were 48 definitions. Yet everyone we meet 'knows' (within a particular society) what religion is, although obviously the term does not mean the same to everyone.

One definition that can be broadly applied across many belief systems and, indeed, to the fundamental meaning systems of a secular society as well is that used by Geertz (1968), who has produced a working definition of religion as follows:

> A system of symbols which acts to establish powerful, pervasive, and long-lasting moods and motivations in men by formulating conceptions of a general order of existence and clothing these conceptions with such an aura of factuality that the moods and motivations seem uniquely realistic. (p.643)

Another definition was used by Oser (in Fowler *et al.* 1992, p.37), this time relating to religious consciousness 'in terms of persons' constructions of their relationship with an Ultimate Being', the focus being on capturing the human–divine relationship. This relationship is described as a 'dynamic, interactional cognitive activity by which a person copes with contingencies, gives religious meaning to situations, interprets religious messages, and engages in prayer'. This perspective, Oser says, is an holistic structure, used by the individual for solving problems 'encountered in life through religious categories' (p.38). The concept being examined in Oser's study is thus restrictive, admitting only those who relate through religion to an Ultimate Being in some way. I am well aware of the many older people living in the community who have no religious base to their lives, yet these same people do have a spiritual dimension. Therefore any definition of religion must be inclusive of that group. Oser, like Fowler, acknowledges that the person's religious structure develops through life. It is noted though that this definition of 'religion' is not as inclusive as that of 'faith' developed by Fowler in his work.

## Is religion relevant in the secular society of the twenty-first century?

Greeley (1973, p.60) wrote that religion is not concerned basically with disembodied appearances of reality, or abstract matters, or the givenness of reality, or the political situation: 'It is concerned with the Ultimate on which reality rests'. And, Greeley writes, by answering the most basic questions that humans can ask, religion can provide an interpretation and shape with which to approach daily life.

Religion, then, is an important way in which humans work out their faith or their spiritual dimension of being. What is that reality for older adults, and how do older people relate to religion these days? Answers to these questions may to some extent illuminate the dimension of the spiritual for older adults.

### 'I'm not really religious'

First, what do we mean by 'being religious'? Often people will say to me, 'I'm not really religious', particularly when they know I am a priest. Geertz (1975) says religious activities can be described as a persisting tendency to perform certain sorts of acts and to experience certain sorts of feelings in particular circumstances. He takes 'being religious' to mean being motivated by religion. As well, he sees this as being susceptible to certain moods, for which 'worshipful' might be one.

In the latter part of the twentieth century and into the twenty-first, people are at last beginning to recognise this issue, with a renewed search for the spiritual. The undue emphasis on the individual in society has given way to the need for connections with others in meaningful relationships. The need for a sense of community is stirring in our highly technologised world. Also stirring is the need people are beginning to recognise, as a longing for connection with a Being outside themselves. For many this takes the form of relationship with a loving God, while for others it may be a desire to achieve wealth, or power, or prestige in work or in the arts, or any number of other human activities.

Greeley (1982, p.9) stated that there exists 'a bitter and useless controversy in the sociology of religion about what religion is'. The argument centres on whether there needs to be 'an explicit "transcendental" or "superempirical" referent for a belief system to be religious'. Greeley suggests that ideologies such as Marxism and feminism or psychoanalysis can become basic belief systems for people, and these then take on 'a sacred and transcendental quality which makes them indistinguishable from religion' (p.10).

## Faith: what is meant by this term?

The second term to be considered here is 'faith'. Faith means different things to different people. One might say, 'I have faith in Jesus Christ', another might say, 'I have faith in the goodness of humanity'. How do we define it? Is faith the same as spirituality? Fowler (1986) in his stages of faith development (p.26), gave this definition of faith:

The process of constitutive-knowing

underlying a person's composition and maintenance of a comprehensive frame (or frames) or meaning

generated from the person's attachments or commitments to centers of supraordinate value which have power to unify his or her experiences of the world

thereby endowing the relationships, contexts, and patterns of everyday life, past and future, with significance.

Fowler's definition is broad and all-encompassing, it recognises the human capacity for constructing meanings and interacting in relationships as well as relating to the transcendent. It is evident that Fowler is using his definition as a structure for faith, not a content of faith. His definition allows for considerable breadth of content. In fact, his definition provides for an orientation to or commitment of living.

There is more to write on 'faith' and Fowler's recent research in this area, and this is presented further in Chapter 8, under 'The spiritual journey in ageing'.

## Spirituality defined

And so to 'spirituality'. While it is commonly recognised that humans do have a spiritual dimension to their lives, precise definition of this is less exact, and even more complex is the way the spiritual dimension is expressed by the individual (Report of the Social Policy Committee of the Board for Social Responsibility, 1990). Fischer (1985) comments that spirituality is the deepest dimension of all life.

So how is the spiritual dimension to be understood? In the Hebrew sense of *ruach*, spirit is the breath of life, that which enlivens the human being, this same spirit that was involved in the Creation (Gen.). Thayer (1985) says the Hebrew concept of spirit is the 'human capacity for participation in and responsiveness to the essential dynamism of the transcendent' (p.45). Moltmann (1992) writes that 'Literally, spirituality means life in God's Spirit, and a living relationship with God's Spirit' (p.83). The Greek *pneuma* encompasses the meaning of wind, breath, energy and dynamic reality, while the Greek perspective of spirit, used in New Testament times, was often as a contrast to flesh: spirit, linked with the divine; flesh, linked with the profane or lesser things of life. This view sets up a clear dichotomy, a separation of spirit and the body. Against this Moltmann (1992) writes that:

> If according to the Christian hope 'the transfiguration of the body' consists of the raising from death to eternal life, then it is already experienced here and now in the Spirit of life, which interpenetrates body and soul and awakens all our vital powers. Eternal love transfigures the body. As 'love's body', the body comes alive, receiving and giving life. (p.95)

In this understanding of spirituality lies a wholeness of body and soul, a creativeness, a new freedom in life, with possibilities and opportunities, the spiritual that adds vitality to life. This 'Spirit of life' Moltmann speaks of is God's Spirit that acts to enliven the human body and soul and bring wholeness to humans, acknowledging the interrelationship between body, mind and spirit.

Others, too, suggest a much closer relationship between spirit and the physical body. In this view, spirit has been defined as a basic human drive for relationship with the transcendent (Carson 1989).

Thibault (1995) says spirituality refers to a particular spiritual style in which the individual seeks to work out their sense of meaning and relationship. She further develops this to say that in a strictly religious sense, the spiritual is the way a person works out their relationship with God and the values and activities that are related to that. It could also be said that the spiritual is what gives depth and meaning to life, and that the spiritual dimension is worked out in both the horizontal dimension, in relationships with others, and also in the vertical, so to speak, of relationship with God, or in some sense of the other, the unexplainable.

There are a number of definitions of human spirituality. I shall outline and examine a number of these demonstrating the process of choice for a definition here. First, that of von Balthasar (1965):

> Spirituality is a modern notion which may be defined as: that basic practical or existential attitude of man which is the consequence and expression of the way in which he understands his religion – or more generally, his ethically committed-existence; the way in which he acts and reacts habitually throughout his life according to his objective and ultimate insights and decisions. (p.5)

Features of this definition include a practice of the person that is habitual and is derived from a world view. This world view is based on ultimate meanings that the individual holds. It is wider than the understanding of a practice of religion, and indeed can be applied to people who do not exhibit a religious faith. This definition suggests, but does not make explicit, the possibility of changing spirituality through the lifespan.

A second definition is that of de Guibert (1986):

> The word 'spirituality' can designate many objects. First, it can mean the personal interior life of a man, or the thought on which that life is more habitually nourished, or forms of prayer or various practices, or special graces which sustain and develop that life. Second, the word can signify the manner of directing others which this or that person employs in his ministry, the principles he teaches, the means of training he employs, and the particular goals he points out or suggests. Third and last, the word often means the spiritual doctrine formulated in the person's writings, or the doctrinal synthesis of matters pertaining to the spiritual life which he expounded, insinuated, or took for granted in his writings, or which at least we can draw from his pages. (p.2)

Guibert's definition pictures a habitual stance, oriented to religious practices, and an interior life. It gives a sense of the richness of expression of
human spirituality. While the first part of this definition may include secular
spirituality, the intent is unclear. If we are to acknowledge the presence of the
spiritual dimension within all human beings, as is being done in this study,
then any definition used must include the possibility of spirituality in all
people. An important aspect of Guibert's definition is the acknowledgement
that there is a continuity of the spiritual, a deposit that is handed on from
generation to generation, a part of the community, as well as of each
individual.

Holmes (in Thayer 1985, p.54), has outlined a five-point definition of
spirituality:

> a human capacity for relationship with that which 'transcends sense
> phenomena' the subject perceives this relationship as an expanded or
> heightened consciousness, independent of the subject's efforts. This is
> grounded in the historical setting and exhibits itself in creative actions in
> the world.

Holmes' definition is rich, but an important aspect of spirituality is relationship with other human beings; this may be implicit within the definition,
but lacks that further aspect that is needed to describe the fullness of human
spirituality. Holmes's definition also lacks a clear indication of the habitual
nature of human spirituality.

Labun (1988) emphasises the relational component of spirituality. First,
spirituality is seen as an aspect of the whole person which is related to and
integrated with all components of the person's functioning and expression.
Second, spirituality is expressed through interpersonal relationships and
through a transcendent relationship with another realm. Third, Labun says
that spirituality involves relationships and produces behaviours and feelings
showing the existence of love, faith, hope and trust, giving meaning to life
and reason for being.

Still further, spiritual well-being has been defined by the National
Interfaith Coalition on Aging (NICA) in North America, 1972. At a special
workshop to reach a consensus of the meaning of 'spiritual well-being' they
produced this definition: 'Spiritual well-being is the affirmation of life in a
relationship with God, self, community and environment that nurtures and
celebrates wholeness.'

This definition promotes an ideal to move towards in ageing and
spirituality. The achievement of spiritual well-being, however, is not a state

to reach, but a process and a continued movement towards wholeness that has the potential to continue throughout human life. Moberg (1990) remarked that despite the broad applicability of this definition, it had failed to make a significant impact on the field of gerontology and geriatrics.

### Religion, faith or spirituality?

Considering the terms religion, faith and spirituality, I have decided to use 'spirituality' here as understanding of the term spirituality is broader than the term 'religion' in most common current use. This is of importance for the sample of older people interviewed in this study, as the word 'religion' often means simply 'going to church'. Second, although spirituality has a similar meaning to faith, as defined by Fowler (1981) the word spirituality is more widely understood in the health and psychology literature, while it is also in common usage within the fields of pastoral theology and pastoral care.

For this study, 'spirituality' as defined draws from several of the definitions above, recognising, first, the human need for ultimate meaning in each person, whether this is fulfilled through relationship with God or some sense of another, or whether some other sense of meaning becomes the guiding force within the individual's life. Human spirituality must also involve relationship with other people. Spirituality is a part of every human being, it is what differentiates humans from other animal species. There is a real need to have a definition of spirituality that is inclusive of all religious groups and of the secular.

It is appropriate to consider spirituality as having two components, a broad, generic component and a specific component. The generic component is that which lies at the core of each human's being. It is that which searches and yearns for relationship in life and for meaning in existence. Individual humans may find this need addressed in all sorts of situations in life, in love, in joy, in suffering, and in pain and loss. Ashbrook (1996, p.74) says that 'Beyond the self of culture lies the soul in God, the core of each person's being'.

The specific component of spirituality is understood as the way each individual works out their spirituality in their lives. This may be in the practice of a particular religion, it may be through relationship with other people and in community, through work or through particular centres of meaning and interests in life.

The operational definition used in this study takes into account the main characteristics of the sample of older people interviewed, of Christians and others who acknowledge no faith or denominational affiliation.

The definition of spirituality used in this study is:

> That which lies at the core of each person's being, an essential dimension which brings meaning to life. It is acknowledged that spirituality is not constituted only by religious practices, but must be understood more broadly, as relationship with God, however God or ultimate meaning is perceived by the person, and in relationship with other people. (MacKinlay 1998, p.36)

## The spiritual dimension and health

Many people in current Western society do not give much credence to the spiritual dimension either in themselves or others. It is becoming increasingly recognised in the nursing literature (Carson 1989; Highfield 1981, 1989; MacKinlay 1992; Ronaldson 1997) as well as in the specialised literature on ageing (Kimble 1995; Koenig 1994; Seeber 1990) that the spiritual dimension is critical to the well-being of human beings. It seems that spiritual well-being is basic even to healthy psychosocial functioning.

The relationship between healthy adjustment to ageing and religious involvement has been studied, with a number of studies demonstrating a positive relationship between them (for example, Moberg 1968). Even so, the question of attendance at church services may miss the real life issues for the elderly; for example, how does faith relate to the realities experienced in the ageing process? As Moberg (1968) put it, it is difficult to know whether those who are well adjusted engage in many religious activities, whether those who engage in many religious activities are assisted to good adjustment in ageing, or whether religiosity bears little relation to spirituality in the elderly.

A certain degree of denial of the spiritual in the face of a highly developed profile in the physical and biological sciences during this and the last century has left many people without the strategies for achieving (w)holistic well-being. In many ways we have become alienated from the spiritual; there is a great need to redress this alienation in our lives. The search for spiritual wholeness is a life-long search for each human. Each person has to find wholeness in their own way, some may even fail to find wholeness by the end of their lives. It is contended that health is a complex interaction between biophysiological, psychosocial and spiritual dimensions of the human being.

During recent years a great deal of research has focused on the psychosocial dimension of humans, considering personal interactions, personality and the psychosocial needs of humans. Erikson *et al.* (1986) described the final psychosocial developmental stage of the human lifespan as integrity versus despair. In his earlier writings he had focused on the psychosocial dimension, but in this later book, the product of interviews with octogenarians who had been a part of his longitudinal studies and written when he was in his late seventies, he has included the spiritual dimension.

Psychosocial research has been valuable in addressing the inadequacies in these dimensions which we so often experience. But it seems that we have not reached an adequate state of knowledge by working in those dimensions alone. The spiritual dimension looms as a great untapped region for many, both health professionals and the elderly themselves.

Early research into the spiritual dimension in nursing, in a study of oncology nurses' perception of spiritual needs, has shown (Highfield 1981, 1989) that nurses often failed to distinguish between the spiritual and psychosocial dimensions of patient needs.

A study based on Highfield, carried out with frail elderly people in the Australian Capital Territory (ACT), resulted in change of nursing practice for a number of nurses who participated in the study (MacKinlay 1992). This may have been due to a greater sensitisation of the participants in the study to the spiritual dimension. It may also have been because the nurses involved, who were studying in a continuing education course in gerontological nursing, actually had the time to sit and listen with their patients. The changes in nursing practice were reported by the nurses, who were using a journal-writing and reflective method of recording clinical experience.

Comments showed the nurses to be more aware of the need for meaning in the ageing person's life. It showed them to be more self-aware in their nursing practice. It showed them considering residents' needs in a new light. This included a joint search for meaning which took place with elderly people, their relatives and nurses, to overcome disabilities and pain and to bring meaning into the lives of some very frail elderly people (MacKinlay 1992).

It could well be said that this was a new dimension of nursing which seemed to be emerging during the study. This new dimension was that of the nurse as a spiritual facilitator or *meaning maker* for the frail elderly person (MacKinlay 1997).

Now the spiritual dimension is one which many nurses have either acknowledged as being the sole domain of clergy; or, at best, have felt ill prepared to intervene in. Yet it seems in reality that there is a gulf between the nurse's role and the clergy's role. In many instances neither group of carers is adequately meeting the spiritual needs of patients. This study sets out to examine this gap between the roles, thus outcomes of the study address both nursing and clergy aspects of intervention. Obviously, the pastoral care role is one that is close to the material of this study. The spiritual role is not confined to nurses and clergy, but also has wider implications for those involved in social care and social work as well.

## Psychosocial development in ageing

An understanding of what is happening in spirituality in ageing can be gained through first studying the contributions from psychosocial development and faith development. A number of researchers have made important contributions to the knowledge of psychosocial development in ageing. One important caution made by Neugarten (1968) is that researchers should be careful not to assume the same close links between the biological and psychological in adulthood as in youth. This is probably even more important to remember in later adulthood. Neugarten has said of the 'middle' years of life: 'probably the decade of the fifties for most persons represent an important turning point, with the restructuring of time and the formulation of new perspectives of self, time and death' (Neugarten 1968, p.141). These tasks of middle life noted by Neugarten are also tasks of finding meaning, and are therefore part of the spiritual work of ageing as well. Are these tasks that continue into the later years of life? It would seem to be so. This study seeks to answer this by specifically considering the spiritual dimension of independently living older adults.

Neugarten (1968) notes that introspection increases noticeably at this time; there is a move to increased 'interiority'. In a sense, it seems that the middle years have moved since the late 1960s. Perhaps now, with our increased longevity, it is necessary to reconsider just where those middle years are within the lifespan. Perhaps the 30 to 50 years grouping of the late 1960s should give way to a 40 to 60, perhaps 65, years now, keeping in mind of course that chronological age is increasingly irrelevant as people grow older.

## Erikson's psychosocial stages of ageing

Erikson has marked the psychosocial developmental stage of the elderly person as that of integrity versus despair (Erikson *et al.* 1986). It is important to realise that, although this has been designated the final stage of psychosocial development, it is not isolated from the preceding stages, as Erikson *et al.* (1986) makes clear:

> It is through this last stage that the life cycle weaves back on itself in its entirety, ultimately integrating maturing forms of hope, will, purpose, competence, fidelity, love, and care, into a comprehensive sense of wisdom. (p.56)

For Erikson (1986), at each developmental stage the individual is both re-experiencing the tensions that were inadequately integrated when they were focal, and engaging in the yet to come of the new stage of development. Thus, when the person reaches the final stage of development, they still have to re-experience, for example, earlier stages of psychosocial development, and bring these into balance in the struggle for integrity versus despair. Fortunately, the final stage is not isolated from those that preceded it; allowing the possibility of revisiting earlier stages through life review to deal with earlier issues that have not been completed, or were dealt with appropriately at the time.

Erikson wrote that through the lifespan, each person has to some extent, anticipated the 'finality' of old age. Each person has, to some extent, experienced a sense of an existential dread of 'not-being', at the same time as they continue to integrate other parts of their behaviours and life stages. A fact to be faced in the later years is that more life has already been lived than is left to be lived. The past is, in fact, 'inalterable', while the future is still unknown. How does one approach the remaining years? Is it with a sense of satisfaction over the time already lived? Or with a sense of dread of what is to come? The sense of wisdom is set into this final stage, where the person seeks towards integrity or, on the other hand, declines into despair.

## Peck's ageing stages

Peck (1968), working from Erikson's eighth stage, ego integrity versus despair, and considering that this stage could cover a timespan of some forty years of adult life, suggested it might be more useful to divide it into more discrete stages. As a result he set forward stages for middle age and for old age. At that time life expectancy was not as great as it is now, and life expectancy continues to extend rapidly, particularly in the over 85 year olds. The effect of this is to extend that later life period covered by Erikson's stages even further, perhaps to fifty or more years. As well, there have been a number of social changes and health status changes in the general population since that time. However, there are some aspects of Peck's developmental stages in later adulthood that are certainly worth considering.

First, is *ego differentiation versus work-role preoccupation*. The specific issue Peck identified here was vocational retirement for men, usually in their sixties. In the last decade or so voluntary redundancies for many men, often in their fifties, and maybe even younger, have complicated this stage. The effect is perhaps to make it an even more important stage to navigate. As well, more women are in full-time work than thirty years ago. But the issue Peck (1968) identified in this stage, is a

> general, crucial shift in the value system by which the retiring individual can reappraise and redefine his worth, and can take satisfaction in a broader range of role activities than just his long-time specific work role. (p.91)

He suggests the chief question might be: Am I a worthwhile person? (without that work-related identity).

Loss of meaning for older men in society is a very real problem if current suicide rates for older men can be taken as an indicator (Hassan 1995; Klinger 1999). Until now the transition for women between roles of homemaker-career woman and retirement have been less marked. This may change as gender-based roles become more diffused.

The second task of ageing, according to Peck, is *body transcendence versus body preoccupation*. He writes that with increasing age there is a well-recorded 'decline in resistance to illness, a decline in recuperative powers and increasing experience with bodily aches and pains' (Peck 1968, p.91). He suggests that for older people who have relied on physical well-being, 'this may be the gravest, most mortal of all insults'. He says that for 'many people those elder years seem to move in a decreasing spiral, centred around their growing preoccupation with the state of their bodies'. On the other hand, it seems to be the case for many others, who also experience the same kinds of physical disabilities in ageing, to find life satisfaction and meaning in spite of these disabilities. As Peck says: 'In their value system, social and mental sources of pleasure and self-respect may transcend physical comfort alone' (p.91). It is reasonable to assume that in the changes in health status which have accompanied increases in longevity in the last few decades, this stage has probably been pushed back to a later period of life for many.

The concept of body transcendence versus body preoccupation, touching into, as it does, ultimate meaning in life, would seem to be not only of significance from a psychosocial perspective but also of great significance when viewed from within the spiritual dimension. As older adults begin to experience the loss of physical power and well-being, they are thrown against a sense of their purpose in life, and questions such as 'why am I here?'; 'has it all been worthwhile?' begin to press more insistently upon the individual. These are questions of life meaning. Questions such as these push the person to ask the next question, 'What do I do? What should I be in the rest of my life?'. Such questions are essentially of a spiritual nature.

Peck's postulated third stage of psychosocial ageing is termed *ego transcendence versus ego preoccupation*. Peck (1968) remarked that one of the 'new and crucial facts of old age is the appearance of the certain prospect of personal death'. For younger people, death comes unexpectedly, but older people know it must come. Peck points to ways of constructive living in generosity and unselfishness to provide a way to face the prospect of death. Of human achievements and relationships he says contributions to the culture, family and friends 'may, indeed, be the only knowable kind of self-perpetuation after death' (p.91). This is one way to approach the concept of transcendence in ageing. Another is the teaching of the Christian gospel, through which the last enemy of humankind, death, has been defeated (1 Cor. 15:26). Christians believe that Jesus died and was resurrected from the dead by God, overcoming the power of death. Thus the belief in the resurrection of Jesus removes the sense of meaninglessness and hopelessness from human lives; Christian hope does not confront death as the final, intractable problem of life (Bauckham 1995) but hope begins with the promise of new life (transformed life) here and in the future through the resurrection. Thus, for Christians, ego transcendence is possible through the resurrection of Jesus.

This psychosocial perspective may be just as legitimately treated as a spiritual perspective where meaning in life and being able to see beyond the present with a sense of hope enable the person to shift focus from themselves and the fear of annihilation and death, to achieve ego transcendence. Peck acknowledges this adaptive stage as one requiring 'deep, active effort to make life more secure, more meaningful, or happier for the people who will go on after one dies' (p.91). Peck suggests that 'this kind of adaptation...may well be the most crucial achievement of the elder years'. An alternative view sees ego transcendence as grace, and thus of letting go, in order to move on.

At what chronological age these stages occur may vary markedly. Indeed, marrying and having a family later in life, the onset of chronic illness, or even earlier retirement may tend to shift the timing of these stages forward or backward along the lifespan for the particular person. Thus it can be seen that how and where a person is in their life development stage is not tied to chronological age alone, and may be only marginally influenced by it.

In many ways there is close interaction between the psychosocial and the spiritual dimensions. Both are crucial aspects of human development right across the lifespan, and the importance of this development does not diminish in the later years of life.

## Summary

In this chapter use of the terms 'religion', 'faith' and 'spirituality' have been examined, and a choice to use the term 'spiritual' in this study has been made. This choice is based on the chosen area for study, that of independently living older adults; the term spirituality seems to be more widely accepted and understood within this group. As well, the term spirituality is more widely understood within health, psychology, pastoral theology and pastoral care literature and practice. Spirituality is used in this study in a generic sense, but the focus of the study is on spirituality in Christians and other older people who do not acknowledge an affiliation with a faith group.

The relationship between the spiritual dimension, ageing and health has been examined. It is apparent from an examination of empirical studies that much more is known of the psychosocial dimension of ageing than the spiritual. This is an important area for further study.

# CHAPTER 4

# Meaning in life

## Spiritual development in ageing

### Meaning in ageing

Spirituality as defined in this study recognises the sphere of ultimate meaning in people's lives; the meaning which arises from the core of one's being.

Erikson's (1968; Erikson *et al.* 1986) concept of integrity versus despair seems correctly to accept the assumption that a task of ageing is to make sense of this life and our part in it; finding meaning is a critical element of what it is to be human. Clements (1990) considers two parts in the process of ageing: that of the years leading to the fourth quarter of life, and then the development that takes place in the final quarter of life.

### Meaning making

Rhodes and Reuther (in Ashbrook 1996) note that feminist theology takes the validity of one's own experience as the starting point of meaning making. This approach needs to be distinguished from the individuation of Western civilisation that asserts the autonomy and rights of the individual. Rather, it is in the experience of connecting between people, the so-called horizontal aspect of spiritual relationship, in which people make meaning. Thus we reflect who we are in relation to others; this hermeneutic comes from feminist theology.

Ashbrook makes the valid point that we do need community, and that this is a part of our making of self-identity and a means of making meaning in our lives: 'The belief of self-versus-others or self apart-from-others simply is a snare and delusion. Identity and intimacy are simultaneous and sequential, from the beginning and throughout the life cycle' (Ashbrook 1996, p.106). He suggests that there can be no alienating distance between people if we are to really be alive.

However, this view must not be taken to its extreme, that is, to deny the need for relationship with God, or a sense of transcendence or the otherness in one's life. The views of Ashbrook are important views, but are only one aspect of the equation: we need both God and human relationships. For some, relationship with others may be or become less important, while others have a far greater need for community.

## Spirituality in ageing

In Chapter 3 spirituality was considered in relation to psychosocial development and to health. Now it is asked, does spirituality change over the lifespan? Is the spiritual dimension, as is the psychosocial, subject to developmental changes over the lifespan? Is there a universal component to spirituality, for all people, of all religions and none? Do all people follow the same developmental stages?

If we take spirituality as that which lies at the core of the person's being, the most important and deepest thing in a person's life, then it becomes apparent that, as a person in older age becomes increasingly aware of the immanence of death, then a search for meaning in that life becomes an important factor for that person. We have been well aware of this over many years, in the naturally occurring reminiscences of the elderly and the desire to tell their life story to make sense of their life history. This it seems is not simply a desire to talk about old times, but an important task of ageing, part of preparing for death, of making sense of life in this world.

### Changes in spirituality in ageing

Regardless of the way of viewing age-related changes to spirituality, a number of authors have recognised the presence of such changes. Fischer (1985) writes of a necessary 'letting go' in order to be able to move forward; this she sees as the capacity to affirm life in the face of death. In a similar vein, Clements (1990) writes that a potential crisis of meaning comes in the young old, taking the form of, in some cases, conversion, or in more frequent cases, stripping or shedding. This process of shedding, he says, can be seen as a means of acquiring spiritual maturity in advancing years; but, he goes on, it does not necessarily result in greater spiritual integration – it may, on the contrary, lead to challenges that are not met.

Clements (1990) describes the process of 'stripping away' as the taking from the individual:

> those cultural and social values learned and practised in the earlier years...by the same society that had taught them and the same society that had rewarded their attainment in the younger years. (p.61)

This description is not incompatible with the disengagement theory set forth by Cummings and Henry (Havighurst *et al.* 1968). Here two options for successful psychosocial ageing are set forth. The one, the so-called activity theory, says older people respond to losing former roles such as work and parenting by substituting other roles. The other, the disengagement theory, sees the observed behavioural changes of ageing as being a mutual withdrawing from former social roles – 'mutual' meaning that it is accepted both by the older persons and by the society at large, and is of mutual benefit to the individual and society. Here Clements (1990) is suggesting a spiritual withdrawal from society in the process of ageing. What he is describing is somewhat different from the psychosocial perspective.

This process of 'stripping away' is described by Clements (1990) for the 'person formed by the Christian tradition…as a sacramental process of "emptying that leads to God"'. The stripping, he says, leads to 'an emptiness that signifies an inward and spiritual grace at the core'. On the other hand, he says, an emptiness that lacks any sacramental meaning may also be revealed. 'In either case, the emptiness that has always been present is now revealed in stark nakedness, no longer hidden by the social and cultural props that society has taken away.' This description of spiritual development in ageing has parallels within mysticism.

This may be a time when the older person struggles to relinquish past roles, things they may no longer be capable of doing, and comes to an acceptance of God in their lives. This last stage seems to be moving towards reaching a connectedness with God and preparing for 'going home' (MacKinlay 1997).

For 'able-old' people Vogel (1995, p.82) sees vocation in old age as a time to focus on the life journey, of focusing on faith 'in ways that make the world a better place'. She writes: 'It is a time for exploring issues and questions. No questions should be seen as off limits, and *living into the questions* can be experienced as more helpful than being given someone else's answers.' Vogel further suggests this to be a time of 'sharing family stories and traditions and for *binding the generations.*' (p.83). Thus it would seem that there are still tasks to be achieved in living into the later years.

### Spiritual development and meaning making in ageing: time left to live

Neugarten noted a change in time perspective among older adults of a transition from time since birth to time left to live (Neugarten 1968).

Frankl's (1984) ontology of time holds that 'having been' is still a mode of being, perhaps even the safest mode, particularly for older people. Frankl wrote of individuals having transitional meanings earlier in life, and coming to ultimate meanings in ageing. Butler (1963, in Neugarten 1968) also noted the stimulus to increased use of reminiscence could well be a time shift, a growing perception of shortness of time until death.

The concept of time is changing for older people. How individuals respond to this realisation of changing time may influence their sense of involvement with life and their sense of hope as they face that future. It is suggested that older adults may reach a point at which they become more attuned to facing the end of life; a sense, perhaps, of running out of time, and this sense may provoke a heightened search for final meanings within the individual. The person coming to this realisation has choices: to face the reality of time, or to deny; to continue to grow spiritually, or to stagnate; the opportunity for developing spiritual integrity and hope, or for final despair. It is in each case a personal decision.

Frankl (1984) wrote of his observations of experiences in the prison camps of the Second World War (p.59): 'As the inner life of the prisoner tended to become more intense, he also experienced the beauty of art and nature as never before.' And further, (p.87) Frankl wrote of the conditions of utter devastation in the camps, where the inmates suffered through lack of sleep, insufficient food and mental stress. Even then, he wrote, people had choices in how they reacted and behaved. It was clear that choices were still being made, the results of 'inner decisions', not of the camp influences alone.

Based on his observations, Frankl became convinced that, even under the most horrific circumstances, a person can decide what will become of him/herself, mentally and spiritually, and can maintain personal dignity in the events, even in a concentration camp. How the individual does this may still give the opportunity to add a deeper meaning to the person's life, perhaps to face troubles with courage, unselfishness and dignity. The alternative, Frankl says, is to lose basic human dignity and act more as an animal (Frankl 1984).

Frankl (1984, p.101) continues to explain the potential focus of meaning within the human being:

> This uniqueness and singleness which distinguishes each individual and gives a meaning to his existence has a bearing on creative work as much as it does on human love… [one who realises that] He knows the 'why' for his existence, and will be able to bear almost any 'how'.

Thus Frankl (p. 104) is able to say that: 'human life, under any circumstances, never ceases to have a meaning, and that this infinite meaning of life includes suffering and dying, privation and death.'

It seems that in later life there is for many people a conscious and deliberate search for meaning in life. Frankl (1984) writes (p. 121) of a will to meaning as distinct from the Freudian pleasure principle, or will to pleasure. He states, 'Man's (*sic*) search for meaning is the primary motivation in his life and not a "secondary rationalisation" or "instinctual drive"'. Frankl further states that:

> this meaning is unique and specific in that it must and can be fulfilled by him alone; only then does it achieve a significance which will satisfy his own *will* to meaning... Man, however, is able to live and even to die for the sake of his ideals and values. (p. 121)

There is no time within the human life cycle where there is greater variability between individuals than there is in ageing. The process of ageing will bring joy for some and suffering for others, yet how this is responded to by the individual will vary greatly and is part of the individual response to meaning that Frankl has written about. Each person's meaning is ultimately their own. This brings with it a responsibility for living life to one's potential. Yet, at the same time, each person is a part of a community and meanings grow out of community as well.

By way of explaining our spiritual life journeys, and coming to understand the final meanings of our lives, Frankl (1984) writes of watching a movie, and recognising that it is made up of:

> thousands upon thousands of individual pictures, and each of them carries a meaning, yet the meaning of the whole film cannot be seen before its last sequence is shown. However, we cannot understand the whole film without having first understood each of its components, each of the individual pictures. Isn't it the same with life? Doesn't the final meaning of life, too, reveal itself, if at all, only at its end, on the verge of death? And doesn't this final meaning, too, depend on whether or not the potential meaning of each single situation has been actualised to the best of the respective individual's knowledge and belief? (p. 168)

In this sense Frankl speaks of the sacredness of human life, of its specialness, and the regard we must take of life, even in the seemingly most hopeless of cases. His words illuminate the journey of life, how meaning is created, of all the pieces of one's life, but also, how it is only in the seeing of the whole that final meaning can be arrived at. In the current 'throw-away' society, his words bring a refreshing world view to the possibilities in the meaning of human life.

## Transcendence and the spiritual

When exploring the domain of the spiritual there remains an extra component, that of the transcendent, the mystery of otherness, the ultimate that lies beyond human understanding.

Moody (1995) uses the term 'spiritually advanced' to describe some older people from a cross-cultural study he reports conducted by Thomas. Moody asks if late-life spirituality is to be considered as a task of integrating the self, that is, bringing to wholeness or incorporating the earlier remembered self. Or, on the other hand, can it be loss or stripping of a 'personal history in favour of self-transcendence'? (p.92).

Just what is transcendence? According to Bellah (1969, p.85), in traditional theological terms, 'Transcendence is an attribute of God that indicates he is outside and independent of the world'. Perhaps, for application to our Western society today, his interpretation of transcendence may be an appreciation of a reality that is independent of ourselves, our societies and our cultures. Bellah notes that the main 'inner' dimension of transcendent reality has always been an inner experience of fulfilment rather than of need. The feelings that accompany it are of wholeness, rightness, and well-being. The experience is often acknowledged to be a conventional religious phenomenon but it seems that many people experience such experiences in a secular sense as well.

Frankl (1984) explains transcendence in the mode of the human need to search for meaning, to take responsibility, to reach outwards from themselves, to connect with others and with their environments. He says that human beings are incomplete in themselves, but in need of relationship with others. Self-transcendence requires that an individual 'forgets himself' and his/her interest is directed towards another. He says the more one is able to achieve this the more human one becomes. From a Christian perspective, this ultimate other is God, and the term transcendence is used in this context to refer to God being more than and outside the created world (Stott 1992). Frankl uses the term 'self-actualisation' of Maslow's (1970) hierarchy of human needs to describe this process of self-transcendence, remarking it is not 'an attainable aim at all,...the more one would strive for it, the more he would miss it' (Frankl 1984, p.133). That is, self-actualisation is only possible as a part of self-transcendence.

Self-transcendence may be regarded as part of the development tasks of ageing. Various authors, including Bellah (1969) and Fowler (1981), have referred to what Maslow has termed 'peak experiences' as examples of such transcendent experiences.

## Spirituality and mysticism in ageing

The practice of mysticism is one way in which people may seek to strip all other things in life away, to reach a close and intimate relationship with the living God.

Mysticism is defined by Moody (1995) as 'the deepening and intensification of the spiritual life to its utmost point' (p.99). It is unclear in this definition whether he sees mysticism as being an end state or a process. He distinguishes between spiritual development and cognitive development in later life, saying, 'the goal of spiritual growth in later life has nothing to do with 'late life learning' or enlarging the mind through travel, study, reflection, or even psychotherapy' (p.93). All of these activities, he writes, only replace one kind of mental activity with another.

Moody asserts that it is unwise to make mysticism the source of a one-sided '"pursuit of happiness" or "life-satisfaction," as gerontology would have it' (p.95). It must be noted that the central tradition of mysticism is, above all, a stripping away of illusion or consolation in favour of divine reality itself: 'Not my will, but yours be done' (Lk 22: 42b).

Moody raises an important issue in the process of ageing. It seems there is a real need for older people to be able to share the negative aspects of their lives too, by working through experiences of, for example, guilt, remorse, the fear of death or loss of cognitive function, so that spiritual growth and wholeness can occur. Too often, Moody says, counselling has sought to eliminate negative emotions, rather than supporting a person in walking through the grief, the loss and fears that might be a part of later life.

While the mystic tradition has always been seen as giving a supreme insight into the ultimate meaning of human existence, it is acknowledged that the mystical way is probably not open to everyone. There are many people who are not attracted to such a way; indeed, it may be that particular personality types have more affinity with mysticism than others. Even if, as most mystics have described their developing consciousness, as ways of moving 'towards wisdom as an integration of thought and feeling,' (Moody 1995, p.96) seeking wisdom through mysticism may not appeal to all.

Mysticism, while much neglected in twentieth-century Christianity, may yet have an important contribution to make in the spiritual development of older adults in the process of working from provisional meanings of life to final meanings. It would seem that the mystic process is related to the development of transcendence in ageing.

Moody (1995) offers a challenge to all engaged in research into ageing at this time:

> Taking mysticism and ageing seriously would mean a very far-reaching reassessment of the possible meaning of old age. One can think of old age as a kind of 'natural monastery' in which earlier roles, attachments, and pleasures are stripped away. From the monastic viewpoint, isolation is not 'loneliness,' nor is 'disengagement' a lack of charitable concern for the world, as the career of Thomas Merton demonstrated. To think of ageing in this way is very different from the celebratory revisioning of the life-course so common today as gerontologists try to remake the condition of the 'young-old' into a kind of extended middle age full of vigour, sexuality, curiosity, contributive roles, and all the rest. The mystical tradition offers a very different language and a very different ideal for the second half of life. (p.96)

A number of questions arise from Moody's writings. First, is mysticism a way of life that should be fostered more widely among older adults? Further, can aspects of mysticism be taken and used effectively in assisting numbers of elderly people to enrich their lives by coming to a deeper understanding of who they are and why they are and have been here on earth?

But what is the relationship between mysticism and personality type? Perhaps it is specifically people with certain personality types, for example, introvert types, who are attracted to and can benefit most from mysticism. Thus, it would not be appropriate to introduce it on a wide scale into our society. However, it may be that certain strategies used in mysticism may be developed with benefit for most older people. Spiritual autobiography is one of those strategies that may be developed and used far more widely.

## Reminiscence/Life review in ageing

How do elderly people perceive value and meaning in their lives? Meaning in life continues to be important into older adulthood. There are still developmental tasks in the psychosocial and spiritual dimensions right until the point of death. Reminiscence and review of life form an important aspect of this. Moody (1995), writing of mysticism, says that people may seek to integrate the mystical counter-tradition into the framework of ageing and the life journey, making it part of the continuing life story.

> A common approach to late-life mysticism takes the form of autobiography where the mystical quest is part of a spiritual journey. Today there is growing interest in reminiscence and life-review; some writers even speak of 'spiritual life-review' in the sense of an examination of conscience or repentance. The idea of life-review must be traced back originally to Protestant spirituality, and the spiritual significance of life-review has clear importance for ageing. (p.94)

Of spiritual autobiography Morgan (1995) says, 'a hunger exists (among older adults) for a spirituality focused on meaning-making, that goes beyond what is offered by traditional religious structures' (p.3). Among the elderly residents of nursing homes interviewed as part of a study of spiritual needs (MacKinlay 1992) the frail elderly informants were, for the most part, only too eager to share their spiritual journeys. For many, they ack-nowledged, it was the first time they had been able to share their fears and longings with someone willing to take the time to listen. In fact, it seemed that while they had been able to share the good things from their previous lives it was more difficult to share the griefs and fears.

The terms 'reminiscence', 'life review' and 'spiritual autobiography' are sometimes used in different ways by different authors. The subtle dis-tinctions between the terms and their functions in ageing are illuminated below.

Much work has been done in reminiscence and life review in the past couple of decades. Story telling as therapy is becoming increasingly recog-nised in health-related fields (Gustafson 1994). Story is an important aspect for many ageing people. In the past, it is probable that older people were given more opportunities to reminisce, as this was a way of passing knowledge and wisdom from one generation to another. Gutmann (1987, in Bornat 1994) argues that Western societies have lost a sense of culture.

Reminiscence has been identified as both a valuable and often naturally occurring phenomenon of ageing. Neugarten remarked on the degree of increasing use of reflection and restructuring of experience engaged in by middle aged persons. In one study (Neugarten 1968) she suggested that this may be a preliminary to the reminiscence that occurs in older adults. A number of studies during the past two decades have focused on reminiscence from a life-review perspective as individual therapy and, probably more frequently, as group work (Bornat 1994; Haight and Webster 1995). Reminiscence has been studied mostly from a psychological perspective. It seems less has been done from a spiritual perspective.

Reminiscence may be a critical part of ageing, connected with Erikson's (1986) final stage of psychosocial ageing: integrity versus despair. Coleman (1994) studied naturally occurring reminiscence. Wong and Watt (in Bornat 1994), considered types of reminiscence, distinguishing six different forms: integrative, instrumental, narrative, transmissive, escapist and obsessive.

Erikson *et al.* (1986) found with his interviews of octogenarians (p.69) that as his informants distilled from their past what they viewed as essential to their future, many turned to religion, both in the context of their current beliefs and those held over a lifetime. For them, religion has been a force around which life's decisions and work had been taken. He saw them being able to face the future, that may hold many uncertainties, in the context of their religious beliefs. Some of his group spoke of the importance of attending church, regardless of whether they attended or not.

A ground-breaking paper on the place of reminiscence in ageing was written by Robert Butler in 1963. He recognised from his clinical experience as a psychiatrist and from the literature that reminiscence was not just a regression into early life by older people unable to face the present. In his paper Butler distinguished between the process of life review and reminiscence, saying that life review is a looking-back process, set in motion by looking forward to death, and it potentially proceeds towards personality reorganisation. On the other hand, he says that reminiscence is a part of life review, but the two are not synonymous, a view supported by Burnside (1988). Burnside noted that nurses have not differentiated between the two terms, and the differences are poorly understood.

Butler (1963) proposed that reminiscence in older adults is a universal phenomenon, that it 'contributes to the occurrence of certain late-life disorders, particularly depression, and that it participates in the evolution of such characteristics as candour, serenity, and wisdom among certain of the aged' (p.486). Thus the outcome of this stage may be either integrity or a sense of despair, as Erikson *et al.* (1986) has recognised.

Prior to the time of Butler's (1963) writing, reminiscence in aged people had been regarded a symptom of psychological dysfunction. At best it was viewed as a means of escapism from the reality of ageing. Butler, however, postulated that reminiscence in ageing is 'characterised by the progressive return to consciousness of past experiences, and, particularly, the resurgence of unresolved conflicts; simultaneously, and normally, these revived experiences and conflicts can be surveyed and reintegrated' (p.487). Butler saw the impetus for reminiscence to be the realisation of approaching death, and the realisation of one's own vulnerability. Further, he saw it as affected by the lifelong unfolding of the individual's character.

### Outcomes of reminiscence and life review

Butler (1963) noted that in his experience life review may proceed without obvious outward signs; at other times, perhaps because there are more unresolved life conflicts, it is much more apparent. In its milder form nostalgia and mild regret may be seen, while in the more severe form anxiety, guilt, despair and depression may be evident. In the extreme it may even end in suicide.

Coleman (1986) noted in his work that a number of his sample had referred to unpleasant feelings associated with reminiscence as well as to having experienced pleasant feelings. He described four categories of reminiscers: those who reminiscence, those who were non-reminiscers and, within each of these groups, reminiscers who found it valuable and those who did not; and, for the non-reminiscers, those who saw no point in reminiscing and those who were troubled and avoided any reminiscence. Coleman found those who were troubled by memories had lower morale than the other groups. Coleman's (1986) study appeared to focus more on the use and value of reminiscence as a strategy rather than as a developmental task of ageing, as in this study. His work is thus of importance to understanding the manner in which older people have been using reminiscence naturally.

### Using life review or reminiscence

There appears to be some confusion regarding the two terms and the application of the modalities in practice (Burnside et al. 1994). Burnside (1988) states that life review should be conducted by qualified therapists, having a background in special education, gerontology and usually one other discipline such as psychiatry, psychogeriatric nursing, pastoral counselling, clinical psychology or social work. Of reminiscence she notes that it may include 'bits and pieces of a life' (p.668). The listener need not be a professional. Burnside regards reminiscence as a psychosocial intervention, and life review as a psychoanalytically based intervention. Further, she notes that reminiscence may not focus on meaning, whereas life review does, and it assists the individuals in the resolution of conflicts and guilt, and may help to prepare the person for death.

Therefore, according to Burnside (1994, p.164) life review is regarded as a developmental stage of ageing, while reminiscence cannot be such because of its overall lack of specificity, that is, it may be focused or may not, depending on the circumstances. Burnside notes that 29 types of reminiscence, some overlapping, have been identified. The benefits depend on the type.

## Functions of reminiscence and life review

Life review can be regarded as a developmental task of ageing (Kimble 1990, p.124): 'Life review provides a configuration, a mosaic of meaning in our lives, and facilitates the next stage which includes death.' Further, Kimble notes that life review is a normal and natural activity of humans; it is seen in every culture. Spiritual life review, with other techniques, enable individuals to express their life in terms of a relationship with God (Ellor *et al.* 1990).

In Burnside *et al.*'s (1994) review of empirical studies (p.166) she noted that one function of reminiscence is to reduce a sense of vulnerability in the individual. Burnside (1988) states that reminiscence work is a 'modality in which nurses excel' (p.646). At this time Burnside reviewed nine research projects on reminiscence carried out by nurses. Six of these were conducted using residents of nursing homes, one a day care centre, and the last, older people attending a nursing clinic. None of these considered life review specifically from a spiritual perspective.

According to Coleman (1986) there are four functions of reminiscence: the review of life, the story-telling role, the creation of a meaningful myth and the maintenance of self-esteem (p.14). When the spiritual dimension is considered, it appears there is yet another function of reminiscence, that of meaning making. While this may closely resemble the creation of meaningful myth, it would appear to go deeper than that, to the core of ultimate meaning for the particular person; it is a summation of who they are and why they have been here.

Coleman suggests that the sense of a well-lived earlier life may be important in helping the older person facing decreasing capabilities in ageing to accept their present status in life. Again, this may be related to Erikson *et al.*'s (1986) development of integrity in ageing. But while identity maintenance may be important, it seems that, from the spiritual perspective, it becomes more than that. It seems that the life review is a seeking to deal with past events and experiences and to seek wholeness in life, to seek ultimate meanings in life and to come to a completion of living. Thus it is a case of not only identity maintenance but also spiritual growth and final meaning of life. In the process, the person may well come to a sense of self-worth and integrity.

Erikson et al. (1986), in a study of octogenarians, noted that many of the participants, on reflection over their lives, expressed satisfaction with the choices they had made in marriage, how they had raised their children and the kinds of work they had done. They made the point, however, that present satisfaction with past life didn't mean lifelong contentment. The researchers were able to verify this from data of earlier studies with the same individuals, with evidence of 'profound unhappiness and restlessness' in earlier times. They suggested a number of possibilities for these findings: first, that they were bringing 'a sense of integrity into scale with a sense of despair'; second, perhaps this was a process of 'pseudo-integration', that is, the construction of a satisfactory life view arrived at by denying elements from the past found unacceptable. As well, they suggested informants may have wanted to maintain a measure of privacy from interviewers they may have regarded as strangers. Here it is hard to see this as being so, in view of the fact that these people had been involved with research for many years and had apparently already divulged considerable personal information. Finally, they suggested that these omissions may reflect a lifelong process of 'reintegration and recasting' in which past events have taken on new meanings and have been put into perspective with the whole of life experience. There is a sense too that the individual has come to an acceptance of the inability to alter things now past – in a sense a decision made in the wisdom of ageing.

A further term used in this area is 'guided autobiography'. Birren and Deutchman (1994) say that a positive relationship has been found between the amount of reminiscence and the degree of ego integrity (or self-integration) achieved. They write that guided autobiography enables the older person to recall and relive a wide range of personal experiences; this too is a way for older people to see how much they have survived and transcended during their lives. Birren and Deutchman point to the value of guided autobiographies being conducted through groups. A valuable part and by-product of the group work can be the overcoming of loneliness by the establishment of new relationships through the group process.

For those who do not have a positive outlook towards reminiscence, Coleman (1986) suggests that short-term counselling may be helpful to people whose thoughts are dominated by regretful memories. Indeed, it is important to consider that while often it is not possible to change the circumstances of ageing, the individual's perception of their circumstances based on their past *can* be changed. For some this may include blame for past actions, or guilt, justified or unjustified. In some instances negative memories may be highlighted by depression. For those who are bereaved and show a 'persistent inhibited or painful reminiscence…[it] is a good indicator of the need for grief therapy' (Coleman 1986, p.158). He has further made note of the value of reminiscence used in psychogeriatric institutions, leading to greater socialisation of those involved, including higher self-esteem and behavioural improvements.

Coleman (1986) suggests the counsellor needs to hear the person out, to provide the necessary catharsis and to finally assist the person to move from a sense of guilt to one of forgiveness. This moves into the arena of the spiritual dimension; underlying the psychosocial is the spiritual with its core values of acceptance and forgiveness. So guilt should be addressed not only from the psychosocial, but also with strategies from the spiritual, perhaps of a religious and ritual nature. Coleman notes the importance of the Christian confession in this regard.

Much has been done in recent years to develop group work in reminiscence, both within institutions and in independent living situations (Coleman 1986; Bornat 1994; Burnside 1994). While noting that life review has become a familiar concept in the study of ageing in recent years, Coleman (1994) commented that the value of life review counselling has yet to be determined. Still, he notes that the satisfaction gained by many who participate in reminiscence is beyond doubt. He notes four points to be highlighted in types of reminiscence: finding positive memories; confronting painful memories; empowering memories inhibited by grief; and encouraging non-narcissistic memories. Spiritual autobiography can effectively include such types and then explore final life meanings through these.

Kimble (1990, p.120) says, 'The individual is accepted as one responsible for his or her life story and the telling of it'. Allowing the person to tell their story, being with the person and listening are vital components of pastoral care. In the telling of the story, the person may express memories of unfulfilled self-expectations. Guilt may be a result of such perceived failures of earlier life. Memories of guilt, but also memories of positive aspects of the past are carried forward.

## The possibilities of suicide

Butler (1963) considered that some older people facing their past life events may find these too distressing to cope with and too difficult to communicate to others, saying: 'It is often extremely difficult for the reviewer to communicate his insights because of the unacceptability to him' (p.491). It may also be difficult for this individual to comprehend the meaning of these events. Butler noted that in the most tragic of cases the people may feel there is no other way but suicide, and this may in some way account for the raised rates of suicide in older age.

Currently suicide rates are higher for the oldest males, those more than 85 years of age, having increased from 37.0 to 50.0 per 100 000 in the ten years to 1990 (Hassan 1995, p.67). Hassan writes that preliminary evidence from South Australia suggests that for older people, particularly men, suicide is often planned and rational. Further, 'Suicide for many of them means not an unwillingness to live or inability to live but a willingness to die'. The fact that they have survived to old age demonstrates their will to live to an old age; but it is suggested by Hassan that the economic, psychosocial and health problems of old age 'become unbearable' (p.66); perhaps these in turn become spiritual distress in the older person. In the light of Butler's comments above, it would seem that the spiritual dimension is also important in the decisions of such older people to commit suicide.

## A move to further work with spiritual life review

Kimble (1990) describes life review as a 'phenomenological approach in seeking to understand the "lived world" of a person'. Each of us has a unique experience of life, not lived by any other person. We can, as it were, only be privileged to catch glimpses of the 'lived world' of another human being. The spiritual focus of life review in particular, 'Chronicles not only a person's encounter with life, but with God... The patterns of our lives are shaped by the meaning we give to what we remember' (Kimble 1990, p.125). Further, Kimble writes that we continue to 'create' ourselves until the very point of our death.

So far, much of the work in life review has focused on the psychological and comparatively little on the spiritual or faith journey aspect. Some of the case material presented by Coleman (1986) has included material of a religious nature or on meaning in life, but a conscious presentation of the spiritual has not been demonstrated in his work. In contrast, both Kimble *et al.* (1995) and Clements (1990) have examined the spiritual life review and described it as a task of ageing. As well, Morgan (1995, p.3) notes that the faith dimension has often been missed in the life review process. He suggests that religious communities have a 'unique responsibility' to address the spiritual needs of older adults. Morgan emphasises the importance to the church community of the sharing and preserving of the stories of older people, remarking that the use of these stories may help churches to become 'communities full of vibrant life' (p.4).

An important difference between the life review of psychosocial interest, or the identity-maintaining reminiscence and the spiritual life review or, as it is sometimes called, the spiritual autobiography is that the spiritual dimension brings the elements of the story into a view of where God has been present in that story. For example, where does the person connect with that particular experience? Where is/was God in a particular experience? What needs are there for reconciliation with others, with God? For confession? For forgiveness? It is in this context that this study seeks to explore the spirituality of older adults.

## Learning in later life

Life review, although a naturally occurring phenomenon for many older people, may still need affirmation and development in the context of society of the twenty-first century. Some older people may well need to learn the skills necessary for effective life review, and in particular for spiritual life review. Of course, learning in later life is not restricted to life review, important as that may be. There are many opportunities for learning and growing spiritually for older adults today. The overall aim for learning in later life stated by Vogel (1984) is the nurture of spiritual well-being as it can be enabled through religious education (p.144).

One organisation that seems to have set out to provide for the specific learning needs of older adults is the Shepherd Center of North America. They set out to provide specific ministry for older adults living independently in the community, in Kansas City. They identified four areas for intervention with these older adults (over 65 years). First, the need for life maintenance; second, life enrichment; third, life reconstruction; and fourth, life transcendence (Vogel 1984).

## Summary

*The literature in this chapter has been examined to explore the place of meaning in life for older adults with an emphasis on the relationship between spiritual development and meaning making in ageing. The important concept of transcendence and the spiritual dimension has been considered in the light of mysticism as another way of understanding the development of increasing interiority in older adults. While the ability to come to terms with and transcend the difficulties of life is probably an important aspect of ageing, and mysticism may be one way of developing these skills, it is acknowledged that for a number of reasons mysticism is not an option for everyone.*

*The importance and widespread use of reminiscence in ageing was examined, clarifying the terms of reminiscence, life review, spiritual autobiography and life review therapy. The application and usefulness of these concepts in caring for older adults was outlined from the literature. The wealth of available literature on the psychological aspects of these areas, but the lack of empirical material on the spiritual aspect highlights the need for further study, to examine the spiritual component in reminiscence, and life review and the relationship of these with the development of spiritual integrity in ageing.*

# CHAPTER 5

# Types of ultimate meaning and images of God

## Ultimate meaning

In this study in-depth interviews were used to tap into themes of ultimate meaning for these older adults. Ultimate meaning for each person was, as spirituality is defined for this study, 'that which lies at the core of one's being', in other words what the individual attached most meaning to in their lives.

The material from in-depth interviews in this study allowed an exploration of each person's image of God, or sense of the other, as well as other aspects of spirituality. A life review of each person's spiritual and religious development was included in the interviews. It is contended that the image a person has of God (or gods), or indeed, the absence of such images, will play an important part in the whole of life experience for that individual. Several questions were raised in the review of the literature. Does a person's image of God change across a lifespan? How might the God image held by the person be related to or, in the absence of such images, what other factors might be relevant to, the hope that an older person may claim in difficulties, such as suffering, loss, and/or facing death?

## Images of God

The image we each have of God is most likely formed by our life experiences and learning in childhood. Greeley (1973) suggests our image of God is conditioned by the circumstances of life, and in particular by culture. It is helpful to consider the images of God from an anthropological stance, as it brings to awareness the variety of images of God held by different cultures. The images held in general are those that are consistent with the understanding of the people for a particular culture. The image of God held by individuals includes an image of God's attitude towards them. These images are drawn out in the myths of the culture. Greeley notes some of these myths, including the nature religions, where the religious rites must be carried out perfectly to placate the gods so that punishment will not follow. The forgetful god who would help humans, if he remembered, needs rites performed to remind him of his relationship with humans. Yet another divine attitude is described by Greeley (1969) as the tragic tradition, where:

> the gods are seen as implacably bent on keeping man in his place, and man becomes a powerless plaything subject to the whims of the gods. Then there is the deistic god who set the whole operation of the universe in motion but then apparently lost interest in the project to busy himself about other things. (p.102)

Further, Greeley notes: 'The final stage of the deity is the Jewish and Christian one in which God is a jealous lover seen as intervening in history in pursuit of man with whom he has for some reason become emotionally involved' (1969, p.102). In a multicultural society such as Australia in the early twenty-first century, it would seem reasonable to suppose that individuals could hold a variety of images of God, depending on their cultural origins and also on their life experiences and religious education. A variety of images of God may even exist among Christians of various denominations, as well as for different religious faiths and sects. The image of God that a person holds in a post-industrial society may be coloured by scientific beliefs and myths based on the media and hearsay information about a particular religion as well as personal experience.

## Ultimate meaning in life

The first theme arose naturally from the line of questioning on spirituality, or ultimate meaning, in life of each individual. Each person was asked: 'Who or what gives greatest or deepest meaning to your life?' Most people were able to isolate this ultimate meaning to one or two components, for instance, God and relationship with others. Often this 'other' was a spouse, if there was one. This theme arose readily from the data, as not one of the informants denied having meaning in their lives. In fact, some really wanted to expand on the topic of meaning. Some of the informants acknowledged multiple centres of meaning in their lives, such as relationship with others, music, art, the environment. A sense of 'otherness' was also acknowledged by a number of informants. It is not surprising that there was a high level of response to this question of human meaning, because humans are characterised by their ability and propensity to attach meaning to objects and people in their lives.

Meaning is both a function of learning taken on from socialisation into the particular culture, and the individual's interaction with that. Meaning is open to review and change at different points of the lifespan.

In understanding the spiritual dimension it has been said that people attach provisional meanings to events in their lives as these occur, but that in the process of ageing these meanings are re-examined in the light of further growth and learning across the lifespan and final, or ultimate, meanings are constructed (Frankl 1984). Thus in the latter part of the lifespan, as people are coming to a stage of review of meanings and reframing of meanings, reminiscence becomes common and can be regarded as a normal part of ageing. It has been said that reminiscence is a developmental task of the final part of life, and in particular of the spiritual dimension.

It would seem that final meanings continue to be adjusted and re-formed right until the point of death. Thus it is evident that none of the informants in this study had reached end or final meanings when interviewed; it must therefore be acknowledged that further refinement and development related to their spiritual dimension would continue for each of these respondents.

## Image of God or sense of other

The responses varied widely. I had deliberately chosen to include a range of informants, from some who had a close relationship with God to others who did not acknowledge the existence of God. Included is the way they articulate their image of God and how they respond to this. As the informants in this study were either from a Christian background or had no major faith affiliation at the time of interview, the image of God focused on here is in line with informant information. Thus what is described here is a Christian dimension, or for other informants a non deity-centred dimension of ultimate meaning in the individual's life.

From earliest times humans have sought to bring God into their own image, to produce a God of a size that is comfortable. To name God was a concern of Old Testament times: for example, Moses, who asked God 'If they [the people] ask me, What is his name? What shall I say to them?' (Exod. 3: 13) and Jacob, 'Please tell me your name' (Gen. 32: 29). Their requests were not fulfilled, at least not in the ways they asked. In a post-industrial, multifaith and multicultural society there are many images to be had of God, including that there is no God. The stories of the informants in this study exhibit a variety of God images, as one might expect.

The searching that some of the informants have engaged in at an intellectual level shows the difficulty of really understanding who God is even by a lifetime of intellectual activity. Just when they seem to grasp one picture of God, they are confronted by another. Carroll and Dyckman (1986) say that in Christian spirituality in mid life the task is to discard our images and definitions of God because we cannot contain or control God with any words we would use in description. The informants in this study have already moved through mid life. Some have acknowledged their own experiences and difficulties of trying to confine God to an image, while others seem to have accepted the possibility of living with a degree of mystery and a changing image of God. Yet, for all this, the very human search for meaning continues.

## A personal relationship with Jesus

Ten informants acknowledged some type of personal relationship with Jesus (not all of these are discussed under this heading). Most of these informants acknowledged making a personal commitment to 'give their lives to Jesus' at some point.

Sylvia made a personal commitment to Jesus at age 14 years. Now, she says, she has a daily walk with God that is not only a comfort but also a guide and support. Doris, who like several others in the study came to a personal commitment in mid life said that deepest meaning for her is 'in my relationship with God, through Jesus...it seems to be the backdrop to my whole life' and:

> for me God is just that loving one, who cares about me, who loves me, who's given me all that I have, that's close to me, and I see God a lot through creation, and all that's around me, and people.

Edith has a personal relationship with God and she explained: 'I can sit down and talk to God'. Her prayer is addressed to Jesus. She questions the place of evil in the world and how this may fit with her idea of God (interview soon after the Port Arthur Massacre) acknowledging a lack of answers. This woman had many regrets from earlier life, but following a cardiac arrest she turned around in her attitudes and her faith. She now regularly attends church and 'doesn't hate anymore'.

*A God of love*

For others the central image of God was as a God of love. As the Christian message sets forward a strong focus on the love of God, it could be expected that more informants would have spoken of this aspect of God. For a number it was implicit in their stories of the relationship they had with God, through Jesus, but few spoke explicitly of God's love.

Hugh described a profound spiritual element in life. He continually searches for meaning in life, and to know God. But, he says, 'God is unknowable, I don't see any evidence of God in the world. The last evidence of God appearing in the world…was Christ'. Of the existence of a personal god he says, 'I can't say that, although I pray to a personal God sometimes, hoping someone's listening'. He remarked that the spiritual force in the world is love.

This man continues to intentionally search to know more of God, more about God. His search is a deep and largely cognitive search. He described having an image of a spiritual force of love; this image also contained a sense of mystery.

*Creator God*

A number of the informants described God as a creator God. George said 'I mean all that [creation and the universe and God's part in it] is impossible, so you say to yourself, the whole thing is impossible, and yet I mean I choose to believe that it's there.'

Eva also is aware of a creator God: 'God is not in long flowing robes and a white beard, God is life.' She sees God in everything, 'plants, the trees, the ground, the earth… God is part of the world, is the world.' 'And if you hurt that – you're hurting Him.' She also saw God returning as a judge. This woman, at 83, has not attended church for many years; she has developed an image of God that underpins her everyday life, an image she has built through a great deal of reading in a variety of areas, including Christian, Buddhist and general secular literature. She holds a complex understanding of God that includes God as Creator.

Mary also spoke of God as creator: 'well there must have been a creator, I just know, now well, he'd have to take me and surprise me…the world really is a beautiful place'. This woman has never had any contact with a church, she remembers her family living very 'religiously', and not being allowed to go to the pictures or do things others children did. She remembers her father reading the Bible to them at home. She has developed a deep spirituality in later life, tied mainly to her love of nature and concern for other people.

## A God of strength and power

Another image of God is that of a God of strength and power. Vera acknowledged God as a source of strength in her life. She had a deep sense of God acting in her life at particular times of crisis and expressed gratitude to God for her well-being.

Yet another aspect of God that fits with strength and power is the greatness and majesty of God. Lisa expressed a sense of awe of God: 'And I find it uncomfortable to talk about God, just any time. In a way, I've always thought God is too great to be brought into trite things, and this I've always found uncomfortable.'

George recognises there is someone in charge: 'It is Providence that has the hand in what happens to us.' This man continues to read and study about his faith; he also acknowledges the power of God.

Ann reported her image of God: 'He's an all-powerful being' and 'the only real insight we get into God is from Christ'. 'If you believe in Christ, you have to believe in what he said about God.' She also expressed her gratitude to God: 'I think you should thank God for what you've got.'

## A simple acceptance of God

These informants have not seemed to want to question God, nor to study and search for understanding of God. Yet they seemed to accept God as being there. They seemed able to accept the presence of God without the cognitive search that some other informants made. Dawn said that she didn't want to get into theology, while Daisy described God as 'just like a security blanket, more than anything, something to hang on to'.

Stan expressed a simple, unquestioning faith. He said he believes God exists, he believes in Jesus Christ. He sees God in control and doesn't question his faith. This informant was a widower and discussed even his recent loss of his wife in very objective and factual terms.

Dawn says that faith gives her real meaning in life and her simple acceptance is evident in these remarks:

> Well, I felt things got so bad in my life, especially after my mother died, which is 28 years this year. I'd be at a really low point and I used to say to myself, well if God wants me to keep going He will, and He did.

Her image of God: 'Well it's a strong spirit isn't it? It's a spiritual thing...
that's passed down into the world, from suffering... Christ died for us, and
that was the ultimate sacrifice and someone was prepared to do that, so, you
know...' She went on: 'I find that religion, theology, suffering's not
something I get into.'

### God is there, but what in fact is it?

A number of informants found it very difficult to articulate a concept of an
image of God. Lisa says it is hard to define God, yet she has a sense of God
being there. She turns to God, 'not just when I want something'. She accepts
the existence of Christ: 'God is there, but what in fact is it?'. Win finds there
is a sense of both acceptance and mystery for her in her belief, as she
acknowledges a sense of awe of God and God as Creator. Her support comes
ultimately from God.

### Distant from God

These informants recognised no personal relationship with God, in fact,
there was a sense of distance between them and God.

Flora says she feels distant from God and keeps God in the background;
this seems to be since her husband died. On the other hand, she remarked: 'I
would never ever say that I didn't believe, I couldn't cope with that at all,
perhaps I'm one of these people that keep God in the background for when I
need him, which is not very good.' She explained: 'I had great faith until my
husband was ill, he was only 49 when he was first taken ill and we knew the
cards were on the table, that he'd only live about five years, and I began to
wonder then...'. She asked: 'What exactly is the meaning of faith? What is it
that you can hang onto? I mean why are we here? I don't believe it all just
happened. I don't know how it happened, but I don't know.'

Mary sees religion as the cause of wars. Her childhood teaching:

Dad read the Bible and everything...but I was never game to ask, and I
thought since nobody's been back to tell us what is in this, I mean, they say
Jesus Christ came back. Then there are so many different religions in the
world now aren't there, it really makes you, it can make you a bit sceptical.

### A God of my own

In the present multicultural and multifaith society a number of the older
people in this study have lived their lives outside the organised church. One

of these is Helen. She seems to have reached a point now where she has constructed her own religion, a combination of different backgrounds, including various Eastern religions. A parallel to this can be seen in 'Sheilaism' written of by Bellah *et al.* (1985), where the evidence is that individualism is resulting in people constructing their own religions. This informant feels she is 'in church all the time because God's within me, why do I need to go to church and listen to a sermon from the Bible that I can read myself and…that is the stage I've got to'. This type of belief is at the same time both inclusive, in that it is tolerant of all religions, and exclusive, as it is so individualistic that it cannot be truly shared by any other person.

Helen explained that she believes we are all 'sparks of the divine fire … everybody, every soul…is a portion of God's mind…'. Further, she says, 'God is the great spirit, now basically our energy comes from that, but on a grander scale' and 'I conceive God primarily as the first cause of thought…'. She acknowledged a belief in angels: 'I think we've all got guardian angels'. And of Jesus she said, 'I think you know that Jesus was mostly to teach us to love and that the kingdom of heaven is within us'. This informant had studied widely. Coming from a church background as a child, in a rural community, she has had little contact with any formal religion in adulthood but she has continued to read very widely.

### A philosophy of life, no concept of God, responsibility for well-being rests with the individual

Still others saw themselves as being self-sufficient and having no need for a God or source outside themselves in their lives. Ultimate meaning for them came in other ways, including the need for being strong within themselves.

Since her husband became ill Betty has been re-evaluating meaning in her life. She has no real concept of God. She says her idea of God is more a philosophy of life, based on an upbringing that included the Christian ethic. Her concept of afterlife is remembering people after they have died.

Beryl also seemed to live from a philosophy of life. She said her energy comes from being healthy, and from her friends, family and the activities she is 'immersed' in. She says she does not allow fears to surface. 'If there were a real crisis…you don't have any power over that.' She remarked that she doesn't like weddings or funerals. This informant has a definite sense of her own responsibility for her well-being in life. She does not believe in God. She said: 'Well I have a being…there is a personality there, and a lot of it's in response to others, as people see you, but a lot of it is in what you are yourself.' In relation to a concept of God she acknowledged the complexities of life and the mystery of being:

> In the rational thinking you know sort of first causes and this sort of thing. I mean one can contemplate that but as far as you know, beneficent or maleficent being no, no being. I don't think anybody knows, I mean neither scientists, theologians or [anyone] you know… I think we're just here and, in an enormous universe and what's always puzzling and rather paradoxical is that we are so small and so insignificant and yet every person, not only me I mean every person is so complex.

Another informant, Diane, struggling to find an image of God, said: 'I don't know what it is, but there's something out there that's some force that we just don't understand.' She added, 'I sometimes feel I'd like to believe.'

Even these informants who did not want to acknowledge a god, did acknowledge some sense of being that they could not fully understand, and perhaps even here there is room for care of the spiritual dimension, meeting such people at their point of need.

## Ultimate meaning: family/environment/arts/work

Respondents stated they found their main source of meaning in life from a number of aspects, some from God, others from relationships, through nature and the environment, some from the arts, and others still through their work. These aspects are examined in Chapter 7, 'Response to the Ultimate'. Meaning through human relationship seemed to be a major theme for most of the informants, therefore it is treated as a separate theme.

## The images of God identified in this study: pastoral implications

In working with older adults it is vital to discover where each individual is on their journey of faith, to ask what is the image of God held by that person. This is important both to avoid the mistake of projecting one's own belief system on to another and, second, one can never be sure what kind of faith or philosophy guides an individual's life unless one first takes the opportunity to find out.

A further crucial point is made here. As the spiritual dimension is a critical aspect of the life journey for so many older adults, it is vitally important for health carers working with older people to be aware of their own spirituality so that they may avoid the danger of projecting their own belief system, or lack of a belief system, on to those they care for. It can only be from a point of self-awareness that health professionals can effectively assist older people to both identify their spiritual needs and to address these needs.

### The individual's image of God and health care

It seems that the image of God held by each individual is an important starting place, both for that person and for any health-related care. The God image will underlie the hopes and attitudes the person brings to any new situation, be it a situational crisis or a developmental stage in life. In a way this could be described as one's spiritual portfolio, and it consists of much more than simply having a religious affiliation or not.

This God image will colour the opportunities open to the individual. The person who has an intimate relationship with a loving God will tend to be able to let go more of personal difficulties, while a person who believes in a punitive God will tend to see punishment as part of life and perhaps believe that there is no way out from things that they have done in the past that they perceive were wrong. Such individuals may find it impossible to deal with issues of guilt. Forgiveness is an important factor related to healing for those with a belief system that acknowledges such a possibility, for example Christianity.

### No image of God

Some informants had no image of God or a god. For some there was a philosophy of life, perhaps built on a Christian ethic, for others there was no concept of 'otherness' or god at all. The position of these individuals also needs to be considered in providing for pastoral care. These people still struggle with meaning in life, because they are human beings and life meaning is common to all people.

### Other sources of ultimate meaning in informants' lives

A higher being may not be the source of ultimate meaning for some informants. Most informants considered relationship with others to give ultimate meaning to their lives. Some acknowledged multiple centres of meaning. For some, in this study, nature and the environment were important; for others, music, writing, reading and the arts formed important aspects of ultimate meaning.

It is noted that work was not one of the forms of ultimate meaning for any of this group. Some of these people had enjoyed most interesting and rewarding careers prior to retiring; but none of these were mentioned as the source of ultimate meaning for members of this group, although one former academic still kept in touch with the latest developments in her field of study. The group was small, thus too much cannot be made of this finding. It would be interesting to see whether other older people, who do choose to work into later life, find meaning in life continues to be drawn from work or vocation. It seems that in an ageing society this may become so, for some at least. This too could be an area for further study. It would probably be preferable to wait until further effects of changing health status and changing roles in older people are evident in larger numbers of older people in society.

## *Summary*

*Images of God, or sense of 'other', varied greatly among this group of informants. It is important not to make assumptions of the personal belief systems of others at any point in the lifespan, and particularly so in older adults. Each faith journey is an individual one; the way older people respond to the Ultimate depends on so many factors. These factors include: their initial teaching within their family of origin; their experiences as children, including early formal education and exposure to religious education; their life experiences, including relationships their family experiences, work, and leisure activities. And as important in forming their image of God as anything else are the types of crises they have encountered in life and their responses to them.*

*Those who work with older adults need to be spiritually self-aware, avoiding projecting their own beliefs on to those they care for. Further, they need to be able to meet the individual at his or her point of need.*

# CHAPTER 6

# Response to ultimate meaning in life

## Religious

### Response to ultimate meaning

No study of spirituality would be complete without considering the religious dimension of spirituality. Religious practices form an important aspect of how people respond to the Ultimate in their lives. However, it must be stated that religious practices do not constitute the whole of human spirituality. Indeed, many people do not follow any overtly religious practices in their lives, but they may still acknowledge their spiritual dimension, worked out in other ways.

How do people respond to ultimate meaning? Augustine wrote that this search is ultimately one that culminates in finding God. 'The human heart is restless until it finds its rest in thee' (Augustine, Confessions Book 1, in Chadwick 1991).

Modern-day psychological study seems to recognise this same search, the need for affirmation and completeness. Erikson (1968, p.714) writes of the human need for 'regular and mutual affirmation and certification' which, he says, exists in the infant and continues through life. This search for reality, meaning and connection with ultimate reality is acknowledged as a universal human characteristic.

How do people respond to ultimate meaning? It is a response that moves necessarily from within the person to another in some way. The use of ritual is one way that humans may respond to what has ultimate meaning for them. The terms 'ritual' and 'ritualisation' need exploring, for use in this study.

Erikson (1968) sees ritualisation on the one hand, as a process that begins with mother–child interactions, such as facial expressions and response to these, and on the other as a need, that, once aroused, 'will reassert itself in every stage of life as a hunger for ever new, ever more formalised and more widely shared ritualisation and rituals which repeat such face-to-face "recognition" of the hoped for' (p.714).

Once having come to an understanding of meaning in one's life, then meaning is attached to various symbols, which become representative of meaning for that person. This is particularly important for the spiritual dimension, where evidence of meaning is often internalised. Thus the person wishes to make a response to what it is that brings meaning into their life. Various objects come to represent this meaning and, over a period of time, the object itself may trigger the experience which it represents.

Meaning is both a function of learning taken on from socialisation into the particular culture and the individual's interaction with that. Meaning is open to review and change at different points of the lifespan. An important aspect of meaning for many people is found in rituals that may be of a religious or secular nature.

## Studies of religious practices

Ellor and Bracki (1995, p.153) commented that a critique of studies of religiosity showed a lack of adequate definitions that could be used to guide research. They found that often the terms religion, religious and religiosity were used indiscriminately 'to refer to some type of behaviour or feeling that can be associated with religion'. They suggested a second problem of the research was that defining and understanding of religion varied according to the professional orientation of the individual.

For all this, interest and involvement in religious activities is a legitimate area for study, and in many respects practice of religion may be a fairly close measure of spirituality. In other ways, however, for older adults the relationship may not be so close. It may be that a person's interest and involvement in religious activities may be governed more by availability of opportunities for participation than interest, particularly for frail elderly people. Thus studies may show that there is diminished practice of religion by older adults, when in fact this is not an indication of a lessened importance of religion or the spiritual dimension. Rather, it is an indication of a lessened ability and perhaps a lessened desire to engage in formal religious activities, for a number of reasons.

Religiosity studies have tended to show that belief in God becomes stronger in older people. A Gallup survey (1976), in Harris (1990) reported that 96 per cent of older respondents said they believed in God. It is difficult to determine whether differences in religious beliefs occur across the lifespan, as most studies have used cross-sectional data rather than following one age cohort in a longitudinal study. Results of these studies tend to be misleading, as religious belief in any particular group may be influenced by factors of social and historical circumstances of the cohort as well as the factors in the ageing process itself.

One longitudinal study conducted over an 18-year period (Blazer and Palmore 1976, in Harris 1990) measured religious activity including church attendance, listening to church services on the radio, watching religious programmes on TV and reading the Bible. They found that religious attitudes remained fairly stable over time.

For study of the ritualistic dimension of religion, two types of religious activity have been defined: organisational and non-organisational (Harris 1990). Palmore (1987), in Harris (1990), found no ageing effect on church attendance (organisational activities). However, a decline in church attendance does occur with increasing disability in elderly people. Ainlay and Smith (1984) and Mindel and Vaughan (1978) in Harris (1990) suggest that these declines may be offset by increases in the non-organisational activities. These activities include religious radio and TV, Bible reading and prayer. A survey (Harris 1990) conducted by a religious radio station in the USA found that 27 per cent of their listeners were over seventy years of age. Another study, into Bible reading habits, found 38 per cent of people at senior centres reported reading the Bible or other religious material on a daily basis. Nearly 95 per cent of older people reported praying. Markides *et al.* (1987), in Schaie and Willis (1991), in a longitudinal study, supported the findings that church attendance decreased among older adults, while participation in activities such as private prayer remained stable.

These studies were of USA origin. In Australia studies show that older people, (over sixty years) are more likely to be members of a church and to pray regularly, as well as to have claimed some supernatural experience (Kaldor 1987). It is worth noting that it is not known what proportion of this group of people sixty years and over was in the frail aged group.

## Being religious and church attendance

There certainly has been a decline in church attendance for most major religious denominations in Australia in recent decades (Hughes 1993). Does that mean that religion is less important to society? Are there differences in the older population? Indeed, many say that society is becoming more secular and that religion is not as important as it used to be, although this is not shown by the numbers not stating a religion in the Australian census figures, (always an optional question). Since 1911 the figures have varied between a low of 2.7 per cent in 1911, to a high of 12.8 per cent in 1933 and 10.2 per cent in 1991 (Hughes 1993). It is difficult to know what people mean by their identification of a denomination or religion on a census form in any case; it may be simply a sense of affiliation with a particular religious group, without ever attending church, or it may mean regular involvement. In the 1991 census 12.9 per cent of the population stated they had no religion. The 'no religion' group was weakest among the over fifty age group. And even three-quarters of the 'no religion' group surveyed in the National Social Science Survey (Hughes 1993) said they believed there was a God. Thus it is difficult to be certain of how important religion is in the current society, and further, how important it may be to older Australians.

Bellah *et al.* (1985, pp.246–247) writes of the growing separation between church, state, families and individuals in North America, noting that it was perhaps a natural stage of development of society for this to happen. The importance of individuation is stressed but, writes Bellah, 'Absolute independence is a false ideal. It delivers not the autonomy it promises but loneliness and vulnerability instead'. While this may not present problems to younger adults, at least some older adults may find the concept of independence increasingly difficult to maintain.

Frail older adults may be physically isolated from their church and community by a society that emphasises continued independent living, resulting in not only social isolation but spiritual isolation as well.

If religion can be understood as a meaning system by which humans relate to each other and to the transcendent in their lives, a way by which they make sense of their very existence, then to be deprived of the language needed to mediate at the interface between themselves, society and ultimate reality will have major implications for both individuals and the wider society. It must be asked, how significant is this issue? Are the current cohort of older people part of this issue too? What changes are there in the needs of older people for meeting their religious needs, changes that may have arisen due to the changes of the wider society?

It is human to want to respond to what has meaning in life for each of us. To some degree this is a natural aspect of what it is to be human; to some extent this becomes a conscious reaching out in response to meaning in our lives. This meaning may be connected with something that we perceive to be greater than ourselves, that is, 'otherness'.

## Symbols of meaning

The words 'ultimate' and 'otherness' are both ways of expressing something of great importance and something which lies beyond full human understanding. For all our advances in the fields of science and technology this century, it has not been possible to push the barriers back on human understanding of either 'ultimate' or 'otherness'. Yet, the very fact that something comes to be 'other' is because humans have assigned symbolic meaning to it (Greeley 1973). Ashbrook (1996, p.141) drew out the significance of the symbol making as naming: 'To name something is to bring it into consciousness – to bring it into being – and thereby connect it to that which makes sense. We are more for having named it and are empowered by having been able to name it.'

It seems appropriate to reach an agreed understanding of 'symbol' before we proceed further. The sacred symbols of a people, says Geertz (1968), from an anthropological view, function to synthesise their ethos, that includes the tone, character and quality of their life, with its moral, aesthetic style and mood, indeed, their world view. The concept of culture adhered to by Geertz (1975), denotes:

> an historically transmitted pattern of meanings embodied in symbols, a system of inherited conceptions expressed in symbolic forms by means of which men communicate, perpetuate, and develop the knowledge about and attitudes towards life. (p.89)

This view of meaning of a people is so inclusive that it permeates all that the community is. That is, the symbols of a culture 'name' or point to the meanings, those things that make the culture what it is. It also includes the concept of ritual. In this view, there is connection between secular and sacred; in fact, the secular can be imbued with sacred power by the people.

Over time symbols can change and new things can become symbolic for the community. There is a strong sense in which the symbols of a people are not an individual matter, but a corporate matter whereby a people are able to communicate their deepest-held meanings of life one to another, and in that context the use of symbols and ritual is of whole community importance.

For older adults, it is asked, how is this mediated? In a postmodern society, are the symbols of older people even known and understood across the society? If they are not, is it a case of the older adults having to learn, as part of the ageing process, to accept new symbols for the sacred in life? Or should there be an attempt to deliberately continue to examine and uphold the existing symbols and rituals of this society, particularly those relevant to older adults, for meaning and continuity of society? Aspects of liturgy may be important in this regard.

## Symbol making

'Man is the being who is capable of creating symbols, and a being in need of symbols' (Frankl 1990, in Kimble 1990, p.116). Bellah (1969) comments that, being human, it is only possible to think in symbols, and it is only possible for humans to make sense of any experience through the use of symbols. Meaning for humans is mediated through the use of symbols. What then is the place of symbols in human being and activity?

A religion is as good as its symbols.

> The force of a religion in supporting social values rests then on the ability of its symbols to formulate a world-view in which those values as well as the forces opposing their realisation are fundamental ingredients. (Geertz 1968, p.422)

And further, man is a 'symbolising, conceptualising, meaning-seeking animal', (p.422) and religion is his attempt to symbolise the ultimate reality. A religion will be effective precisely to the extent that its symbols are effective.

An important contribution is made to understanding meaning in ageing through the work of symbolic interactionism. This discipline also provides a basis for the in-depth interviewing used in this study. A central concept of symbolic interactionism is the distinctiveness of human behaviour and interaction as it is performed through the 'medium of symbols and their meanings' (Manis and Meltzer 1978, p.6). They make the point that humans make choices in how they respond to stimuli on the basis of meanings they have attached to the stimuli. These meanings they see as socially derived through interaction with others, that is, it is a community-wide activity of assignment of meaning. Thus the meaning of symbols is arrived at over a period of time by consensus within a community, which is congruent with the concept of cultural development of symbols already discussed in this chapter.

Geertz (1975) notes that for those able to accept their usefulness in their lives, religious symbols:

> provide a cosmic guarantee not only for their ability to comprehend the world, but also, comprehending it, to give a precision to their feeling, a definition to their emotions which enables them, morosely or joyfully, grimly or cavalierly, to endure it. (p.104)

In the postmodern society symbols of meaning have come under intense scrutiny as to their relevance to the community and individuals within that community. With increasing emphasis on individualism in the wider society, it is becoming increasingly difficult to retain the meaning of symbols that once were used as visible signs of identity and purpose in life.

Hay (1982) asks, have religious symbols lost or changed their meaning? Have they in fact disappeared? Writing from the perspective in the UK in the 1980s he seemed to think they have. This sense of meaninglessness, and the renewed concurrent search for meaning in the society at this time, may well be associated with this. But Hay says there is a deeper question than a preoccupation with institutions and symbols. An emphasis on these, he says, may blind us to 'the claim of religious people that there is a sacred dimension to human experience which is prior to all symbols' (p.69). The meaning and use of symbols appears as an extra tension for older adults, some of whom may find it difficult to come to terms with the shifting focus and uncertainty of the present society.

Thus care is necessary in understanding the meaning and usefulness of symbols. Geertz (1975) says that meaning may only be 'stored' in symbols; these religious symbols:

> dramatised in rituals or related in myths, are felt to sum up, for those for whom they are resonant, what is known about the way the world is, the quality of emotional life it supports, and the way one ought to behave while in it. (p.127)

Put this way, symbols would seem to provide a framework for living. Symbols an older person has held dear for many years may be particularly important to them when other aspects of life seem to be changing and out of control. Appropriate use of symbols in ritual may be especially valuable for frail older people and for people who have dementia, it may well be a way of enabling them to connect with something outside themselves.

## How did the people in this study respond to meaning?

The theme of meaning in life was clearly identified from the data. As the centres of meaning varied among the informants, so too did the ways in which they responded to ultimate meaning. This theme has a number of categories, including religious activities such as church attendance, prayer, Scripture and meditation. Relationship was an important source of meaning, including spouse, children and grandchildren, and group membership. Music, art, the environment and a number of other activities including writing and gardening also were important in bringing meaning to the lives of these older adults.

The way in which people attach meaning and respond to the ultimate in their lives modifies their sense of hope. The degree to which they develop wisdom as part of the ageing process, their satisfaction in relationships and their sense of self-sufficiency or vulnerability are also derived from the sense of ultimacy in their lives and their response to that.

The generic model representing themes raised by participants in this study (Figure 2.1) attempts to explain the interaction between each of these dimensions in human spirituality. It can be applied to describe spirituality for any particular individual, according to their view of ultimate meaning.

## Gender differences in church attendance, prayer and religious experience

There are well-recognised differences in gender church attendance patterns (Kaldor 1994). Greeley and Durkin (1984) studied factors involved in attendance at Mass in a group of young Catholic women (between 18 and 30 years of age). They then compared these findings with data collected in the National Opinion Research Center (NORC) on a wider age group of people.

They found that 'feminist' and 'not feminist' women differed in their likelihood of attending church regularly. Those who attended more frequently were likely to have a mother who went to work before their daughters were six years of age and who attended church; and the informant was more likely to attend regularly if her image of women was influenced by feminism, enhanced by attending college (university), and attendance depended on the image that the woman holds of the church now. A powerful image of God, expressed as a closeness of relationship with God and, in particular, a recognition of God as Lover may override variables.

We should note that the subjects in Greeley's studies were all young women. However, it is worth considering the family patterns reported for these women, to see if they shed any light on attendance patterns for the group of older women in the current study.

## Religious practice: worship

*Patterns of church attendance and possible background to these*

Of the 24 older people interviewed in-depth, 11 attend church regularly while 13 don't attend or rarely attend. Questions raised and answered in part through the in-depth interviews included: Why do people keep going to church? Does it satisfy their spiritual needs?; Are these needs perhaps satisfied by other means?

Various informants raised a number of factors that impeded their ability in some way to meet their spiritual needs. It is noted that these informants were all living independently in the community, and were for the most part reasonably healthy third agers.

It seems that, in ageing, there are probably a number of variables operating, including disabilities and transport difficulties, that may make it hard for these older people to attend church services. As well, an increasing move towards interiority may produce changes in worship habits, perhaps making private prayer more important than corporate worship.

*Factors among informants which prevent meeting of spiritual needs as the person would like*

These include:

1. lack of mobility

2. transport difficulties

3. diminished energy levels

4. incontinence

5. dementia (none of the informants had dementia, but eight mentioned it as a fear).

At least one of the factors listed was found in each of the informants. This shows the tremendous variation of disabilities that older adults experience and still manage to function reasonably well in independent living. Any of these disabilities can interfere with the meeting of spiritual needs. For those who want to attend worship, it may mean that they are unable to get to a place of worship to actually attend a church service. For some, it means not being able to participate fully in a service of worship, through sensory deficits or from lack of energy, to stay awake and concentrate for a whole service. These disabilities are even more prevalent in the population of older adults in long-term residential care. Any planning of worship services must take such issues into account.

### Attenders

Lisa, Doris, Edith and Ann are all Catholics and are all critical of the Catholic Church. However, they all currently attend church. Doris is currently actively involved in her church (she takes communion to the sick). Ann said the deepest thing in her life is the practice of her religion, particularly the Mass. She reported having a good church upbringing.

Edith told how as a young child she had a number of unhappy experiences associated with the Church and with attending a church school. Edith had spent some years not attending church. She had vivid recollections of some incidents and of some of the nuns, both good and bad. She had felt alienated from the Church in early adulthood. She has started going to church (Catholic) regularly again after many years of non-attendance. She said: 'Since I've been going to church I've felt, yes, I am a different person. I feel as if it's filling a need in my life that was lacking.' She said that in the last few months and weeks she had started to laugh again. She also remarked that she had separated her spiritual dimension from the Church, in which she seems to be saying that while she doesn't agree with all the Church does, she is still willing to be involved and worship on a regular basis.

These findings were examined to see if there is any trend towards patterns of church attendance that are similar to Greeley's (1984) work. He noted that anger expressed by some Catholic women may be related to a church that no longer exists in the same way they remember it; that it has changed, but that they don't want to know that it has changed. It is noted that the criticism directed at the Church by Catholic women in that study varied between informants.

It is possible that, for this group, life experience, faith stage and wisdom may have become important factors in church attendance. Greeley and Durkin (1984) noted that if the woman's image of the present Church is linked to her past image of God, then the woman can only be protected from 'anger' towards the Church should she hold a strong image of God. It would also be worth examining the childhood experiences of these older women to see what differences there were between their experiences and those of the younger group of women.

Vera, Angela and Dawn are Anglicans and currently attend church. Vera attends church and plays the organ, which she enjoys. Angela noted that Church has always been a part of her life. In her early life she admitted to being an 'habitual' church attender, that is, she regularly attended church, but it had no meaning for her before her conversion at 55 years of age. Although Dawn says church has lost its meaning for her, she still attends. It might well be asked why she does still attend, and it would seem one reason may be her sense of isolation. Church still provides some sort of community for her, even though she says she feels herself isolated from others at church due to her single status.

Carol, Win and Ben attend the Uniting Church of Australia. Carol has never left the Church. She has changed denomination on a number of occasions as she has shopped around to find a church where she can feel comfortable. She still attends church services on a regular basis (weekly). Win is active in her church community, through her Church, and is an active church goer.

Ben spoke of his early church involvement:

It's always been there right there from the, I mean my sisters believed, my father believed, they took me to church, we learnt at Sunday school, it went right through although when I was a POW there wasn't any church for three and a half years or anything like that but I, I do believe it was the prayers that brought me through.

He still attends church regularly. He says he goes to church to get fulfilment, 'But then you've got to take that back out with you'. He sees his worship and his living of his faith on a daily basis as being strongly connected.

Sylvia questions the degree of change happening in the Church (Church of Christ) at present: 'I just feel that the church is allowing itself to be influenced by the secular world.' She still attends but sometimes wonders why she still does.

### Non-attenders

The reasons for non-attendance were varied. Lack of mobility and transport were two reasons; however, it is noted that one of the most disabled in the study attended church every week. Other reasons given for not attending were being unhappy with the type of services and just not wanting to go to church anymore. For instance, Hugh finds formal church doesn't play a big part in his life. It cannot be assumed that those who do not attend church do not engage in other non-organisational religious behaviours. As can be seen from the informants in this study, they respond in a number of other ways to otherness and the spiritual.

Flora watches a religious programme, *Songs of Praise*, on TV. She rarely attends church now. If she does go it is with one of her daughters: 'I don't really feel I need to go to church.' Talking of what she doesn't like about church services these days she said: 'You've got to shake one another's hands, well I'm not like that. I'm probably a bit of a loner really.'

George also watches religious programmes on Sunday mornings, and later in the day. 'I mean that *Songs of Praise* on the ABC, I wouldn't miss that.' He said: 'I rarely go to church these days, that doesn't concern me in the least.' This informant also spoke of his love of church buildings, particularly in England. At this point in his life this man appears to be moving to a more internal and non-organisational form of worship. He had been a regular church attender earlier in life.

Beryl was the most adamant of all the informants in her response to church attendance. She went to church three times when she was 11; after this, she remarked, she didn't want to hear any more 'fairy stories'. Her parents were atheists.

Diane said she stopped attending church when she was a teenager. She was very critical of the standard of preaching when she had attended church. However, she did turn to the church for support when her husband had cancer, and until he died. She does not attend church now. People often become more aware of their spiritual needs during times of crisis, and it seemed this was the case for Diane. It would be interesting to know whether her spiritual dimension becomes more important to her as she continues to age.

Eva told me simply, early in the interview: 'I'm not into religion.' When I asked her, 'What do you mean by religion?' she replied, 'Well, going to church and being a do-gooder, but you don't mean it.'[1] She said that the church had changed since she knew it (as a young woman) and she saw 'no meaning in it' now. Eva's understanding of religion is quite different to that of Geertz (1975), who wrote that 'being religious' means being motivated by religion, and being susceptible to certain moods, of which 'worshipful' might be one. There is a sense in which Eva is responding to something she sees as superficial and hypocritical, but at the same time her use of the word 'religious' seems to be not unusual in current society.

In other instances, increasing disability in either the individual or their partner may make it difficult to get to church. Daisy and her husband were in this situation. She said: 'I think religion is man made, God didn't make lots of churches for people to belong to' (meaning the different denominations). She and her husband don't attend church anymore. Daisy's husband has severe arthritis.

> Actually I think it's mostly laziness; it's much more difficult to get up in the morning, well not get, we get up but to get going, and we also say yes we will go back but somehow we don't get there. Well [husband] sort of gets up and he can't move so...

This woman had been involved in church activities until about ten years ago; but it seems that her husband's disability is a real factor now in her non-attendance.

Sally is another one who never misses *Songs of Praise* on TV on Sundays. She said: 'Whatever I'm doing I stop and I sing the hymns.' She remarked, 'Well I could get to a church and if I made up my mind to walk I could walk but all I have to do is to ring up the church people and they'll pick me up.' This informant did not mention that it would be about twenty minutes walk from her home to the church and a fair part of this uphill. She has asthma, and seems quite short of breath even moving about her home, so it might not be really feasible for her to walk to church anyway.

From a different perspective the decline in church attendance and emphasis on individuation in society has had some rather interesting effects in the religious/spiritual development of some people. Bellah *et al.* (1985) writing of the North American scene, noted:

> Most Americans see religion as something individual, prior to any organisational involvement. For many, such as Sheila Larson [an informant in his study] it remains entirely individual. Where it does involve organisational commitment, the primary context is the local church. (p.226)

Bellah *et al.*'s (1985) findings would seem to fit the experience in Australia for some as well. His anecdote on Sheila is pertinent.

> One person we interviewed has actually named her religion [she calls it her 'faith']... after herself... She is a young nurse who has received a good deal of therapy and who describes her faith as 'Sheilaism'. 'I believe in God. I'm not a religious fanatic. I can't remember the last time I went to church. My faith has carried me a long way. It's Sheilaism. Just my own little voice.' Sheila's faith has some tenets beyond belief in God, though not many. In defining 'my own Sheilaism', she said: 'It's just try to love yourself and be gentle with yourself. You know, I guess, take care of each other. I think He would want

us to take care of each other.' Like many others, Sheila would be willing to endorse few more specific injunctions. (p.221)

The author suggests Sheila's position is representative of many in America. From data collected in this Australian study the picture appears remarkably similar here, too. For example, Helen, who says she feels she is 'in church all the time because God's within me, why do I need to go to church and listen to a sermon from the Bible that I can read myself?' This woman had constructed her own religion, a mixture of Christianity and Eastern religions. She demonstrates a deep sense of spirituality which is very much her own.

## Liturgy/Music in worship

Liturgy is an important way in which humans may respond to otherness or the numinous, to reach out to God. For others the sharing of rituals of a secular nature may be more important. Erikson (1968) sees this process of ritualisation contributing to a pervasive element, the 'numinous'. Erikson sees both the infantile sense of ritualisation and the adult ritual as parts of a 'functional whole', that is, a 'cultural version of human existence' (Erikson 1968, p.715). Shils (1968) makes the comment that ritual has become less compelling for numbers of people because of hostility towards rituals connected with 'hieratic, monarchical, and aristocratic structures of authority' (p.747). Nevertheless, ritual still seems to survive, thirty years on from Shils's writing, perhaps in a slightly more self-conscious way in Western society. Ritual is examined in this study with relevance to the part it plays in the expressions of spirituality in older adults.

It was interesting that as many comments on liturgy came from informants who never attend church as from those who attend regularly. It was a point on which most people seemed to have an opinion. There were no questions directly asked on liturgy in the in-depth interviews. The frequency of informant comments on church services may have been because they connected my being a priest with church services.

Religious traditions were an important part of worship for a number of informants. It is interesting that some who do not attend church have very strong ideas about what traditions should be kept. For instance, Eva said changing of religious dress, for example nuns' habits, removed some of the mystique. She felt these traditions were important, remarking (of nuns), 'they've given up a life, in our religion they've taken away the mystique and that is wrong with the world'. (This woman was not a Catholic.) In a sense Eva seemed to be responding to the mystery of 'otherness' that she associated with the church and with the spiritual. It was still there for her, even though she no longer took part in religious practices. There were others like her, too.

It is noted that a number who did not attend church anymore said they always watched *Songs of Praise*. Some were critical of newer types of music used in worship, and yet seemed to enjoy the wide variety of music presented in *Songs of Praise*.

Flora doesn't like the familiarity expressed in church services these days. Her main experience of worship was of the Church of England services pre-1970s. This would seem to be consistent with Greeley's (1984) conclusions that some of his sample were responding to a type of church that no longer existed. It is interesting that this woman liked to visit churches and sit quietly, but not while a service was going on.

Vera finds liturgies of the church helpful, but she has some concerns about modern translations, particularly when used in liturgy. Sometimes, she said, she finds the forms 'helpful, and sometimes modern translations are not', she finds herself listening to the words of the prayer and asking, 'Why did they choose that word?' She feels that way with music, too, and raises a concern about losing 'what is good and proven and sound for the sake of something new and glossy and which only lasts two or three years'. She continues to play the organ at church, and enjoys that.

Her comments would probably be echoed by many older people, who seem to feel comfortable with the forms of worship they have grown up with. Ann is one of those. She said that the deepest thing in life for her is the practice of her religion, particularly the mass. Of changes she said: 'I grew up with the Latin mass...and I'm not sure that all the changes have been wonderful but it doesn't change my view that the core is still the same.'

Sylvia was another who found worship a very personal activity. As she commented, worship is an individual thing for her, between her and God. She said she does not like the 'greeting' during the service, she finds it distracting from worship, saying it is unnecessary 'when a fellowship cup of tea is offered at the conclusion of the service'. She would prefer a more meditative type of service. This finding is consistent with an increasing sense of interiority in ageing.

Music, too, is an important part of liturgy. Ben noted that singing means a lot to him, 'especially in the church life'. He doesn't like modern church music, finding more depth in words of older hymns. He remembered with joy some of the times at church when he was a child:

> Thanksgiving was another place where there'd been all the fruit and labour in front of the altar, you know, bring your pumpkins, and your wheat would be in the aisles attached to the end of the pews. These things, they were great because it meant something.

He remarked on the importance of symbolism in liturgy for him: going to the altar rail and kneeling to receive Communion. 'You see, I like…you going and kneeling at the rail, you taking yourself to God, it doesn't just come to you.' They don't do that in the church he currently attends, but he keeps going.

George said he liked going to church as a young adult 'more for the music than for any belief'. Doris spoke of the importance of special festivals of the church year and the ritual surrounding these. She shared how these festivals are marked by the small group of which she is a member. On special occasions the group involves the families of members. Doris was experiencing these special festivals both within the formal liturgical setting and within her small group.

Edith sings in a church choir, which she regards as a special experience, 'singing in praise to God', while Diane, who does not currently attend church, said she finds liturgy can get repetitive and meaningless.

Do other activities, such as prayer and watching TV, or listening to the radio, give enough input to satisfy the individual's response to the Ultimate and adequately address spiritual needs? Catering for the different worship needs of people presents practical difficulties in designing liturgy that is suitable for all age groups. It underlines the benefits of planning church services with the particular needs of specific age groups in mind, but it must also be said that older people, as well as younger ones, may have a wide range of the types of liturgy that appeal to them.

Provision of appropriate liturgy also involves taking church *to* older frail people who cannot leave their homes to attend church services.

## Prayer

Private prayer forms a part of the lives of 18 informants, while six of the informants did not pray at all. A changing in type of praying over the years was noted by a number of informants, mostly moving to more informal prayer and praying more often.

*Gender differences in prayer*

Hay (1982) noticed that women were more likely to hold traditional beliefs and to pray daily, noting that there were variations between denominations. According to Greeley (1982) both older men and women pray more than young men and women. The increase in older women's prayer is even 'sharper' than the increase in older men's prayer. Greeley suggests the reason for this may be that 'the socio-emotional role of women makes them the "praying specialists" in the family'. This was found among the older people in this study, too. Women seemed to use prayer more often than men, and also to feel more comfortable about praying, some noting how their type of prayer had changed over the years, particularly in becoming more informal. Some seemed almost apologetic about this and seemed to be wondering if their prayer should be more formal. This seemed particularly so for some who had not developed their faith as adults, and perhaps remembered set prayers that were learnt by heart.[2] On the other hand, Lisa continues to keep habits of religious practice developed early in life, for example daily prayer, especially keeping to the time of day when she prays.

*Women's prayer*

Types of prayer were also interesting, particularly the use by some widows of their deceased husband's photo as a focus for prayer, either praying or talking to him through the photo, or using him as a mediator with God.

Flora said that she started lighting candles after her husband died. She said she found that, while others needed people around them, she needed to be on her own. She likes to light candles in a church, any church, anywhere. She feels close to her husband when she does. She doesn't know why. Flora said there was something special about the light. Flora had told me earlier that she does not pray, so I asked her what does she feel when she lights the candle. She said she sits, thinks, remembers, and gives thanks for all the good things that have happened in her life. I suggested that this is prayer, and she readily said 'Yes'.

Carol said prayer has been a regular part of her life for many years. She says she often prays spontaneously, once or even several times a day. Vera said: 'I pray on a regular basis, but I'd have to say that quite often it's meaningless. It's my fault, not His, my fault.' She says she lives each day as it comes, and frequently asks (presumably from God) for strength.

Sylvia says she constantly prays for her family. This informant expressed many concerns about her adult children. Angela was also a member of a long-term study group and prayer was an important part of her group.

Ann said she likes to pray. On most days, this could be several times during the day. She noted that her prayer has changed over the years and is less formalised now. She suggested that she may have more time to pray now. 'Perhaps I've got more things to pray about, but prayer has become more important in my life, certainly than it used to be.' She still says the rosary, but is not so keen on it as she used to be. She still maintains though that the rosary is important, and says, 'It's been so highly recommended'. Edith also prays and says the rosary every night.

Diane questions her motives in prayer, as she feels she only prays when she wants something (even if it is not for herself) and feels that is hypocritical. She says she doesn't 'actively' pray.

A different perspective was taken by Sally who said: 'I get my comfort from praying to God and speaking to (deceased husband), that might not be the right thing to say. Then I say I'm sorry, it's God I should be speaking to first, I'm talking to you first, I said well maybe you could just lead Him in and tell Him.' Regarding prayer, she said that she is concerned that she is always asking God for something. She prays more when she is sick. She said she asks her dead husband to intercede for her: 'I was praying to God and (husband): please help me to get better and all this you see, and then when I feel better I feel, dear, thankful.'

Helen, who has constructed her own belief system, said:

> I visualise that I have a direct link to God my creator, my Father creator, only if I find I can't cope myself; only in dire or extreme circumstances or to help somebody else would I ask for guidance and help. I think you don't have to do it more than once, you don't need repetitive prayer.

She does not pray so much as meditate, and believes that you should pray once only for anything and it will be answered.

### Men's prayer

It seems in this study that three of the four men pray. There did seem to be gender differences between this small sample of men's prayer and the sample of women's prayer. These differences were in line with the differences reported in other research. George said he prays mainly for others, rarely for himself, and he is not sure of the efficacy of prayer, while Hugh says he often prays now:

> It all depends on what you call prayer, of course, it's difficult to define… So I think of this idea of God who intercedes in human affairs, and whom we pray to at church, to save the Queen and so forth, all these things, and we might intercede to and so on, in our prayers. I think that really is a vain hope … So a personal God, I can't say that, although I pray to a personal God sometimes. Hoping someone's listening.

When asked how he defines prayer, he said, 'I don't address my remarks to someone who's listening up there. I think that's an absurd idea, my concept of prayer is mainly addressing my thoughts to my loved ones, and a very general expression of goodwill.'

It is interesting that Hugh does still sometimes pray, even when he seems not to acknowledge the efficacy of prayer. Perhaps part of that stems from his early life, and experience of religious life. In contrast, Ben says that it was prayer that got him through the most difficult parts of his life.

### Reading the Bible and other religious literature

Eight informants mentioned Bible reading, five finding it useful, while three specifically stated their difficulties with accepting or using the Bible. It seems that in some way a number of the informants had difficulties really comprehending the contents of the Bible. Is that because they had not had the opportunity for guidance in reading it? Some showed evidence of a deep understanding of Scripture. It is unclear whether this is an example of grace, of the ability to understand Scripture, or whether the answer lies in other directions. Some older adults may appreciate an opportunity to read and study the Bible, or even to have the Bible read to them; this may help to clarify misunderstandings of Scripture. Others may enjoy the opportunity to be involved in other reading, not related to religious material.

George reads the Bible and is very knowledgeable of Scripture. 'I read the Bible, in all sort of forms a great deal, and you know sometimes I'm really taken you know, by what I read (and) re-read.' Reading of other religious books is also important to him.

Vera spoke of her belief in Scripture:

> Well again, I don't take an absolutely literal view of the writings in the Bible. They express a truth. Genesis expresses a truth and it's not a literal one and it doesn't worry me at all that Science says that this is the way the

world began. What I find even more difficult is to suggest that it all happened by chance. Now that is a far bigger thing for me to swallow than to swallow the existence of God. You know, it looks to me as if there's a guiding imagination principle, whatever you like to call it, I call it God, behind all this.

She has carefully thought through and discussed her stance on this. She has a clear understanding and response to the God of her understanding. She noted however that she preferred some of the older translations of Scripture and liturgy. She has a sense for the way the words are, they are familiar and a comfort. She finds new words cause her to focus on the words, rather than the meaning behind them.

Clergy and pastoral carers should be careful in choosing versions of the Bible that will be familiar for frail older people, but at the same time be sure to check with older people so that what they choose is appropriate.

Doris emphasised the importance of prayer and study of Scripture in the small group of which she was a part. Continued Bible and other studies are a great source of learning and fellowship for older people.

However, not all would want to read the Bible. Ann, for example, was one who found reading the Bible not at all to her liking: 'I used to try and read the Bible but it was just so violent, it turned me off.' Dawn also expressed some apprehension of study of the Bible: 'I don't go into Bible study because it starts me thinking too deeply and it worries me you know, you know what I mean, it's way, it's beyond my comprehension.' For still others, it is there just in case. Daisy remarked: 'It's (the Bible) always on the head of my bed but I, I wouldn't say I read it everyday or anything like that and, ah, but it's there.'

Helen, largely self-taught in religious literature said: 'On a grander scale I conceive God primarily as the first cause as thought, instead of the Bible saying in the beginning was the word, how can he have any word without the thought behind it, so I think that is the first error.' This woman has read widely, and has an understanding of the 'Word' that could be near the understanding expressed in the Bible, although she does not seem to realise that.

A great variety of responses to reading the Bible or other religious books has been revealed among informants in this study, probably reflective of the wider community. It must be remembered that this group of older people were still independently living, had few serious sight problems and were not dependent on others to provide for their reading needs. This will not be the case for the more frail residents of nursing homes.

## Other ways of responding to ultimate meanings

Seven mentioned regular reading of other religious and general books. Five were involved in religious studies of various types, mainly in small groups. Three used meditation, two Christian and one of an Eastern type.

### Study

Carol was involved in individual study in spirituality, which included work on dreams, on a Jungian basis. She had attended a number of courses in these areas during the last few years. Eva talked about how her image of God had changed over the years, largely, she thought, due to her wide reading.

### Meditation

Helen, Carol and Win use meditation regularly. Carol attends a weekly Christian meditation group. She said that she didn't spend nearly enough time in meditation. Win also goes to a Christian meditation group and finds this very helpful, while Helen uses a combination of Eastern types. She says that meditation is important to her and she receives answers to problems through meditation. She describes herself as more often meditating these days than praying.

## Summary

*Response to the Ultimate, or what it is that brings meaning into an older person's life, formed an important part of each informant's story. Human beings are, after all, 'meaning makers'. Thus this aspect of the spiritual dimension is an important area for intervention in providing effective services in aged care.*

*The independent living older adults in this study were mostly able to address their own needs related to their individual responses to what was ultimate in their lives.*

*It was seen that non-organisational as well as organisational religious activities were important to these informants. A number of the people in this study were using spiritual strategies of a non-organisational nature on a regular basis, such as meditation and small study groups. The existence of these groups is probably not widely known among this age group and it is likely that many more older people would benefit greatly from these activities. Such activities could be more widely used and encouraged in parishes and other community settings.*

*It is vital that health professionals, clergy and care workers for the elderly are familiar with the variety of ways that older people may respond to what is meaningful in their lives, both in religious content and in other ways, such as music, art and the environment.*

## Notes

1   An excerpt from Eva's story appears in *Journal of Religious Gerontology* (forthcoming).
2   In the researcher's experience it is often the set prayers that are remembered and connected with by people who have dementia. A concern is that there is much less emphasis on teaching prayers by rote these days, that the deposit of learnt prayer will not be there if it is required later in life.

# CHAPTER 7

# *Response to the Ultimate*

## *Meaning through experience and activity*

### The concept of 'otherness' or the 'numinous'

There were accounts of various ways in which informants found meaning in life, in addition to those already outlined in Chapter 6. A number of informants spoke of deep and special experiences of a spiritual nature at one or more points in their lives. In each case the informant voluntarily shared the account with me: I did not at any point ask an informant about spiritual experiences. It appears that experiences of 'otherness' and responses of a religious or spiritual nature are not uncommon. I have included this material because of its obvious importance to those who shared it with me.

There are times when people find it difficult to express an experience, something which lies outside their knowledge and ability to explain. Some seem more prone to such experiences than others. In some such experiences people express a sense of 'not of this world' or something mysterious that seems to break through into their world. It is something that seems external to the person's understood world view. One way of describing these experiences is 'otherness,' another is to refer to the 'numinous', that is the holy or sacred. *The Macquarie Dictionary* (1981) defines 'numinous' as pertaining to a deity, a divine power or spirit, or arousing elevated or religious feelings. Otto (1952, p.12) asserted that the numinous 'can only be suggested by means of the special way in which it is reflected in the mind in terms of feeling. It is such that it grips or stirs the human mind with this and that determinate affective state'. Otto describes this as the

> deepest and most fundamental element in all strong and sincerely felt religious emotion. Faith unto salvation, trust, love, all these are there. But over and above these is an element which may also on occasion, quite apart from them, profoundly affect us and occupy the mind with a wellnigh bewildering strength. [for example, it may be found]…in sudden, strong ebullitions of personal piety and the frames of mind such ebullitions evince, in the fixed and ordered solemnities of rites and liturgies, and again in the atmosphere that clings to old religious monuments and buildings, to temples and to churches. If we do so we shall find we are dealing with

something for which there is only one appropriate expression, '*mysterium tremendum*'. (p.12)

This sense of otherness then may take many forms, and human responses to the numinous are also varied. How are we to understand 'otherness'? Otto (1952, p.26) describes it as the 'wholly other', that is, that which is quite beyond the sphere of the usual, the intelligible and the familiar, which therefore falls quite outside the limits of the 'canny', and is contrasted with it, filling the mind with blank wonder and astonishment.

Other manifestations of this tendency of the feeling of the 'mysterious' are noted by Otto (1952), that people may be attracted to objects and aspects of experience that cannot be fully understood by the individual. He notes:

It finds its most unqualified expression in the spell exercised by the only half intelligible or wholly unintelligible language of devotion, and in the unquestionably real enhancement of the awe of the worshipper which this produces. Instances of this are the ancient traditional expressions still retained despite their obscurity, in our Bible and hymnals; the special emotional virtue attaching to words like 'Hallelujah', *Kyrie eleison*, 'Selah', just because they are 'wholly other' and convey no clear meaning; the Latin in the service of the Mass, felt by the Catholic to be, not a necessary evil, but something especially holy; the Sanskrit in the Buddhist Mass of China and Japan;…and many other similar cases. (p.64)

It is apparent that experiences of otherness are universal and have been part of the human condition for as far back as we have records. There are many examples in the Old Testament, including Isaiah's vision in the Temple, the book of the prophet Ezekiel contains a number of such accounts, the book of Daniel and, within the New Testament, the book of Revelation. In a more recent study Greeley (1982) discussed the perception of 'otherness' in his and McCready's research.

Times and places of otherness are 'sacraments' in the sense that they represent situations and circumstances in which 'otherness' reveals itself… Sociologists more modestly will be content with saying that a number of things seem capable of triggering experiences of grace and then in their residual images representing and articulating that experience. (pp.79–80)

The sense of otherness or the numinous is something that seems to elicit a response from human beings (Otto 1952; Hardy 1979). The response varies according to both the stimulus and the situation of the individual. For some there is a sense of awe in the presence of something beyond human comprehension. One response to the Ultimate is to worship. The practices of religious activities are a way in which people will respond to the Ultimate.

People have been fascinated by the sense of 'otherness' and accounts of mystical and transcendent experiences. Hardy (1979), working in England, collected together over 4000 first-hand accounts illustrating a 'deep awareness of a benevolent non-physical power which appears to be partly or wholly beyond, and far greater than, the individual self' (p.1). These accounts have come from people living in a society where scientific knowledge casts doubt on any such experience of 'otherness' or transcendence.

The characteristics of these experiences have been, first, that they are unlike any other type of experience of that individual; second, the experiences are not necessarily 'religious' and have been reported by adherents of religious faiths and by atheists and agnostics too. Children as well as adults were among those reporting the experiences. In common for all of them was the conviction that there is another dimension to life (Hardy 1979). Further, Hay (1982, pp.118–19) gave figures for those who responded to a survey asking 'Have you ever been aware of or influenced by a presence or a power?' The researchers found that 36 per cent of the sample of people in Britain said 'Yes'. This was near the figure for the USA sample responding to the same question: 35 per cent. They were surprised because they had thought that having such experiences would be linked to church attendance, and they had assumed a lower British response as three to four times as many Americans as Britons were regular church attenders.

Thus, an important aspect of this is that researchers in these two major studies found large numbers of people had reported experiencing some sense of 'otherness', and this experience went very much wider than those who were regular church attenders. These experiences of 'otherness' are a part of human spirituality. Neglecting the spiritual dimension in older people is to ignore an important part of the human being, a part that needs acknowledgement as a legitimate component of human experience.

McCready and Greeley (Greeley 1982) found in their research that intense religious experiences were triggered by events that are listed below, in order of frequency of mention: listening to music; prayer; beauties of nature such as sunset; moments of quiet reflection; attending a church service; listening to a sermon; watching little children; reading the Bible; being alone in church; reading a poem or a novel; childbirth; sexual lovemaking; one's own creative work; looking at a painting; physical exercise. Hardy's (1979) research produced a similar list of antecedents or triggers to experiences, with a few additions: happiness, illness, the prospect of death, the death of others and crises in personal relations.

Greeley (1982) notes that for most people, these experiences are arrived at by grace, shaped by their 'rational, if not philosophical concepts of God which they have derived from their religious heritage'. He admits it seems possible for the concept to arise before the experience, but often the experience 'explodes' beyond the concept. Since human experience of the spiritual through transcendence would seem to be part of the possible repertoire of experiences available to most, if not all, human beings, these experiences should be present in a sample of older adults as well. The way people respond to the numinous and to 'otherness' in their lives may vary tremendously, for some people religious ritual or liturgy is particularly important. This is an important expression of human spirituality.

## Ways in which 'otherness' or the numinous are expressed

The arts form an avenue for the expression of otherness or the numinous. Otto (1952) wrote extensively on this topic.

> In the arts nearly everywhere the most effective means of representing the numinous is 'the sublime'. This is especially true of architecture, in which it would appear to have first been realised. One can hardly escape the idea that this feeling for expression must have begun to awaken far back in the remote Megalithic Age. (pp.65–6)

Otto referred to the experience of a '"downright magical" impression' and notes: 'We feel we can detect the special characteristic of this "magical" note in art with fair assurance even under the most varying conditions and in the most diverse relationships.' This experience, he said, could be found through a building, a song, a formula, a succession of gestures or musical notes or, in particular, certain manifestations or ornamental and decorative art, symbols, and emblems.

Writing of Gothic architecture of the West, Otto (1952, p.67) remarked that it was the 'most numinous of all types of art'. The sense of the experiential is well brought out in this description:

> The semi-darkness that glimmers in vaulted halls, or beneath the branches of a lofty forest glade, strangely quickened and stirred by the mysterious play of half-lights, has always spoken eloquently to the soul, and the builders of temples, mosques, and churches have made full use of it. (p.68)

In her essay on art and imagination, Harris (1986) emphasises the central role of spirit in faith and of the importance of symbols and imagination in the life of faith. Art is seen as a vehicle for 'otherness', a way of symbolising the numinous. She writes of other forms of knowing:

> other media are also appropriate: sound, as in music; silence, as in prayer; stone and wood, as in sculpture; shape, line, the human body itself. Such forms, other than offering understanding discursively or conversationally, project experience metaphorically and symbolically. These forms preserve multiple interpretation and enable us to know what is not amenable to discourse – to know, in contrast to discourse, unspeakable things. (pp.117–18)

It is noted that Harris also speaks of silence as a vehicle for otherness. This may be expressed through prayer or in meditation, or contemplative prayer. These forms of knowing are ways in which the deepest things of life may be understood. For instance, the concepts of guilt, forgiveness, death, reconciliation, resurrection, love and faith, while not primary concepts, 'are primarily human realities, best understood in immediacy and involvement' (p.118).

### The significance of church buildings

Otto (1952) has written of the well-known significance of church buildings. Church buildings were important for a number of informants. Flora responded to the architecture of the buildings, especially the older church buildings of England. There was a sense of awe about her experience, it was a very personal experience, and she did not feel this when she was with a lot of other people. In a way, she has a very individualistic response to the 'holy', preferring to sit quietly in a church building rather than in a church service. George, too, said he would travel to visit churches, particularly while he lived in England, and remarked how the buildings interested him.

Diane, although she does not normally attend church, has some special experiences of being in church buildings. She related some of these from her travels overseas, and one is described here:

> And for some reason I wondered if it was worthwhile saying a little prayer for [her sick god-daughter], there's enough of me there somewhere that says, there's something out there, there's someone out there, no matter what form it takes. The whole place was so beautiful, the walls of the church were timbered up just a short way in places, but the rest of it was in rock. The

ceiling is glass with copper wound round it and coiled round it. It has magnificent wood in the copper beams and there are windows, the altar is a piece of the rock, the sun strikes through, right on to the altar at a particular time, through these windows that come down. And they've left the natural water just seeping down the walls, and orchids and ferns grow. It is the most amazing place. That was a very emotional experience. I went to another church, I've been to a lot of churches…

This woman's sense of awe and the holy are readily apparent in this anecdote; there was something very touching for her in the experience. She was brought up within a church-going family, but no longer has any connections with the church, yet there is still something within her that responds to the holy.

## Meaning through music

It is noted that five informants were members of a music group, and formed a special sub-group for the theme meaning in life, where a common interest seems to bind them together. They have a leader who is enthusiastic and energetic, and about their own age. He strongly encouraged his group members to take part in this study. Thus there is a stronger than otherwise to be expected place for music in the lives of these informants. It is interesting, however, to note that others not in that group also responded well to music, reporting that singing, playing and listening to music is a part of the meaning in their lives; for some it is very much a way of connecting to 'otherness' and the transcendent, and at the least music brings a sense of meaning to many of those interviewed.

Hugh seemed to encapsulate the feelings of a number of informants as he spoke of an interior world that we may experience saying: 'We have certain windows on that, one is music, another is poetry, another is nature… It really is a window on another world, another world of beauty, of a spiritual element.' He contends that music is not necessarily a spiritual experience, but more likely an emotional one. 'I don't define music as a spiritual experience, perhaps I'm wrong. Although it has a powerful spiritual meaning to me.'

For Flora, while she has expressed a distance from God, meaning for her has come through music, which has always been special. She shared this interest with her husband before he died. In fact, she still feels close to her husband through music, even though he has been dead for some years. She reminisced on their sharing of musical experiences:

Well I'll give you one example. Just before he died, a registered nurse brought in her transistor and put on FM and there was a Mozart piano concerto being played... He couldn't talk but I did say to him, do you know what it is? And I could tell by the look in his eyes that he did, and really I think...every time I hear that you know.

Carol likes to read and listen to classical music. Vera says that meaning in life for her comes from good music, good drama and good writing. She regards these as being inspired by God, whether they are of a religious nature or not.

### Art

Lisa is learning to paint, something she had wanted to do for a long time. She enjoys it and is totally absorbed in the art:

I decided to fulfil one of my sort of unachieved ambitions, I've always wanted to learn to paint... I went to an art school here and entered a course in still-life painting, and I enjoyed [it] enormously, the complete absorption in something, which means that you stop thinking about anything else, just focusing on that.

Obviously, painting provides a source of meaning for her, but to what extent could this be addressing the spiritual needs of this woman? Is there a sense of 'otherness' in this activity? It would seem that it is a source of deep involvement and satisfaction in the process of the activity. As well, she was gaining an insight into herself, and perhaps, a new self-awareness:

Apart from the doing of it, I suddenly realised I was learning something about myself, which I didn't know was there, and that was that I could become absorbed completely in something which was not concerned with anything external... I mean, if you are trying to draw an object, you are concerned in, it's a form of communication, I suppose, in a way. Also, it's absolutely fascinating.

Fowler (1986, p.288) described an experience he had of aesthetic hunger on entering an art gallery, which he expressed as a hunger for beauty and, even more, a hunger for 'images and forms that could touch deep places in the spirit, healing, energising, and giving it new life'. This informant's experience in the art classes could perhaps be in this realm. There was no mention of a religious theme in either instance. However, it seems most probable that the human being can and does respond to experiences of beauty and creativity such as art. And this can be a 'peak experience', a touching into the soul of some kind of 'otherness'.

## Writing

Five of the informants have been involved in writing, two have had work published, in their later years. Each of them seems to enjoy this activity a great deal. Some of the writing involves reminiscence and history, and it is probably a valuable venture for both the individual and for the community.

## The environment

A love of nature, the environment, or creation was important for most of the informants. A number spoke of the joy of gardening, or of being able to go into the bush, the mountains or sea. In fact Carol found meaning 'only from nature, from trees and places like the Botanical Gardens, and where you can get away from people'. This informant has a deep relationship with God, yet she expressed finding meaning through creation and the environment. Perhaps this can be seen as meaning through a creator God.

Doris said: 'I think I'm conscious of creation around me and the beauty around me, certainly in people, my friends, I see all those things as good. Watched over by the Lord being the best thing.' Angela spoke of the changes she was experiencing now as she grows older: 'The mountains...they seem to be sharper than they used to be.'

On the other hand Win spoke of her awareness of creation around her and said she looked for 'little miracles every day'.

> That little tree, how did it know it was autumn – usually things when they start growing are green, this had little autumn leaves on, it was only, it was one of the seeds from one of the trees round here, how did that tree know that it was autumn? That's my miracle for the day.

Diane finds meaning in being out in the wilderness. One of her greatest joys was putting her feet on the Antarctic for the first time, an incredible emotional and spiritual experience for her. Helen spoke of peak experiences in life for her as 'beauty all around us, and look for beauty, strive to be happy, joy from nature and seeing something grow in the garden'.

Mary said behind her love of painting lies a love of nature. She likes to be with people, and 'I like to think that even my painting gives people encouragement'. For this woman there has been a mid-life blossoming, a realisation of talents she did not know she had, and a new freedom to use them. These she has developed and used wisely, often for the benefit of others. This fits with Neugarten's (1968) observations of changes in mid life.

### Experience of 'otherness'

According to Hardy (1979), Hay (1982) and Greeley (1982) experiences of 'otherness', or intense religious experiences were not uncommon in the studies they performed in North America and the United Kingdom. Six of the informants in this study volunteered experiences which could only be described as experiences of 'otherness'. None of my questions asked for this type of information. This was one aspect that a number of informants clearly identified as part of spirituality.

George spoke of an experience at the time of his father's death: 'And then, one early morning, it seemed to me that my wireless went on, a light or something, and that was that, and then [his sister] rang me a few hours later and said "Dad's dead", and she said, "twenty past one or something" and that was really the time I had the strange experience.'

One man recounted a mystical experience he had as young man, where all his future life was mapped out before him, all of which had since happened, including who he would marry, the work he would do and a book he would write.

Angela described a powerful spiritual experience: 'And there was the oddest thing, I was suddenly filled with this entire, completely filled with light, this very strong light, I was full of it, and I was so overwhelmed by it...'. Another informant, Edith whose husband died about four years before, shared how one night she had observed something that she described as a glow moving around the bedroom. She said that at times she had a real sense of her husband being there with her.

Eva said she remembered her husband calling her, saying her name, saying 'I'm sorry' just before he died. He was in hospital and she was at home when she heard him call. Later, when they came to give her a message to come to the hospital, she knew already that he was dead.

Helen spoke of a number of religious experiences:

but...I had some extraordinary experiences where I felt that I knew that somebody who had passed over and wanted to get a message through … some messages, word came through me, almost as if I was overshadowed, of words that I wouldn't normally use.

Her religious experiences include sensitivity to people's auras. Helen has constructed her own religion.

What do these experiences demonstrate? These experiences were obviously important to these informants who, in each case, seemed to look for affirmation from me, and there were comments like 'I couldn't just talk to anybody about that'. There is not a lot written about such experiences. Hay (1982, p.121) remarked that they had thought older people may be more likely to have such experiences, although he noted in their UK sample that education may have been a confounding variable. Indications were that those of higher social class and who were better educated were more likely to have religious experiences. This is an interesting area, and one in which, it seems, perhaps people don't always feel comfortable to share with others. Only two of these informants who spoke of 'otherness' regularly attend church.

### Summary

*The experiences described in this section outline how various of the informants in this study have responded to the ultimate, or connected with events or things that were particularly deep and significant for them. For some, the experiences were of joy, or of peace, of awe, of bringing fulfilment and meaning, or of a sense of connecting with something or someone outside themselves. At a deep level, on occasion, mystery meets with human experience. Being in church buildings, particularly Gothic buildings, was described as being a special experience by some. Response through music, the arts and in particular painting were important to a number.*

*Knowledge of this variety of ways of responding to the Ultimate in older people's lives may be of assistance in supporting them in responding to what is ultimate in their lives, be it church services, prayer, meditation, or music, art or the environment. Sensitivity to people's experiences of 'otherness' is also important in the work of pastoral carers, noting that a number of informants remarked that they would not share accounts of such experiences 'with just anyone'.*

# CHAPTER 8

# The spiritual journey in ageing

## Faith and spiritual development in later life

Is there actually a spiritual journey that carries through into ageing? In recent years there has been a growing interest and discussion regarding changes in spirituality across the lifespan. The most prolific author in this field has been Fowler and his work has generated a great deal of discussion during the last couple of decades (Harris 1986; Koenig 1994; Parks 1992; Shulik 1992). Although he has talked of 'faith development' rather than 'spiritual development', I have chosen to include his work here as his definition of faith is close to the definition of spirituality I have used in this study.

### Fowler and stages of faith development

According to Fowler (1981) there are stages of faith development across the lifespan just as there are stages of psychosocial development. But it would seem that not everyone progresses through all these stages. Fowler asserts that everyone has a faith which, when defined in the broadest of terms, is to be understood largely as meaning in life. His model of faith is one that allows for a universal understanding of faith and provides a structure that can be applied to any faith or religion; that is, he has presented a structure, not a content, of faith. In a sense his presentation of the paradigm is that of a generic faith, which could be applied equally well to Christianity, to other major world religions, or to humanism. Fowler, in the process of developing his stages of faith development model, has tested it on people of different faiths, on people who acknowledged no faith, and on different ethnic, educational and socioeconomic groups.

Fowler (1986) writes: '*Faith* has to do with the making, maintenance, and transformation of human meaning' (p.15). Fowler goes on to state that he believes faith to be a human universal, and 'most often, it comes to expression and accountability through the symbols, rituals, and beliefs of particular religious traditions'. Further, he states:

the major religious communities are the living repositories of the faith expressions of countless peoples in the past and present. These elements form traditions. They can serve to awaken and express the faith of people in the present. But faith is not always religious in the cultural or institutional sense. Many persons in our time weave and paint their meaning-canvases in communities other than religious, and often with symbols or stories which have no direct relationship to traditions of group piety or religious worship. (p.16)

In a multicultural society it is understandable that there will be many different ways of weaving and painting the meaning-canvas of life. When considering the spiritual, or perhaps the faith, needs of older adults, it is necessary to have an understanding of what such meaning-canvases might look like.

Fowler (1986) sees faith as *relational*, saying that faith begins, for the infant, within relationship, leading to developing trust in another person. Loyalty develops in return for trust, that is, the relationship is reciprocal. Loyalty is:

an active mode of knowing and being in which we relate to others and form communities with those with whom we share common loyalties to supra-ordinate centers of value and power...in which we grasp our relatedness to others and...power(s) and value(s) which unify and give character to an ultimate environment. (p.19)

He also sees faith *as a way of knowing*: 'Faith is a way of being, arising out of a way of *seeing* and *knowing*.' Fowler says, that faith 'is a knowing which involves both reason and feeling; both rationality and passionality...the challenge is to recognise that meaning-making, as a constructive movement, is prior to and generative of both reason and emotion' (p.21). It involves *constitutive-knowing*: 'the knowing that composes or establishes both the known and the knower in relation to the known'. Faith has to do with the learning of moral-knowing as well.

Fowler (1986) has described seven stages of faith development (p.32):

0   Undifferentiated

i   Intuitive-projective

ii   Mythic-literal

iii   Synthetic-conventional

   iv   Individuative-reflective

   v    Paradoxical-consolidative or conjunctive faith

   vi   Universalising

He described these stages following in-depth interviews of a large sample of people (p.359) at different ages across the lifespan. He sees these stages as somewhat related to Piaget, Erikson and Kohlberg's developmental stages but notes that not every person will progress through all stages. In particular, Fowler believes that stage 6, universalising faith, is rare. It appears, according to his findings, that older adults are more likely to be in stages three to five. Only those stages more relevant to the study of older adults are outlined here.

### SYNTHETIC-CONVENTIONAL FAITH

Although this stage is seen as occurring in late childhood, it can also become a terminal stage of faith development; thus some older adults may be at this stage. This stage is seen as being the faith of the community, it's everybody's faith, that is, conformist. The holder of this type is tuned to the expectations and judgements of significant others and has not seen the need to construct his/her own faith stance. It is synthetic in that it lacks analysis, it is accepted without question. This type of faith provides a coherent orientation in the midst of the more complex and diverse range of involvements of school, work and society (Fowler 1981).

### INDIVIDUATIVE-REFLECTIVE FAITH

In stage 4 there is a relocation of authority in the self, resulting in a critical distancing from one's previously held assumptive value system and, second, the emergence of the executive ego (Fowler 1981); that is, the individual will be critical of the advice and knowledge of others. This stage is typical of early adulthood but, again, may be a final stage for some. The transition into this stage may occur at any time from young adulthood onwards.

### PARADOXICAL-CONSOLIDATIVE OR CONJUNCTIVE FAITH

A 'balanced faith, inclusive faith, a both/and faith' (Astley and Francis 1992, p.viii) is rare before thirty. A marked feature of this stage is a 'new openness to others and their world views, and a new ability to keep in tension the paradoxes and polarities of faith and life (p.xxii). A new humility and recognition of interdependence is seen at this stage.

UNIVERSALISING FAITH

The final stage of faith development, universalising faith is said to be rare and only occurs in later life. It has been described as a selfless faith: it involves a relinquishing and transcending of the self.

## Critique of Fowler's stages of faith development

Koenig (1994) has written a rigorous critique of Fowler's theory. He criticises Fowler's work on a number of bases, including, the correlation between cognitive ability and level of faith, saying that the original sample may have been biased and not fully representative. He says that there is a proper place for the acceptance of a simple faith, underscored by Scripture. It would seem, however, that there is allowance for scriptural-based faith in the model, as it is structure, not content that is prescribed.

Koenig was critical of the sampling process used by Fowler, noting that people over the age of 60 years were under-represented in his study (Koenig 1994). However, Fowler (1981) listed the percentage of participants 61 years and over as 17.3 per cent. Of these, 17.8 per cent were male while 16.8 per cent were female. This would appear to be a fair representation of this age group in society, but Koenig is correct in wanting more data on this group to further test the stages for older people. Perhaps, also, there is an over-representation of males in the age group compared with the demographic gender ratio.

Second, Koenig (1994) critiqued the method of selection suggesting that they may not have been representative of the wider community on the basis of educational and intellectual capacity, being drawn from populations in the vicinity of universities and education levels not being presented. He was critical here of the emphasis on the cognitive content of faith. Koenig makes the valid point regarding the difficulty of using an interview schedule based on a cognitive structure of faith development with elderly people, particularly because of the proportion of older adults who have cognitive disabilities.

It would seem that this criticism is based more on the difficulty of making an assessment of the level of a person's faith if they should have dementia, rather than on the possibility that emphasis on assessing the cognitive aspects of faith may seem to produce a decline in faith levels in ageing. Here it may be a case of measuring the wrong criteria. It must also be asked how useful such information would be in a clinical situation. It would seem that the main reason for assessing spirituality and faith in older adults would be to identify needs for spiritual interventions or pastoral care.

It is noted that in Fowler's (1981) study of 359 people only one was found to match with stage 6 faith stage, and this was a male. One would have to consider this description of stage 6 very carefully: does this stage really exist, and is its description adequate? Should we expect more people to reach the higher stages of faith development? Is the way of defining these stages within a cognitive-development framework valid? Further work remains in this fascinating area.

Shulik (1992), using Fowler's (1981) interview schedule, presented further data on 40 elderly men and women, concluding that Fowler's stages of faith development could make a meaningful contribution in the field of ageing. However, no new knowledge of faith development in ageing was added from the use of the Fowler interview schedule in Shulik's study.

### Gender, the faith journey and Gilligan

Parks (1992, p.103) critiques Fowler's (1981) work on the basis of gender, remarking that, based on Gilligan's work, the emphasis in Fowler's stages on individuation rather than on 'relation and the formation of a responsive self' neglects to address critical gender differences in the theory. Harris (1986), too, is critical of what she sees as gender bias in examples of faith stages, noting the reliance of Fowler on Kohlberg's theory of moral development for the development of his theory. She suggests that studies of women's experiences of religious matters, in a similar mode to Gilligan's work, would be fruitful. Fowler, writing in response to her comments in the same publication, notes that his work has been 'in large measure, done in a white man's mode' (p.289).

Gilligan (1993) asks, is human development more properly understood as a process of separation, or of attachment? Gilligan notes that there are documented differences between women and men in the areas of identity and intimacy in young adulthood, confirmed in her research (p.156). She says that men talk of the 'role of separation as it defines and empowers the self', while women talk of 'the ongoing process of attachment that creates and sustains the human community'.

So far there has been little research using women in studying human development and Gilligan (1993) has been critical of this, noting Erikson's emphasis on the study of men's psychosocial development (p.107). Her own work has not included older women and it is uncertain whether her results can be applied to older women, particularly from the view of increasing androgyny in ageing. It may not be a case of either separation or attachment but that both aspects of human development are important. It is important, however, to consider her work in relation to what is occurring for older women in their spiritual development. Can Gilligan's findings be seen in older women too? Is spiritual development going to present different responses in women and men?

Having considered faith, as set forth in the theory developed by Fowler (1981), it is worth noting the relationship between faith, religion and spirituality. Faith as defined by Fowler is closely paralleled by the definition of spirituality used in this study. Understanding the relation between faith and specific religious beliefs and practices is put well by Broughton (1986, p.91): that it is only through specific conversion that faith becomes qualified as 'specifically religious' or is further qualified in terms of a particular denomination.

In spite of understandable criticisms of Fowler's work, it is acknowledged that he has made a highly valuable contribution to knowledge in this field; knowledge that is being continually added to (Dykstra and Parks 1986; Fowler *et al.* 1992; Astley and Francis 1992) since his early publications.

## Consciousness of being on a spiritual journey

Ten of the informants in this study acknowledged making a personal commitment to 'give their lives to Jesus' at some point during their lives. For some it had been a journey reaching from childhood onwards, for others there had been a commitment that began later in life.

Sylvia made a personal commitment to Jesus at age 14 years. Now she says she has a daily walk with God that is not only a comfort, but also a guide and support. She declares a 'very strong acceptance of faith in God', she has 'been able to hold on to that through a lot of personal adversity'. She is 'awestruck by the magnificence…(of creation)…that's the power of my God'. She says she waits to meet God one day.

Doris expressed a deep faith in Jesus, and centres her life on Jesus. She sees Jesus as a close friend. This was not always so, and she described the change which occurred for her in mid life, when she developed a personal relationship with God, through Jesus:

> it was a lot of years later actually, it was in about 1961. I've done a lot of growing up and been married and had children and all that. I think until

then, it [going to church] was a sort of pattern of life. It wasn't that I didn't have a relationship with God, but I really couldn't have called it a relationship. I guess…faith in those early years, for me, was a fear thing I suppose, because that's what it was like, God was up out there, and you know, a big master… But in 1961, I was asked to become a catechist in the state school. We had to do a course of training, and it was a fairly intensive course… All of a sudden, Jesus, and his life, all became real. I could suddenly see he was a person, just like me. Like the rest of us, it wasn't out there.

She described what followed from this course of study:

And that then triggered off something in me, a search, that probably, deep down, I'd always had; but then I began searching more and more, in a growing way. I suppose not immediately, but Jesus became for me a real, a really close friend; someone I felt I really had a deep relationship with.

This change of relationship was a real one that resulted in changed outlook on life and it has persisted since then. Doris noted that her image of God has changed across the lifespan, from that of an impersonal God, 'up out there', tinged with fear, drawn from her childhood experiences and Catholic upbringing. The relationship with Jesus Doris described now is a close and intimate one; there is a sense in which this has become even more important in her widowhood.

Of the spiritual journey through life she says:

maybe, if you're blessed, you come to a stage where it challenges you and you have to, whatever…whatever you come out with at the end, it's your own spirituality you have then, it's not the one that's been passed on to you.

Here Doris acknowledges the necessary step in faith development that requires each individual to make a decision for themselves, in regard to faith. No adult can continue to live on the faith of their parents, no matter how effective that faith is. Each individual has to develop their own sense of what is to be ultimate in their lives, and how they will respond to that. While the expectation is that young adults make such decisions, this is not always so, and it seems that Doris did this later in her life.

She is grateful for the spirituality she has, and she wants to keep it that way. 'I suppose this is part of it, keeping your marbles.' Spirituality for her is also 'a sharing thing. It's sharing with other people. I suppose that's natural enough, because it's sharing it with God in the first place'.

This woman had a real sense of a spiritual journey through her life, she seems able to stand back and consider her life journey and the part her faith has played in it.

Angela, another informant in this sub-category, had a similar experience. Although she said she has always been aware of God, she had been a 'habitual' church goer. She described having a mid-life conversion at 55. After attending a short programme of Christian study, Angela now says of her faith:

> It was like having the blinkers taken off. As if I really heard for the first time. And I thought, why is it that I spent all these years, and I'm hearing. It was at that time that I realised that, I started to believe, really believed.

She now really believes, knows she 'has a Saviour'. She described her relationship with God now:

> I'd like to be able to say he's my life, my whole being, nice-sounding words. I know I'd like to be able to say that. Because I do believe, and when you look around you and you see the beauty of everything. I should be able to do a better job.

And yet, she still seeks to grow in her faith, and she is all too aware of her inadequacies.

## A changing relationship with God

Carol remembered that as a child she had seen God as punitive and distant, and herself as a potential criminal. This view had been encouraged through the teaching of an influential woman in her life, the vicar's wife. From her description, it is unlikely that the informant's perception of God gained through this instruction was as it was meant; rather, it is stressed, this was a small child's perception of it. At one point she made a wire cross which she wore around her neck to remind herself that God was watching her. This image was one that she continued to carry with her until well into her adult life. But now she said, 'I'd describe God as being very all spirit'.

Later in life she became conscious of the development of a personal ongoing spiritual search, 'a real need for developing my spiritual life', which became evident in 1990. Through her search she has come to a new understanding of God. 'I got to know God almost as a person, but not as a man. It couldn't be a person, but both a woman and a man, so therefore it had to be spirit.' She now shows a tolerance to others' views of faith.

This woman, too, seems to have had a later life (at age 67) conversion experience in the manner described by Fowler (1981). Carol's conversion experience is worth considering from a view often espoused in a number of the mainstream Churches, that conversion is most likely to occur in youth, and while that probably is so, certainly a number of older people in this study continue to seek to grow spiritually and had life-changing experiences later in life. Perhaps in later life the journey is even more pressing, because the sense of time is changing, from time left to live to time already lived (Neugarten 1968).

This informant describes a sense of deepening interiority through her study, meditation and prayer life. This deepening sense of interiority has been developing while she has been becoming increasingly frail physically. It is suggested that this is a part of the process of moving from doing to being that occurs with increasing age and perhaps even more so with increasing frailty.

Not all the informants had conversion experiences that they could put a date to. Win clearly expressed her sense of relationship with God when she said, 'I thought it meant that every part of my life needed to be given to God to do what he wanted.' But for her the development of faith was a gradual process, over a number of years from her teenage years, a gradual involvement and realisation. 'It wasn't necessarily just one, one single step.' Her image of God was 'that with God I could do anything, that the impossible was quite possible, you know'. Her faith in God allowed her to gain self-confidence, in marked contrast to another informant, who believed that her understanding of God was what kept her shy and lacking in confidence.

Win now sees God as the creator, 'and the master-mind of the universe'. At the same time she says, 'but I feel I've got to continually look at Jesus and see his sort of interpretation or his attitude towards God as Father'. She further explained her relationship with God by saying, 'I think of God more as a friend. Which is what I think to be why Jesus came: to really to give a different picture of what God was', and 'I think too of God as the Spirit, the Holy Spirit who is in every person'.

This woman too continues to grow in her faith. She still questions God, particularly regarding her daily walk of faith. As she notices physical changes in her life, she asks God how she should handle these, for instance decreasing levels of energy.

Ben's faith journey has also been a gradual one, of growth and development until he has reached a stage where his faith is a central component of his life. A number of difficulties earlier in life have probably helped to shape his belief system, including a divorce and being a prisoner of war.

Ben spoke of his relationship with God: 'Well, He's all encompassing isn't He, and we go to Christ, you're touching deep stuff now. No, no, Christ is the one because Christ died for us and this is it.' Of his faith journey he said: 'I think it…gradually evolved and it just got deeper and deeper as the years went by and, and meant more to me. And you've got to get your priorities right now whether the church means more to you or not, or go the races on Sunday.' This man relied on God in times of great difficulties, for example when he was a prisoner of war and when his marriage broke down. 'There's no one else around to help me.'

### Conversion experience and Fowler's definition

Two informants in this study, Doris and Angela, described coming to a decision in mid-life to accept Jesus as a personal saviour and central in their lives. Another woman described her conversion experience at age 67. These experiences could be classified conversion experiences according to Fowler (1981). He defines conversion as:

> a significant recentering of one's previous conscious or unconscious images of value and power, and the conscious adoption of a new set of master stories in the commitment to reshape one's life in a new community of interpretation and action. (p.281)

Both Doris and Angela described a real change in belief and world views, one speaking of being a 'habitual' church goer before, the other describing a distant relationship with God, perhaps tinged with fear. Changed beliefs included changed behaviours as well. These changed beliefs for each of them included a move that led to adopting a new way of living, new values, a new centre of faith, a 'real' faith, not simply going through the actions. Their faith now meant something completely new. For the former 'habitual' church attender, there was possibly a change in faith stage. Angela had moved from a stage 3 conforming to a habitual worship and belief system, to actively learning and growing in her faith. At the time of interview, it is suggested that she is at stage 5, conjunctive faith. She seems to have come alive to a new set of 'master stories'.

Although Fowler (1981) seems to be saying that people move up through the stages one at a time, I wonder if the outcome of conversion may be one of several things. First, the person may change the content of the faith stage, but not the stage (Fowler, 1981, pp.285–6); second, a change of both content and stage may occur. Fowler also suggests that conversion may precipitate stage change, or stage change may precipitate conversion. Another possibility, not mentioned by Fowler, is that a person may virtually skip one stage, as it appears Doris has done; or perhaps the processing of stage 4 was done almost unconsciously. Maybe the conversion opened this woman to new world possibilities; on the evidence available it seems she has moved from stage 3 straight to stage 5. Doris retains her openness to others, her active participation in the practice of her faith, and her willingness to lovingly accept others different from herself. As well, there is a sense of excitement about life, an engagement with life that is really energising.

## Tolerance of other denominations and religions

Eight informants expressed self-awareness of an increasing tolerance of other denominations and religious faiths as they are growing older. Vera reported a tolerance towards other religions:

> A good Buddhist is probably as acceptable to God as a good Christian, I don't know…maybe, it's not the orthodox Christian view, I don't know. But it's one which enables me to get on with my neighbours. And I mean that in a very literal sense.

Edith shows a tolerance of the faith of others: 'There's only one God you know'. Others spoke of a sense of becoming 'more ecumenical' as they grow older, meaning that they felt more at one with members of other denominations than when they had been younger. It is uncertain whether this is simply a change within themselves, or whether this is a reflection of changing community attitudes among denominations in general.

These views are consistent with paradoxical-consolidative or conjunctive faith as described by Fowler. Thus one-third of those interviewed in-depth in this study could be at stage five of Fowler's stages of faith development.

## Searching for God or a source of meaning

The search for meaning in life was more apparent in the stories of some informants than others. In some instances there is evidence of an increasing interior journey; for some it is a very cognitive search.

Carol is on a journey, a search for meaning in life, an acknowledged journey of faith. She says her energy for living comes from learning new things.

For Lisa, a long-term and deep connection with her own spirituality is evident in her life, in relationships and reflections on faith. She still questions and seeks to continue learning and growing in her faith. Lisa described having a sense of needing to give back some of what has been given to her in her life. She gains self-fulfilment from helping others. She spoke of her life journey and searching:

> I think I was probably just born with a certain sense of an extra dimension, of something bigger than myself, which is there. And I just know it's there. And I think what I've always had is still fundamentally what I have known.

Helga and Mary have a real sense of the spiritual, but don't connect that with the church, or even really with God. Helga has changed in her life search for God. She described her relationship as a young adult.

> I became a real Bible basher. You know they were very radical, I suppose, lipstick, or makeup and dancing and music, were taboo. And because I was brought up in a Scottish heritage, with music and dancing, and fun in your life, you know. And I was this born-again Christian, even though now I realise that my mother was a good sound Christian really, that because, I was packing myself off to heaven, and they [her parents] were going to hell.

This woman has rejected her earlier images of God and has not yet found a right place to be spiritually. She says, 'Of all the religions that I know of, Jesus Christ was the one I can identify with.' She says she has respect for Jesus as teacher: 'he was one of the first great philosophers'. But she doubted he was the Son of God. She sees God as spiritual, 'it's this force, you know', 'it's like something, you can't see, but you can experience it as the truth'. She reports her spiritual support comes through a self-help group. She has relied on the support she has gained through this group both for herself, in her mental health problems and for her daughter, who has schizophrenia.

She says she is working on getting peace of mind, but does not have that yet. She has not found contentment in life: '[I] always want something better than what I've got.' She still searches for a god she can feel right with and has tried a number of different religious groups, without finding one she can feel comfortable with. She currently has no church affiliation at all.

Mary, on the other hand, seems to have found a place of acceptance and peace. She does not have any church background. Mary said that a new beginning started for her 'about 45 or so, I got back into things after being married [divorced]'. In her experience she does not connect spiritual things with church. She went on to say of the spiritual: 'I think that's in yourself, it's something that's in yourself.' She spoke of life as a journey: 'I've always felt that life is quite a trip you know, it's an experience and shouldn't just be wasted.' She believes the religious teaching of her childhood kept her shy and reserved.

Dawn, however, says there are not many satisfying things in her life at present. She spoke of her inner resources, but she has not completely rejected the possibility that responsibility for who she was and what she had achieved in life rested with other people. As she said:

> I think I have learnt to realise in my later years that I am a much stronger person than I ever had any idea of, and if I'd had the confidence, and if somebody had made me realise that at the beginning I could have done marvellous things with my life, that's the biggest regret and when it comes to the crunch I could get up and go on you know.

But now, she is beginning to see that she can make changes in her own life. 'I've done more living since I've retired than I ever did before... Things have much more meaning for me, yes, my life when I was working was awful, quite frankly it was awful.' Dawn is able to look back on her life and acknowledge earlier difficulties. A sense of acceptance is evident here, as she says: 'I have this basic feeling that if I've survived this far, that God has come to the rescue when things have been a lot worse than they are now so, so I'm sure that He will look after me, the last bit.'

Helen says she has been on a 'spiritual quest' for 'most of my life'. Peak experiences in life for her are the 'beauty all around us, and look for beauty, strive to be happy'. She has a great number of books on spiritual matters, on Eastern teachings as well as Western. She feels there is not much difference in the types of spirituality expressed in the writings she has studied: 'They're just different names really, maybe different approaches, but you can simplify it to you know very, very fundamental things in essence.' As she grows older, joys are found in:

> the calls of birds or even the old chooks cackling after they've laid an egg,...friends dropping in occasionally, unexpected phone calls, birthday cards, the Christmas cards pouring in, books, delightful, wonderful books.... There's never time to do all the things I want to do.

## Summary

*Eleven out of 24 informants spoke of a conscious search for meaning as they grew older. A number were finding meaning through human relationship, particularly through grandchildren, and did not seem to seek for any meaning outside this. Why weren't the others in the study conscious of such a search for meaning? Was it because the search for meaning is not a universal human characteristic? This is doubtful in view of the abundance of literature on this topic, from Frankl (1984) onwards. It is possible that the other informants were not so deeply in touch with their spiritual dimension, and were thus not responding to the search for meaning. Perhaps that could be a factor of the society which emphasises the scientific and technological at the expense of the spiritual.*

*One-third (8) of the informants spoke about a spiritual journey or a changing relationship with God over their life journey. Important in this journey is the image of God held by each of the informants, and how this has changed. The image of God held by informants becomes the place from which they respond to life and to others around them; it is an important aspect of the development of hope within the person.*

*While a number of informants noted changes in faith across the lifespan, three in particular had in recent years what could be properly termed (using Fowler's (1981) criteria) conversion experiences. It is perhaps one of the myths of ageing that older people don't change, and that people are not going to be converted in their later years. Two of these women were in mid life, while one was 67, when they had this experience. It has made an important difference to their world view and to their sense of spirituality in ageing. These are pertinent considerations for clergy and pastoral care workers, and are addressed in relation to preparation for these roles discussed in the recommendations from this study.*

# CHAPTER 9

# Perceptions of self-sufficiency and vulnerability in ageing

## Meaning: perceived circumstances and vulnerability

The process of ageing itself, with physical decrements, is well acknowledged (Schneider and Rowe 1990). The problems of arthritis, osteoporosis and fractures, heart disease, dementia, sight and hearing deficits, incontinence and more, all common in older adults, make ageing difficult for large numbers of people. Living alone, lowered energy levels and restricted mobility are other factors in increasing vulnerability in older people.

A major factor for people facing increasing frailty in ageing is, it seems, an anticipation of losing control of their lives, of being unable to make decisions and of increasing dependence on others for their needs. Are these new fears for our current society or are these fears a part of being human? Perhaps fear of increasing vulnerability is more real because ours is a death-denying society.

We need to examine alternatives for human experience and meaning in those who have experienced life-threatening illnesses and major crises in life. People who have lost almost everything in life have often survived against tremendous odds, with a real sense of hope. Frankl (1984) wrote of his experiences in concentration camps during the Second World War, where some survived and others did not, although enduring equally devastating experiences. In these situations, human values shift, the person's identity becomes largely irrelevant and life is stripped of any normal meaning. Frankl asked the question of why some survived while others did not. Hope and transcendence appeared to be vital factors.

## The move from 'doing' to 'being' in ageing

In the current Western societies, identity is derived largely from what one's occupation is; when this is lost, as in ageing, and particularly in increasing frailty, there is no longer an identity available for that person in terms of our normal understanding. What remains is a vulnerable human being. How this vulnerable person experiences life may be a major problem, both for those who are dependent and for those who anticipate dependency.

## Finitude and anxiety

Tillich claims that 'the threat to integrity has its deepest root in the anxiety common to all finite creatures' (Otterness 1995). The anxiety becomes apparent in a perceived separation from God: the threat of 'non-being'.

Otterness (p.439) outlines Tillich's (1963) four principles of sanctification:

1. *Increased awareness:* similar to the wisdom described by Erikson. 'Recognises the ambiguities of life but does not succumb to despair'.

2. *Increased freedom:* from the binding power of the law upon the conscience, can take risks.

3. *Increased relatedness:* power to 'break through the wall of self-seclusion' and establish new and better relationships with others.

4. *The principle of self-transcendence:* 'the recognition that the goals of increased awareness, freedom, and relatedness are only possible when the self continues in relation to the divine source of its being'.

Tillich (1963) also wrote of the power of affirming life and its vital dynamics in spite of ambiguities both within the individual and in others. Sanctification, according to Tillich, is a process, a movement towards maturity, and, he said, the Christian life never reaches a state of perfection.

The description of sanctification provided by Tillich and considered by Otterness (1995) as a way of moving from doing to being is very much like the spiritual journey described by Clements (1990). Yet there are differences between Tillich's move to freedom and new and better relationships and Clement's view on stripping or shedding of roles that relates to the psychosocial theory of disengagement. To use Tillich, or indeed Erikson's (1968) view, the move in ageing is to vital involvement in ageing. Perhaps there does need to be a both/and approach. The real shift from doing to being probably only occurs in frail ageing.

The importance of sanctification and vocation in later life is part of the process of change from doing to being. Of later life, and applicable to this process, Paul wrote: 'So we do not lose heart. Even though our outer nature is wasting away, our inner nature is being renewed day by day' (2 Corinthians 4:16).

Au and Cobb (1995) remark that ageing, considered as a process, is a 'being-towards-death'. As members of a society that clearly values doing beyond being, we must experience certain tensions of meaning as the ability to 'do' recedes and the identity once attached to doing is lost as well. Au and Cobb suggest that the task of shifting from doing to being may be the 'great spiritual task of ageing' (p.449).

The meaninglessness that occurs for some older people may well be because their centre for meaning, being derived purely from the doing component of their lives, is lost in growing older. This is not to say, of course, that 'successful' older age consists entirely of being rather than doing. And many older people continue to do many things effectively, bringing much satisfaction to their lives. Still others will find that the doing is taken away from them due to some disease or illness condition. In all, however, there does appear to be a greater move to 'interiority' in ageing than earlier in life (Bornat 1994; Coleman 1986; Moody 1995).

One problem identified by Au and Cobb (1995) in the doing of older adults is that what they often are able to do is low in public visibility, and thus social recognition of their deeds is lower; they suggest that older people may need to learn to find satisfaction in the doing itself rather than any recognition that may come. While attempting to come to terms with new ways of doing in ageing, it must not be forgotten that it is necessary to focus on becoming and being as well. This is the search for increased interiority, a spiritual developmental task of ageing.

How is this transition made between doing and being? How are the frail and vulnerable older people affirmed? These questions are important and are at least explored with this study of independent older adults even though, due to their level of independence, they were not expected to be frail.

## Perceived vulnerability among the informants

There is a sense in which there is an increased vulnerability in some of these older people, both men and women, even when they are well educated and have strong faith and strong support systems in family and community.

The vulnerability seems to be centred more on things which are outside their control, such as future fears, for example of living alone and of losing control of independent living. Approaching the final stages of their life journey, there may be concerns or fears of failing physical health. Perceived vulnerability seems to be related to anticipated future events. Fear is a feature for some older people. Hulicka (1992) described a fear scale developed and used for fears most frequently endorsed by elderly female community respondents.

This chapter considers the theme of self-sufficiency versus vulnerability. Sub-categories of this include disabilities and the effect of physical ageing, and the transition from doing to being. First, how is the concept of self-sufficiency and vulnerability related to the spiritual dimension? Physical changes of ageing, either as part of the ageing process or as chronic illness conditions of older people will necessarily impinge on the overall well-being of these older adults.

The concept of vulnerability is closely connected with the important enabling concept of transcendence (Frankl 1984). It seems that an aspect of ageing for many people will be the process of learning to transcend the difficulties of a declining physical being and to continue to grow psycho-socially and spiritually. Peck's (1968) stages of psychosocial development in ageing are relevant here, only there is the need to take these stages further to include spiritual development.

Transcendence is a component of both wisdom and of spirituality. Transcendence allows an individual to move from self-centredness to other-centredness. It allows an individual who has multiple chronic illness conditions, or with multiple disabilities, or is otherwise suffering to move beyond these very real difficulties in life, which may block continued spiritual development, to engage life.

The in-depth interviews were a rich source of data for the kinds of health problems these older independently living people experience, and for the ways they are able to live with, and in some cases transcend, the difficulties of everyday life.

## How healthy would you say you are?

An important first question was asked of all 75 participants in the study. Their responses to the question, 'In your perception, how healthy would you say you are?' are shown in Table 9.1. A number who answered this saying they were in good to very good health lived with a number of chronic diseases, for instance diabetes, heart disease, severe arthritis, hip and knee replacements, triple by-pass, etc., yet they regarded themselves as healthy. This illustrates an important factor in ageing; self-perception of health is more than a medical diagnosis. As this study suggests, health in older people is not simply a factor of physical ailments, it is more an interaction between physical, mental and spiritual well-being, involving the ability to transcend the problems an individual may encounter in ageing. Thus the concept of functional capacity becomes an important one in ageing. The real question for each older person is 'How well can I function?', not 'What is my medical condition?'.

### Table 9.1 How healthly would you say you are?

| Self-perception of health | Number | Percentage |
| --- | --- | --- |
| Poor health | 1 | 1.3 |
| Fairly healthy | 11 | 14.7 |
| Moderately healthy | 19 | 25.3 |
| Good health | 29 | 38.7 |
| Very good health | 15 | 20.0 |
| Total | 75 | 100.0 |

## Self-sufficiency versus vulnerability

An important factor for all informants in this study was perceived future vulnerability. All acknowledged their apprehension as they pondered the possibilities of future dependence. There seemed to be a general consensus among those interviewed in-depth that older age came with dependency, loss of self-control and the possibility of mental deterioration. Some had already experienced the effects of physical disabilities and most had some chronic illness; however, the way they functioned in the face of disabilities varied a great deal.

Various individuals expressed fears of the process of dying, but none expressed fear of death itself, even when asked directly. A number have had major surgery in recent years and/or live with chronic illness but still regard themselves as being reasonably healthy. Of particular concern to eight of the

24 who were interviewed in-depth is the possibility of developing Alzheimer's disease. Two informants even spoke of losing control of their lives in this way as being a possible situation warranting suicide or euthanasia.

I have chosen to consider the comments of informants under headings that seem to most accurately reflect their current status regarding self-sufficiency or vulnerability. Some are a complex mixture of self-sufficiency and vulnerability; I have discussed some of these under both headings. Other sub-categories are: fear of increasing frailty; less energy now; disabilities and chronic illness; fear of developing dementia/Alzheimer's disease; memory; and reported transcendence of difficulties.

## Self-sufficiency

Self-sufficiency is highly valued among older adults in Australia (Russell 1981) and other Western societies. Current Australian government policy affirms the caring for older adults in their own homes for as long as possible. Recent developments to bring Community Aged Care Packages to their homes support this. Comments from informants and general community attitude back this policy. Geographically dispersed family structures in this country make it difficult for some frail older adults to receive adequate family support. This group of older people were all functioning well in the community; few used any community supports, and most were able to drive their own cars or use public transport.

Self-sufficiency often involved the individual being able to take part in community activities and belong to various groups. For example, a number of informants were members of the University of the Third Age. They were active both physically and mentally. Among their many activities were music, art, writing, language courses, computer courses, walking, travel, gardening, church activities, meeting with friends, community service, part-time and casual work, and helping others in need.

Being self-sufficient allowed these people freedom on how to use their time; freedom to take part or not be involved in activities as they desired. But for all this, all of them expressed at least a vague sense of the possibility of future vulnerability. Generally there was a range of wellness levels in this group of self-sufficient older people. Of those who reported being self-sufficient, Ann, Beryl and Eva all reported having good health; others lived effectively with chronic illnesses.

Doris is very independent, and at 73 years she has few physical changes of ageing. She doesn't have any fears, but prays each day that the Lord will take away the fears she might have.

Win expressed her frustration at times in trying to remember names: 'I can't remember things, and in particular I can't remember people's names, well, I never have.' She was at one level aware of the fact that this was not a new difficulty she was experiencing, but at the same time seemed to be acknowledging that forgetting is often associated with ageing. Natural forgetting is not strongly associated with normal ageing. Jorm (1987) clearly distinguishes between the ability of elderly people to retain information in short-term memory and that of those who have Alzheimer's disease and whose short-term memory is impaired.

Three informants reported having had successful major surgery. They function very well and seem to have transcended their physical problems.

Ben engages actively with life, and doesn't seem to regard his medical conditions as issues at all. He has a real sense of transcendence. He said: 'Just continue on as I am. Long as I keep reasonable health. I've had a by-pass, I've had a hip replacement and goodness knows, still push the lawn-mower, still do it.' He is very active in assisting other older people, and has a number of interests, including gardening – he has a lovely garden, with lots of flowers, requiring continued work. And he remarked: 'Still do it, still work as long as I can move and go to bed, go to bed and go to sleep and that'd be it, it'd be the nicest way to go. No I got no worries in that respect.'

Edith feels her age doesn't bother her, even though her health has not been good. She seems to do most things she wants. She expresses a deep knowledge of her own body, says she 'knows' when something is wrong, for example her heart. Edith has had a triple by-pass. A cardiac crisis that preceded major surgery was the point of a major life-changing event for her. She has turned her attitudes to life around, saying that she doesn't 'hate anymore'. Again, there is real evidence of transcendence in her life. She, too, actively engages with life and says she is pleased to be alive.

Mary had breast cancer about nine years ago. She seems to have turned this experience around and uses it now for the benefit of others. When she was asked of other regrets in her life she remarked, 'Oh, no, not really, I mean it was a bit bumpy along the way, but then that's what life is isn't it, I suppose.' She has a very positive attitude to life and health. Again, this woman has transcended her life problems, including family difficulties. She is spiritually well, and vitally involved with life.

*Perceived vulnerability*

Some respondents moved between having a sense of self-sufficiency and vulnerability. Carol, the most physically vulnerable in the sample, was waiting for placement in a hostel for frail aged people.

Perceived future vulnerability was by far the greatest concern. A number of these older adults would not be able to count on family members to support them if they became unable to care for themselves. Thus fears of possible loss of control, physically or mentally, would be of real concern to them. I have set the sub-category of fear of dementia separately, as this seems to be an area of special concern on its own. This section concentrates on anticipation of physical problems.

To some informants, the mere contemplation of future frailty was sufficient to make them consider suicide. It is noted that there has been a slight decline in the number of suicides, particularly in the young–old (64–74) group of males in Australia. This has been accompanied by a continuing trend to an increasing number of suicides among the oldest age group, rising for males aged 85 and over between 1980 and 1990 from 37.0 to 50.0 per 100 000 population in Australia (Hassan 1995). Hassan says that suicide in elderly people, as in the young, is 'influenced by a multitude of complex factors including isolation, bereavement, serious physical illness, depression, organic brain disease and poverty' (p.65). Hassan also notes that these factors can make it more difficult for those affected to maintain social integration. It is contended in this study that spiritual factors, too, may be involved in the decision to commit suicide, for instance where a sense of hopelessness exists and the individual cannot justify meaning in further existence through fear of losing control of life, suffering or of developing dementia.

Flora expressed a sense of vulnerability and fear: 'Oh! awful; feelings of getting old and not being able to be independent, look after myself, I really think about that a lot.' She is fearful of losing control of her life, and remarked she has thought of suicide if she felt she could no longer look after herself. She is still young–old (67), and has not experienced many of the physical changes of ageing.

Carol said that she fears disease and falls, and fears intrusion into her life by others. 'Well, right at this very moment I'm going through a fear of the dark...an almost childish fear of the dark [but] it'll be a passing thing.' Moberg (1968) reported that in his experience some elderly patients expressed a fear of the dark. He linked this with increasing frailty in ageing.

This informant was certainly frail, but with extraordinary inner strength. Note that she mentioned, along with her fear of the dark, that she expects that it will pass. A number of other issues were of concern to her as well:

> Because I have osteoporosis I'm inclined to have fractures of the spine, so I'm very limited in what I can do. I don't sit down and worry about it. It's if I wake up in the night, I imagine that I've got a growth, or I've got something wrong, and then I think about you know, what's going to happen to me and I worry a bit about whether there'll be the money to bury me.

She seemed to show evidence of self-transcendence as she spoke of her difficulties. She also demonstrated a real understanding of her own responses to life:

> I worry about my insomnia, I worry about not being able to have a pet, I worry about what people think, I worry about the fact that I don't go to Senior Citizens, and I feel I ought to go to Senior Citizens. I feel I can't say I haven't got support when I don't go to Senior Citizens where I might get support. I worry about not doing 'good'. People tell me I do them good because I'm cheerful. They enjoy being with me, because I'm cheerful, I've got a sense of humour and they find that fairly rare.

She is very conscious of life decisions which have not turned out well for her, yet she is always ready to begin again, even to having moved to where she lives now just a few years ago. She said: 'My life is one long progression of wrong turnings. I can't see anything that I did right, other than retiring, and coming to live in…[her present urban place of residence].'

She has been considering moving into a hostel for the aged as she grows more frail. At one level this woman is very vulnerable, physically and socially, and the social isolation makes it difficult for her to work out her spirituality in relationship with other people. Nevertheless, she has continued to work on her relationship with God and appears to have developed a deep sense of spirituality during this process; from this she seems to draw comfort, peace and the ability to transcend.

George remarked he would much rather be 'taken off tomorrow' than end up in a nursing home. He doesn't want to 'live to 95 and be helpless'. Perceived vulnerability is a factor not only for females, but also for males in the study. For example, this informant related an incident where he had been threatened by some teenage boys while out walking alone. His sense of vulnerability was elicited by a growing awareness of decreasing physical strength and the realisation that he could no longer expect to defend himself physically. Concerned by his increasing physical vulnerability, he has modified his lifestyle; no longer walking alone in places he perceives himself to be at risk and not walking at dusk or later. This man also transcends his physical health problems and lives as effectively as possible within the limits of his physical potential.

Doris exhibits a mixture of self-sufficiency (see comments above under self-sufficiency) and vulnerability. Her sense of vulnerability is mainly related to a potential for vulnerability in the future. She expressed concern for the possibility of losing mobility, or having to give up her home, thus losing her freedom. Although she presently does live alone, fear of living alone does not seem to dominate, but is there in the background. When talking of living alone (not on tape), she said she had her dog for protection.

Doris expressed not a fear, but a dislike of ageism: She had noticed that her self-confidence is easily undermined. On one occasion, she was stereotyped, an incident that had the potential to lock her into an aged passive role that she would want to reject. Vulnerability for this woman and undoubtably others like her is related to a negative picture of ageing, self-identity and self-worth.

Angela still feels inadequate at times. She says she thinks she is 'an absolute failure…probably a lot of people do feel like this about themselves'. She worries about her health and seems very concerned about having had a hysterectomy:

> And then I had quite a sudden, very sudden traumatic operation. And um, it just all sort of went crazy and, I had a total hysterectomy. And that I felt, sort of suddenly I was given this sentence. I thought, suddenly I was thrown into old age.

She perceived the effects of her hysterectomy as: 'suddenly I was thrown into old age'. There seemed to be some fear in that she seemed to see herself as suddenly old. She remarked that she had been a very 'young 55' before her surgery. It seemed her concept of self changed immediately she had the surgery; it seemed to be something outside her control, and tied deeply to her identity. Perhaps her stated love of babies was a sign of her deep connections with her reproductive ability, and the obvious and sudden loss of this threatened her whole identity.

Her passage into 'old age' seemed abrupt and this may have had some implications for her sense of identity. This seemingly was a crisis she had to face suddenly and unprepared. Other informants seemed, in contrast, to experience a gradual realisation of their ageing, and their sense of identity seemed to change little. Angela is fearful of getting cancer and 'things like that'. She expresses fears of ill-health and ageing.

### Fear of increasing frailty: 'I wouldn't like to be off my legs or lose my mind'

Fear of increasing frailty was a concern for many. Associated with this was a definite perception of the consequences of going out of control; this would mean loss of ability to continue living in their own home, perhaps admission to a nursing home, and there was a real fear of this for a number of informants.

The comments related to perceived future vulnerability are obviously tied to the fear of the process of dying, and the fear of having to suffer, expressed by many. This links, too, with the present societal belief in the need to abolish suffering from human experience. As Frankl (1984) has testified suffering is a necessary aspect of human existence at times, but it must be distinguished from unnecessary suffering which of course can never be justified. The argument for legalising active euthanasia is symptomatic of this debate.

There is a sense in which the human being who lives out their full potential of lifespan will probably have to experience frailty and all the things that go with it. There seems to be a tension between not wanting to die and not wanting to suffer. The problem would seem to be solved (in an unrealistic manner) by abolishing ageing. As most people have to live with an ageing body, particularly in an ageing society, it is best that we acknowledge our need to learn to live with ageing. Part of this is going to involve a change of focus from doing to being.

Having to rely on others for one's everyday activities, and a prolonged dying and suffering, were all fears expressed by a number of informants. Mary particularly fears dementia and physical disabilities: of fears, she responded that she 'wouldn't like to be off my legs or lose my mind'. This woman voiced her fears of possible happenings in the future.

Lisa spoke of concerns she has for the future. At present she lives a very full life, but she pondered her position if this should cease to be so:

> I like to communicate with people, and I like to feel that I can share some intellectual enthusiasm, and also that I can help them with whatever problems they happen to have. I suppose there's a dimension of self-fulfilment, also of egotism...I mean, you have to prove to yourself that you can do something. I'm very aware of that. You know everyone needs to do that...probably what I would find most difficult when I really get unable

to do it, is to say to myself, 'What's the good of me now, because I can't do anything, although I found it very interesting a few years ago'.

At one level she seemed to be struggling with the prospect of a future need to move from doing to being; a task that challenges the older people who do become frail. The focus of meaning in life may need to change and future dependency may be a part of this. Lisa affirmed the commonness of this fear of increasing vulnerability, but yet there was also a sense of transcendence in her contemplation of the future, not anxiety.

Hugh, at 70 years, regards himself as in very good health. He seems to have few physical signs of ageing. He has some fears about the process of dying, particularly if he was to suffer severe pain. But, 'I have no fear of death, if I die, I die'. He expressed a sense of vulnerability: 'We've had relatives who've ended up in a dreadful, incapacitated way. I'd hate that to happen.'

Beryl spoke about a recent possible serious diagnosis, which tests later confirmed to be unfounded; she said she had been concerned because 'I don't like pain, I don't think anybody does, and I don't like sickness, and I sort of want to feel strong and anything that just sort of lurks there…it's worrying…'. Beryl also remarked: 'I rely on myself not to be vulnerable.' She stated that the need not to be vulnerable rests with herself. This woman had no belief in any being or power outside herself, thus she took complete responsibility for everything that happened to her in life. This woman also noted that she did not want to think about death.

Daisy fears as she grows older:

you become much more vulnerable and you simply aren't able to cope quite as well as you would like to, probably…because there are just so many strange things happening even in [this community] where you sort of were as secure as could be but you're not anymore.

Daisy was concerned about things she had read or heard about in the media, and expressed her apprehensions regarding these. She lived with her increasingly incapacitated husband. The rural town she lives in is probably no more dangerous than it was some years ago. This is a concern I have heard expressed by other older people as well. It seems to be a statement of their real sense of vulnerability. Doris also expressed similar feelings.

Helen said: 'I think it's rather sad when people get into really advanced age and become dependent on other people.' This woman seemed to be distancing herself from the issues of dependency; it was something that could happen to others, rather than to her.

On the other hand, Dawn seemed to see this possibility especially for herself. She said: 'I worry what will happen when you're not independent and obviously you're not going to be to the end.' She continued:

> I don't look forward to going into community living but I, some people have to look after me presumably unless I, I hope maybe I have a quick and maybe I'll, I'll have a heart attack or something, I wouldn't like a stroke, unless it was a very serious one and it finished you off.

Dawn was yet another who spoke of her fears of future vulnerabilities and possible loss of control. She seemed to hold a view that she is not going to remain independent which has implications for her sense of hope and expectations. It is asked how closely tied are an individual's perceptions of the future and the future reality of these? That is, does it make a difference how she sees the future, with hope or with fear?

## Less energy now

In the process of physical ageing there comes a point at which body energy levels are not so readily replenished. Learning to live within new boundaries of available energy is a real difficulty for a number of older people. Modifications of lifestyle are often needed, and making choices about what is most important in life may be necessary. Energy depletion in extreme old age is characteristic of the frailty seen at this time. It would not be expected that many in this group of older adults living independently in the community would be experiencing these changes as yet, but in fact some were. It is important to note that those who reported decreasing energy levels were coping well; transcendence was a part of this, as well as the ability to let go of things they could not change and to plan other ways of achieving what they really wanted to do.

An important component of the decreasing energy levels may be a turning of the person back into themselves; beginning to make the change from doing to being. In case 'being' is viewed as a static state, it may be more appropriate to speak of the human process of 'becoming', because it is a process continuing until death. Disengagement theory may come into its own here. The findings of Cumming and Henry (1961) of a mutual withdrawing from society by the older person and society from the person may have merit when applied to the state of increasing frailty of extreme old age. In a way everything points to a transition from doing to being at this point of life: less energy, loss of physical power, increasing disabilities, loss of loved ones through death. One might ask, what is left? It is precisely at this point that this transition can begin. This phenomenon is spoken of by Havighurst, Neugarten and Tobin (1968) and the theme is taken up by Clements (1990) in his discussion on shedding and stripping of roles in ageing.

## The transition from doing to being

The informants in this study were, as would be expected, at different points along the ageing process. Some had experienced few physical changes of ageing at the time of interview; others knew what it was like to live with a number of chronic illnesses, most quite successfully. Still others were learning to live with decreased energy levels.

### Decreasing energy levels

Frail older adults and those with terminal illnesses all too frequently experience this phenomenon of having less energy and being unable to do the things they want. The outcome of this can be increasing frustration or a learning to live differently. A realistic goal for these people is to learn to conserve precious energy; to make decisions about what they can do as against what they would like to do. When I first became interested in working with older people in the early 1980s I did not want to acknowledge disengagement theory as being relevant for any older people. I wanted to advocate activity right to the end; the term 'successful' ageing sounded good. But energy depletion does occur for a proportion of older adults, and it is obvious that they can only turn from the doing mode to the being mode. How they are able to accept this transition is important.

So the question is, how can they be assisted in achieving quality of life in such a situation? It is all too difficult for health carers who have not experienced this energy lack to imagine what it is like, and yet it is so important to acknowledge the difficulties experienced by these older people. Energy lack was even an important consideration for some informants in this study of independently living well older adults, where it may be thought it would not be a problem, as none of this group were in need of care and were able to function independently.

## Transcendence

Transcendence may be triggered by increasing vulnerability in ageing, but it is not the only factor involved in the development of transcendence. A sense of approaching the end of the lifespan is probably involved too, as is the continued search for meaning in life, a search that does not diminish in ageing. Other aspects of the phenomenon of transcendence, the shift from doing to being and the development of wisdom are pursued in the relevant chapters.

How can the transition from doing to being be facilitated for those who suffer from increasing frailty and decreased energy levels? More research is needed in this area to provide valuable information about how those who successfully negotiate this difficult area do so. Further studies with frail older adults are of vital importance in this.

Sylvia regrets her lack of energy that prevents her doing things she would like to do and the difficulty of accepting this. The consequences of these changes were noted by Win. She has noticed changing energy levels in herself: 'As I get older I find I can't do the same things that I wanted to do...I find I get a bit stressed because I've got a lot things on my mind and I feel I can't cope sometimes.' She said that the lower energy levels had brought a change within herself, and she found that she was resting too, in God.

Contemplating this change has brought another change, that she is able to accept that she can't do all she wants to. At the same time, she finds it much more difficult to make decisions these days. Win seemed to be making the transition from doing in life to being. This woman has an active faith, she is still involved in a worshipping community and regularly attends a Christian meditation group. She seemed to be changing from engaging in a doing relationship with the world to a life that has a greater sense of interiority.

This is an important component of the spiritual dimension of the ageing process, in line with Peck's (1968) stage of body transcendence versus body preoccupation. The process for Win, of moving from doing to being, is perhaps stimulated by her perception of having less energy and her ability to accept this. Her deep faith and use of Christian meditation have prepared her well for these changes.

Angela said she has less energy, remarking that 'You have more time to dwell on these things', that is, on problems in life, and she sees physical things 'tied up with how you feel physically'. She shows signs of some transcendence over the declining physical self, yet she worries about her health.

Sally said: 'Of course I'm an old lady now, you know.' She has an expectation that she will have less energy because she is ageing and has been sick. She has developed asthma over the last few years and this condition is likely to cause her energy levels to be further decreased.

The importance of setting priorities in daily activities was raised by Dawn, who said:

I have to watch my health all the time, my mental health particularly because if I get too tired, too emotional, if I don't sleep and all that sort of thing I can't cope with the days you know and, and if I don't cope with the days no one else is going to cope with them.

As well, she now has non insulin-dependent diabetes and finds she has to take extra care with her diet, or she has 'no energy'.

## Disabilities and chronic illness

Eleven informants spoke of various chronic conditions that they have or are learning to live with. Mostly their conditions are multiple, yet all of them have a good quality of life and few use any community services. Again, it is important to note that it is not so much the medical diagnosis that is critical, but the individual's functional capacity. The two are not highly related in this group of older adults.

Carol has numerous physical disabilities. At 73 she shows a number of degenerative changes of ageing, more than perhaps could be expected now in her age cohort. She has severe osteoporosis, and has had fractures of the spine which cause a lot of pain and mobility problems. Incontinence has also been a restriction on social activities, including her studies, which she had to give up due to incontinence. Her level of functional independence is declining and her energy levels are reduced a little. She shows a number of physical problems that will make it hard for her to continue living independently for much longer. She is very conscious of this. But yet she appears to be transcending her physical problems and functions to the highest level possible, within her limitations.

Sylvia, at 66 years of age, has severe arthritis which causes marked disability for her. She said she has to rely on her husband's assistance at times when she is physically incapacitated. Even so, she described herself as being in good health.

Stan seems to have no sense of vulnerability. At 74 he had a stroke that left him with slight residual disability. He also has a hearing deficit. He lives alone and is restricted in his ability to travel since his stroke. In spite of being a widower and having the stroke in the last couple of years he seems at peace. There is a sense in which he seems to have transcended his health problems and is coping with his grief.

Betty has noticed it took longer to recuperate than she had expected after an emergency operation recently. She had been well until needing emergency surgery, just a couple of months before this interview. In the last few years she has had both hips replaced, very successfully. She remarked that she and her husband moved from their large home into a retirement unit between the time I first visited some nine months before, mainly because of her husband's increasing frailty.

She feels 'life is more precarious now' because of their age. Both she and her husband have had health problems recently. She expressed fear of ageing, of becoming more vulnerable, and said it was hard to believe it was happening, thinking that her husband will probably die before her and wondering how she will cope.

Diane has severe arthritis and she has required surgery, and didn't know whether she would be able to walk again. The surgery was successful and she is apparently able to do all she wants to now. Eva too has arthritis. She did not mention her diabetes until I prompted her. It is a late-onset diabetes, and she seems to manage it without becoming too worried.

It is not just the informant, but sometimes their spouse who has the chronic condition that may impact on both of them. Daisy found it difficult sometimes making daily adjustments for her husband, whose rheumatoid arthritis is sometimes worse than at others.

## Fear of having dementia/Alzheimer's disease

Dementia was not a topic I mentioned in any of the interviews, but it was raised by eight informants who mentioned a fear of, or at least a hope they would not suffer from, dementia. Their comments highlight the kind of concerns about this disease, considered so devastating by many. It was in this context that the possibility of suicide or euthanasia was mentioned by those who spoke in these terms.

There seemed to be a real perception that people who have Alzheimer's disease are 'non-persons'. And to many this is so. Yet there are glimmers of hope: even in the area of dementia, there is an increasing body of anecdotal information about people who have dementia and who are able to respond to others in various ways. Research in this vital area is beginning, and in this last decade more research is being directed towards ways of reaching into the world of those who have dementia (Goldsmith 1996).

Flora is fearful of losing control of her life, and remarked she has thought of suicide if she felt she could no longer look after herself. Flora is afraid of developing Alzheimer's: her mother is in a nursing home. She joked about Alzheimer's, but it seemed she was seeking to cover her fears.

Vera and Sylvia both had mothers who had Alzheimer's disease. Vera made the point that she sees her mother now as a 'non-person'. She said she would personally have no spiritual problems with euthanasia. Angela said she has a relative who is senile and that she doesn't want to end up 'being a living vegetable'.

Betty remarked: 'Oh, we're all afraid of dependence.' She spoke of a friend who has Alzheimer's and she spoke of her fear of getting it. 'This is you know, half a person in a sense, so I've seen that happening…just only beginning and if that accelerates I think it would be a very big fear, partly dependence, partly you're losing yourself aren't you?'

This seems to be a common fear related to dementia, the combination of the physical dependence and that sense of loss of self. I am not so sure that there is so much a loss of self, *as an inability to communicate what is yourself to others.* At least I believe this is often so, until the very late stages of the disease. Kitwood (1997) and Goldsmith (1996) have outlined new and important ways of improving the quality of life for people who have dementia. More study needs to be done of the spiritual dimension during the progress of dementia. I know of one woman who has early onset Alzheimer's who still retains her deep sense of spirituality, and it is her faith that enables her to function so well (Boden 1998).

It may be that fear of dementia is the bigger of the problems. There seems often to be a conspiracy of silence between the people who have dementia and their carers. This even extends to the Alzheimer's support group literature, that until recently talked about what the carers notice and how to handle it, rather than taking the issues from the viewpoint of the person who has Alzheimer's. Boden (1998) seeks to address some of these issues.

Spirituality in dementia is an area urgently requiring more research so that effective interventions may be developed for spiritual care in nursing and pastoral care for people who have dementia.

## Reported transcendence of difficulties

There are two reasons why I chose to look at vulnerability in ageing: first, because the informants raised that topic often and, second, because I see it as being closely related to the process of ageing, particularly in extreme old age. At that time in life, there is a growing interaction between physical, mental and spiritual dimensions of the individual. While the physical dimension is in decline, there may still be growth in both psychosocial and spiritual dimensions. As the physical deteriorates, the spiritual may move further into transcending the physical disabilities, the fears, the physical limitations, the energy loss, the sensory loss. A number of the informants showed evidence of transcending problems of a physical and/or psycho-social nature.

### *Transcending life's problems*

Carol experiences many problems, of social isolation and physical dis-abilities, yet she seems to transcend these with a wonderful sense of calm and acceptance – resignation would not be the right word; it is not passive.

George was living successfully with a number of chronic conditions, and seemed to be transcending his physical problems.

Doris enjoys meaningful and close relationships with her family and others, and particularly strong bonds exist between members of the small group she belongs to. She seems to face ageing with a sense of integrity and peace; her concerns about possible pain and loss of control which may lie in the future are not pressing and seem not to overly concern her.

Stan, in response to the question, what keeps him going, said: 'It's just old Scots stubbornness.' This was said in the context of his life situation: his wife died about four years ago and he had a stroke recently. He said that he was 'just sort of waiting for death'. Yet he did not appear depressed. He seemed to enjoy his weekly visits to a contact centre, and to have a philosophy of living each day as it comes.

Transcendence is certainly a spiritual process, linked with a developing sense of interiority and integrity; it is the forerunner of wisdom. Those older people who are able to transcend their present difficulties may achieve a real sense of peace and acceptance that passes human understanding. There is a sense in which this concept fits with Frankl's (1984) 'forgetting self'. This concept is that which enables a person to survive through any suffering, to rise above suffering. The question remains, why do some people seem to be able to transcend their difficulties while others cannot? A lack of spiritual resources may be a real difficulty for people who rely on their 'doing' ability as they become older and more frail.

## Ageism and vulnerability

Ageism was not mentioned often by informants, but it was important to Doris, who although she was aware that it was a stereotype of ageing that was being applied, felt that her self-confidence was easily undermined. She felt certain pressures to act according to the expectations of other members of the community that locked her into a stereotyped and limited role as an older woman.

George did not like the term 'senior citizen' as he felt labelled by it. What roles are appropriate for older adults? Should there be defined roles? We are living in a changing society, changing because it is an ageing society. The current cohort of older people are overall more healthy than previous cohorts of elderly people. It seems to me that there are both new opportunities and new challenges for both older people and for the whole of society. How are we going to *be* when we are old? What potentials are still to be tapped? It was first the physical, next the psychosocial and now the spiritual dimensions of growing older that are being addressed.

### Summary

*Self-sufficiency was highly valued by the independently living older people interviewed in this study. All feared future perceived vulnerability as they grew older. Important changes in the ageing process include the transition from doing to being and transcendence of the physical decrements of ageing. Part of this includes learning to live with less energy, a feature of the frailty of old age but noticed already by some of these independent living people. Most of these people lived with more than one chronic illness, maintaining good quality of life. Fear of developing dementia was prominent among these older people.*

CHAPTER 10

# Wisdom and the move from provisional to final meanings

## Wisdom in later life

One of the themes evident in the data from in-depth interviews was that of wisdom. This section considers the concept of wisdom as it appears in the interviews and its relationship to final meanings and the spiritual. I have included material on dying and death in Chapter 11; this material seems particularly relevant to the concept of wisdom in ageing. It may be that the individual's perception of dying and death are related to their development of wisdom and final meanings of life.

Wisdom is understood in this study in a spiritual context, as the ability to discern and construct life meanings appropriately. From the literature it involves both cognitive and emotional aspects. Not so firmly established are the transcendent aspects of wisdom. A definition of wisdom in ageing that recognises the spiritual dimension and which is used in this study is:

> An increased tolerance to uncertainty, a deepening search for meaning in life, including an awareness of the paradoxical and contradictory nature of reality; it involves transcendence of uncertainty and a move from external to internal regulation. (Based on Blanchard-Fields and Norris 1995 p.108)

From wisdom comes the ability to construct one's individual and final life meanings; the spirit grows, finding meaning in being, accepting the inevitable losses of life, and letting go of things that are no longer important. Meaning making in the later years becomes a critical aspect of effective ageing. And it is this search for the final meaning in life which is truly a component of the spiritual dimension.

At the same time, there is acknowledged in this definition a shift from external to internal regulation. This may be seen as the process of individuation, a need not to be concerned by what others think or say about one's behaviour, and the ability to make one's own decisions; in other words, the development of a new sense of freedom in ageing. Yet another component of this is a move to greater interiority in older people, and this too can be seen as part of wisdom. Hope is necessarily a component of this process and is addressed in a separate section, although there is a close relationship between wisdom, hope and final meanings. The choice of this definition is supported by the words of the informants in this study.

## Wisdom in Scripture

The study of wisdom and ageing is not new. Many have studied it over the centuries from a secular perspective while Scripture has many references to ageing and wisdom. The ongoing struggle for meaning in life and the development of wisdom is one that is common to all humankind. The perspective taken in this study is a Christian one in a society that is becoming increasingly secular.

I have chosen not to make a detailed exploration of the wisdom literature of Old Testament times, but rather to focus simply on the biblical presentation of examples. I will then give an overview of relevant research on wisdom from the psychological literature, and then what is available on wisdom in the spiritual dimension.

### An overview of wisdom in the Bible

The Book of Proverbs has much to say about wisdom in general. Actions of wise leaders are described in the Old Testament. Well known is the tale of Solomon judging who is the true mother of a child. But specifically, in relation to ageing in our postmodern world, here are a few examples to ponder. Consider first some verses from the Psalms:

> *Do not caste me off in the time of old age;*
> *Do not forsake me when my strength is spent.*
>
> *(Psalm 71:9)*

and

> *So even to old age and gray hairs*
> *O God, do not forsake me.*
> *Until I proclaim your might*
> *To all the generations to come.*
>
> *(Psalm 71:18)*

The psalmist recognises the vulnerability of frailty in ageing that many older people both fear and experience. It is important to recognise the difficulties of old age as well as the benefits. This passage also recognises the task of older people as repositories of knowledge and wisdom for the next generation, and their responsibility to pass that knowledge on.

> *But I will hope continually,*
> *And will praise you yet more and more.*

*(Psalm 71:14)*

Here the psalmist expresses the persistence of human hope in the face of difficult life situations; this psalm is written in the context of ageing. The words taken from Psalm 90:12:

> *So teach us to count our days*
> *That we may gain a wise heart.*

read as a prayer for the capacity to develop wisdom in later life. From the book of Deuteronomy, 32:7 the author has written:

> *Remember the days of old,*
> *consider the years long past;*
> *ask your father and he will*
> *inform you;*
> *your elders and they will tell you.*

The importance of the link between the generations is stressed here. As in the example above, older people in the Old Testament days were regarded as the repositories of wisdom for the next generation.

In the book of Job (12:12) Job is heard to ask: 'Is wisdom with the aged and understanding in length of days?' We often still equate wisdom and ageing, although the links seem more tenuous in our day.

In the gospel of Luke (2:22 to end), Luke records the story of Simeon and Anna in the Temple. The old age and wisdom of these two is recorded. They are held in respect, their discernment is clearly evident and they have an important place in the gospel account. Both Simeon and Anna are seen as walking in God's grace. In the Epistles of John, and in the book of Revelation, the old man, John, is writing with the wisdom of age.

It seems that our pictures of wisdom have become somewhat faded since the latter part of the twentieth century, and technology seems to have all but superseded wisdom. Can we survive in a society without wisdom? Can technological knowledge take the place of wisdom? Or maybe we have simply shifted the repositories of wisdom? Does wisdom reside with the youth of the world today? Chandler and Holliday (1990, p.129) suggest that in a postmodern world we may have forgotten what wisdom really is, and further, that we may be even unable to recognise real wisdom when we see it in action.

In this study wisdom is considered in part from a psychological perspective, but mainly from a spiritual perspective, taking account of the continuation of development in these aspects of human development across the lifespan.

## Wisdom in a developmental framework

Peck (1968) discussed wisdom as a part of psychological development of middle age. He suggested that as people grow older, that is, reaching their middle years, they become more aware of their declining physical powers and come to realise that life's experience and length of life can be put to effective use in accomplishing more than they had thought possible when younger. Peck, by way of definition, distinguishes wisdom from intellectual capacity as the 'ability to make the most effective choices among the alternatives which intellectual perception and imagination present for one's decision'. He elaborates: the choice making is modified by one's emotional stability and motivation. At his time of writing little research in the psychological area had been done into wisdom. Since then a great deal has been achieved in the study of wisdom in ageing from within the psychological literature (Blanchard-Fields and Norris 1995).

Yet it seems it is necessary to include work from the spiritual dimension to flesh out a better understanding of the concept of wisdom. According to Erikson *et al.* (1986) wisdom is an outcome of the final stage of psychosocial development. It should be asked whether wisdom is to be regarded as linked to a definite final stage of human psychosocial development, or whether it develops over a longer time frame. It is also important to delineate the boundaries of the concept 'wisdom'. Can it most usefully be considered across both psychosocial and spiritual dimensions?

Taking the developmental perspective, the eighth and final psychosocial stage of ageing is described by Erikson *et al.* (1986) in its relation to the earlier stages of development:

> It is through this last stage that the life cycle weaves back on itself in its entirety, ultimately integrating maturing forms of hope, will, purpose, competence, fidelity, love, and care, into a comprehensive sense of wisdom. (pp.55–6)

Thus this final stage of psychosocial development is seen to build on and reshape the meanings of life in relation to all that has gone before and what is now, for that individual. There are possibilities to revisit unresolved problems of years gone by; to come to reconciliation and fulfilment in a reframing of one's life. A time to arrive at final meanings for one's life journey. That is not to say that one should continue to dwell in the past, but to re-visit, reframe, and to move on. A failure to do so may result in a sense of despair for the individual. The successful outcome at this stage of life in Erikson's view is wisdom.

## The spiritual component of wisdom

Blanchard-Fields and Norris (1995) stated that, in all they had discussed of wisdom, a consistent theme emerges: 'the personal quest for meaning of life or finding meaning and purpose in life in order to become whole'. Which is of course the very domain of the spiritual dimension. And yet, as they have considered the psychological literature, they say that little has been done in exploration of the spiritual aspect of wisdom. Blanchard-Fields and Norris suggest this may be because psychologists generally are reluctant to embrace the notion of spirituality; they see this possibly because spirituality represents the developing self, the cognitive self and the transpersonal self.

Returning to Butler's (1963) important early contribution to life review, it is noted that he suggested that a part of life review in ageing is the substantial reorganisation of the personality and that this may help account for the evolution of qualities such as wisdom and serenity evident in some older adults. Although Butler was at this time writing from a psychological view his point about life review is relevant to the spiritual aspect of the process. In the past, Blanchard-Fields and Norris (1995) say, this spiritual formation has been the role of religion, but they are critical of the direction of current organised religion, believing that it may become yet another 'societally-prescribed, external regulation authority' (p.114), failing to properly guide in the self-nurture required for the journey.

The question arises, are many people in current Western societies out of touch with their spiritual selves? If this is so, then the development of wisdom that should occur in later life may too be retarded. Blanchard-Fields and Norris note that a 'sizeable portion of the population does not necessarily exhibit' the qualities of wisdom that characterises adult development and ageing (p.115). They say that many of this older age group, lacking the skills for appropriate spiritual growth in ageing, may have adapted to the society by way of the socially expected and imposed certainties of life, thus retarding the potential for wholeness of development. The possible effect of this would be to have people reaching old age without having achieved their full potential as human beings.

## An approach to wisdom using the spiritual dimension

Research in the area of ageing, wisdom and spirituality is relatively new. One aspect of this study aims to examine wisdom in the context of spirituality within a framework of life review, collecting data from older adults in in-depth interviews.

An important aspect of coming to final meanings is the human need for reconciliation with the Ultimate in each person's life, be that God, or some sense of other, or indeed reconciliation with other people. Reconciliation involves the recognition of wrongdoing, the experience of guilt and the seeking of forgiveness. Guilt was spoken of by a number of the informants.

## Reconciliation/sin/guilt/need for forgiveness: growing into final meanings

One of the aspects of coming to final meanings in life is the need for reconciliation between people, the readiness to acknowledge guilt and wrongdoing, and recognition of the need for forgiveness. In this study, most of these situations relate to factors in human relationship; however, I have chosen to include it in the area on final meanings as it seems often that the need to address such issues only arises in the context of coming to final meanings. A number of the informants spoke of these issues in their lives. Most of those who expressed a sense of guilt over past actions or omissions were concerned because of their actions towards other people.

### Informants differentiate between regrets and guilt

Regrets were seen by informants as sadness or disappointment for things that they had failed to achieve, things that had gone wrong or opportunities missed. On the other hand, guilt was seen as a burden: feeling themselves to be convicted, experiencing remorse, or acknowledging responsibility for wrongdoing or omissions of things they ought to have done.

The informants varied widely in their responses in this area. I directly asked each informant: 'Do you have any regrets or guilts in your life?' To begin with, 50 per cent of informants expressed no sense of guilt at all.

In Hardy's (1979) major study of human spiritual nature, conducted by the Religious Experience Unit in the United Kingdom, he cited one example from those in the sub-category of 'remorse, sense of guilt'. Hardy remarks that finding only 71 respondents out of a total of 3000 in this sub-category was unexpected, noting that accounts of guilt feature so prominently in books of psychiatric case studies. There may be two reasons for the low proportion of respondents who wrote of guilt. First, people who harboured a sense of remorse or guilt may not have regarded this as spiritual experience and therefore did not take part in the survey. Second, Hardy's sample consisted of people who responded to media advertisements and wrote their responses to the centre. A face-to-face in-depth interview presents a very different environment for sharing at a deep level. In contrast, in this study 50 per cent of the informants mentioned guilt related to issues arising from their past. A few articulated their sense of guilt for sins and having a need for forgiveness from God. For the rest, their need for forgiveness was related to human relationships. Guilt was a real concern for a number of informants in this cohort of older adults.

It is also noted that all these informants were independently living older people who for the most part regarded themselves as being in good (54 per cent) or very good health (16.6 per cent). Thus, if guilt is related to the development of final meanings, it may be expected that few of these people would acknowledge their feelings of guilt at this stage. This would be a more likely finding in a sample of frail nursing home residents. Again, the picture may be completely different in a younger age group, whose world view could be expected to be different and who had not yet begun to consider the possibility of mortality in their own lives.

## Belief in God and guilt

In this group belief in God made a difference for some. Five informants who each held deep religious beliefs said that they had no guilt. Five informants spoke of guilt in early life, but they had dealt with this and each of these at the time of interview was a regular church attender. Typical of these was Carol, who remarked that she has worked through a lot of her guilt. Looking back on her life, she said that as a young woman she described herself as feeling 'full of sin'. Now she holds a deep faith and this faith includes regular worship, prayer and Christian meditation. Two of these women were Catholics and both noted that guilt had been part of their early upbringing in the church, as they remembered it. One of these was Lisa, who spoke of her sense of guilt in earlier life:

> I have I think, to a large extent, freed myself from the routine and the sense of guilt which was inherent in the Catholic upbringing, I think, (but) not entirely, I don't think one ever frees oneself entirely of that. Especially if it's been a part of what you knew. But God as opposed to the Church, is just, you might say, a factor of life, so far as I'm concerned.

She now sees life differently and says that guilt is no longer an issue for her. Doris also noted that guilt had been part of religion for her when she was younger. However, she said it was one of the first things she dealt with when she had her spiritual awakening in mid life.

It is frequently claimed that religiosity and guilt are linked. However, in this study there did not seem to be any greater relationship between the two for those with deep religious beliefs than for those who had none. It is also worth noting that the Catholic women in this study who mentioned guilt from their childhood experiences of religion had dealt with their issues of guilt; it was no longer a problem for them. These women had in fact a very effective way of dealing with guilt through the practice of their religion.

### Accepting forgiveness

Another group consists of three informants who believe they are forgiven at an intellectual level, but find it hard to accept at 'heart' or emotional level. Hugh said he has a sense of guilt over some of his behaviour in his younger years. He has struggled with a search for forgiveness (from God), which he has found hard to accept in the context of corporate confession and absolution within the service of holy communion. In the same way, Angela remembers experiencing guilt early in life. She said her new faith has helped her to deal with guilt and regrets, of which there were a lot. She noted that human relationships may be a source of guilt as well. Angela said:

> When you get right down into that very pit, where I did after that operation [in her mid fifties]. I stopped running and, all the old guilts start to pile up on me. And, I think, everybody has them, perhaps don't call them guilts, but other people, you know, guilty about a lot of things. And at that stage, I think, that you feel, that it's impossible to be forgiven, you're so bad.

She now knows she is forgiven, but still says this is easier to know intellectually than in her heart. Dawn also found it very hard to really believe in being forgiven and said: 'Yes, you look back and you think you know how thoughtless you have been about people and then you try and spend the rest of you life making it up…sometimes your guilt interferes with your clear thinking.' She remarked that, in her experience, the place of forgiveness, guilt and faith was 'that in spite of the fact that you feel you're forgiven you still have to pay for it'. She has lots of regrets:

> that my priorities weren't right until I got to a certain stage, [around 50 years], and when I did get to that stage of realising what was wrong, I thought well I haven't got that much time left, changing my priorities now is not going to get me anywhere but at least I'll die knowing that I did try.

Both these women had major changes in outlook in life at about their fifties. They both attend church now. Angela has a strong commitment to her worship and belief system, while Dawn goes to church but seems to go more from habit than from really wanting to attend.

### Deep spirituality: no guilt

Three more informants who show a deep spirituality say they have no guilt. For example, Eva acknowledges past events over which she has regrets, but is realistic in seeing that she did the best she could at that time, in the light of her knowledge and experience then. Regrets are clearly distinguished from guilt in the study.

Helen said mistakes were part of the learning process, 'so I don't have feelings of guilt'. She spoke of her increasing understanding of the need to forgive others, saying: 'It's a long maturing process but hopefully I've mellowed with the years.' Helen had constructed her own belief system that included a god of her own understanding.

### No belief: acknowledged regrets or guilt

A further three informants have no belief and say they have either regrets or guilt. Helga said: 'I feel these awful regrets.' She has not found contentment in life, she said: '[I] always want something better than what I've got.' She does not seem to have been able to deal with her feelings of guilt and regret about her part in her marriage breakdown. She also seems to have difficulties letting go of past hurts and grief; she retains her anger (directed towards God) related to the deaths of her father and sister, some years ago.

Another of these women who have no belief system, Diane, spoke of her guilt over a number of matters: 'No. I have no, no way of resolving them.' She said she carries some guilt for her behaviour towards her mother when she was younger; she had failed to understand things from her mother's perspective.

### Not wanting to discuss regrets or guilt

Only one of the informants did not want to discuss his regrets. Stan seems to have let go of worries in the present, and he did not want to talk about his regrets: 'Well, there's quite a few regrets, but I don't want to voice them actually, it's things that are finished, and as far as I'm concerned, they're finished. So let them stay that way.'

It is important to remember that these older people are individuals, and what might be a valuable intervention for one may be quite unsuitable for another. Health and pastoral care workers must always be sensitive to the spiritual needs of older people. While most of these in this study were very willing to share deeply, their very willingness to take part in this study perhaps classifies them as a particular group. Others of this age group may not have been so willing to share.

Again, it is emphasised that the group of older people involved in this study may respond differently from more frail aged people. The search for final meanings is probably even more critical for this latter group. For example, a sample ($n = 172$) of frail elderly residents of nursing homes interviewed (MacKinlay 1992) all readily shared at a deep level.

### The problem of unresolved guilt

Either real or imagined guilt that cannot be resolved may become a heavy burden for some, and may present a blockage to continued spiritual and emotional development. In some cases spiritual interventions may be required to assist the person to deal effectively with the situation and open the way for further personal growth. In a society where it is becoming more unusual for people to acknowledge guilt, it is important to recognise that this cohort of older people may still experience guilt and may need the assistance of nurses, social workers, pastoral carers or clergy to help them deal with these issues, either in the use of pastoral counselling and/or through confession, absolution and holy communion.

## Wisdom in the informants' stories

All informants demonstrated some degree of wisdom as defined, ranging from the ability to recognise their ways of dealing with problems in the past and how these had changed over time, to evidence of transcendence and change from external to internal regulation in ageing. Informants differed with respect to their level of wisdom according to several factors that form sub-categories of this theme. These areas are considered separately: gender and wisdom, age and wisdom, the person's belief in God and wisdom, loss and wisdom, and those exhibiting an increased tolerance for uncertainty.

## Gender and wisdom

A characteristic of male psychosocial adult development according to the literature has been individuation. Gilligan (1993) has been foremost in the push to rectify this imbalance. Gilligan and others have emphasised the female characteristic of importance of relationship. However, relatively little research has been undertaken in this area in older adults. It is suggested here that older women, in particular, may move more towards a model of androgyny and, as a result, individuation may become a valid component of the psychosocial and spiritual development of ageing. However, gender differences in spiritual development and wisdom are far from clear. It may be that differences seen are more likely to be due to the great variations that develop between individuals as they age, on the basis of life experience (crises and relationship), education and career path, regardless of gender.

The aspect of relationship with God and others is considered further in the sections on both ultimate meanings and on relationship/isolation. It is acknowledged that there is interaction between the various components of the spiritual dimension (see Figure 2.1).

Stan did not talk much about his personal experiences. However, I gained the impression that he had been able to let go of his difficulties and transcend them, as did George and Ben, two more of the four males in the study. The fourth male was younger and still searching for meaning. A lot has been made by some authors of the need to individuate to achieve successful maturity (Fowler 1981; Maslow 1970). On the other hand Gilligan (1993) has noted from her studies that there may be gender differences in the process of moral and faith development; individuation being a particularly male factor, while relationship is a feature of moral and spiritual development in females.

Only one of the four males in this study showed strong individuation, and he had never married and seemed not to desire close relationships. The other three males had a clear sense of their own identity, but functioned best in relationship. The females in the study (20) mostly demonstrated a clear sense of identity, but most also functioned well in relationship (see section on relationship and spirituality). It is asked whether in older people, the same need for individuation exists, and, is it a gender factor? Or does it change across the lifespan? Maybe there is a convergence of the gender factors in the spiritual dimension in the ageing human.

### The men in the study

Two of the men were in long-term relationships. One had never married, another was a widower. Both George and Hugh showed a strong cognitive component of wisdom.

George, who has never married, shows a thorough understanding of his own capabilities including his vulnerabilities. Contemplating his future, he said that he would like to write more, but when he estimated the amount of research needed to be able to write a particular book he had in mind, he said: 'But I realise it wouldn't make any sense at all to attempt it at my age.' He had consciously weighed up the amount of work he would need to do in researching for the particular topic he was interested in writing, and realised that, although he may be capable of doing it, it would be too time consuming and would involve quite a bit of travel and research, so he decided against it.

There is a sense that George was able to make a complex decision, engaging in a problem-solving exercise and armed with a large amount of complex information, including his goals in life, the skills he had as a writer, past experience of the type of research needed for the job, the work required and the possible satisfactions at the end. He was able to make a decision based on cognitive skills, but he also weighed life satisfaction. He was able to stand back from over-involvement in the decision. And the whole was related to his self-identity; his acknowledged need not to have to extend himself, his confidence in and control of the situation, based on a sound knowledge of his own abilities. This man demonstrated a sense of integrity in his decision making at this point in his life, in fact he demonstrated wisdom in his decision making and in his approach to life.

Hugh is still actively engaging with life. He sees his 'role as loving and serving mankind' adding that how we do that is rather difficult. He now shows a deep awareness of the needs of other people, evident in his struggles at being a parent and his joy in seeing his adopted daughter getting her life right.

Hugh spoke of his understanding of motivation and meaning in our lives:

I think all our lives are basically meaningless. It's useless looking for meaning. Our minds are so structured because of our evolutionary role, that we have to see meaning, otherwise we'd all terminate our lives. But when I depart this world, in five, ten, twenty, thirty years, I will be forgotten. Some things, I've written a few books, and they'll be in libraries. Some people will remember me, maybe, and my children will probably revere my memory, and so on, but, like everybody else, my time has come and I've gone. Now what is the meaning of that? I've fulfilled a biological purpose. But we create the meanings I think, and certainly, in my literary work, I created a goal which I achieved and I think I've done what I had to do.

Hugh is able to objectively consider his life and its meaning. While he says that life is 'basically meaningless' he is not depressed, and it is obvious from his involvement in life at present that he finds life far from meaningless. However, his view of life allows him to speak in this way. It seems to be a rather mechanistic view, one that does not seem to *need* relationship and does not involve dependence in any way. Yet he speaks very positively of his marriage and relationships with others. His life is characterised by a continuing search for God, and that is largely an intellectual search. He noted some fears of the process of dying, particularly if he was to suffer severe pain, but he has no fear of death.

His self-appraisal was evident as he said: 'Now I find, as I grow older, I tend to go back in my life, and I contemplate the things that I wasn't a very good sort of person.' He was beginning to be aware of his increasing use of reminiscence. Self-awareness of one's strengths and weaknesses are all important aspects of life review and spiritual growth in ageing, leading to growth in wisdom. In this there is the possibility that people may, through increasing self-awareness, become willing to change and be able to deal effectively with past perceived wrongs in their lives.

In contrast to George and Hugh, Stan shows a simple acceptance of faith and life, and seems happy to make the most he can of his more limited living conditions now. When I asked him where he found meaning in life at present he said: 'I don't really know, I think at the moment, I'm just sort o' waiting for death, put it that way. I mean, I don't know what's going to happen.'

Stan appears to be at peace, and to an extent, seems able to transcend the grief and disappointments of his life. He does not appear at present to be embarking on a deepening search for meaning in his life. However, he does seem to operate from an internal source of regulation. There is wisdom in his attitudes to life, in being able to accept what he cannot change. He is not bitter and seems content with his situation.

Ben, a prisoner of war for three and a half years in the Second World War and divorced, accepts responsibility in life: 'You make your own happiness as you go along, and as long as I can go to church.' He is still actively involved with life. He finds a great deal of satisfaction in assisting at a day care centre for elderly people; community seems to be an important aspect for him.

When asked about fears as he grows older he said: 'No, I have no fears.' Looking back over his life, he said: 'If it wasn't for the prayers of the family and the church I don't think I'd be here today.' His chronic health conditions are transcended and he appears to enjoy living. Acceptance and a simple philosophy of life, based on his active faith, assist him to face the future without fear. There is wisdom evident in his approach to life. Being able to look back on the disappointments in life and put them into perspective, his effective balancing of energies and activities, and living in a balanced and stable relationship now are all aspects of his level of wisdom.

### Women in the study

There was quite a degree of difference in evidence of wisdom between the women in the study. To some extent the differences seemed related to personality and marital relationship. Some women seemed to be more dependent on their husbands and had not actively pursued a deepening of their spirituality. For instance, Daisy expressed an acceptance of life, a letting go and tolerance of uncertainty in life, saying: 'I think as you get older you, you really do have to live day to day.' She sees this as necessary because her husband 'has rheumatoid arthritis which only allows him to do things some days, certainly not others'. Daisy does not seem to have developed a deeper sense of interiority at this stage.

Could it be that Daisy's development is influenced by her marital relationship, that she sees herself more in relationship with her husband than as an individual in her own right? Another married woman interviewed showed a different development of wisdom, Vera showed a clear under-standing of her identity and place in the life journey; this woman has been more active than Daisy in her spiritual searching.

Looking back on her life Vera said she can see patterns in her decisions, 'somebody was pushing me that way, but I couldn't see it at the time'. There is evidence of wisdom, too, where reflecting on her life she says she has developed a new understanding of Genesis: 'You know, eating of the tree of knowledge…the pursuit of knowledge has brought us to the stage where we can destroy the world.' She demonstrated a real understanding of the capabilities and nature of human beings, both for good and bad. She also showed a sense of tolerance towards other people, regardless of their beliefs. Thus there are differences in the ways wisdom is seen to be developing in these two women. So it is not simply marital status that is to be considered.

What about those who live alone? Two of the never-married women (Carol and Win) who discussed belief in God and ageing and wisdom seemed to have developed a much deeper spirituality and wisdom.

Mary, another woman living alone, had breast cancer about nine years ago. She only mentioned this in the context of being able to help and support others. She has a very positive attitude to life and health. This woman had many difficulties through her life, particularly in the earlier years, divorced and bringing up children by herself with few resources. Two of her sons were killed in recent years in accidents. She said: 'I s'pose you get over it, you sort of get over it, but I mean it's always a sad spot, but then you think of all the other things you hear on TV, you know there's lots of people a lot worse off.' Although she has never had a church background she has developed a deep spirituality. She transcends difficulties in her life and works from a centre of internal regulation. Wisdom is evident in her managing of her lifestyle, her ability to let go and see a holistic perspective on life.

Flora, who has lived alone for a number of years, does not seem to be actively searching and growing spiritually. On the whole there were more differences than similarities between these women and their development of wisdom. Further aspects of living alone are discussed in material on social/spiritual isolation.

### Belief in God and wisdom

Is there a relationship between the person's belief in God and the development of wisdom? The definition of wisdom used in this study includes a number of aspects which are important parts of the spiritual development that can occur in ageing, for example an increased tolerance of uncertainty. One of the myths about older people is that they are less tolerant, and that older people become more rigid and do not like change. Yet for those growing in wisdom the opposite seems to be true. Carol is one of the informants who shows evidence of having a deep faith. She has a sense of being able to stand back and evaluate where she has been in her life, and to put her life experiences into perspective.

Wisdom is seen to include an awareness of the paradoxical and contra-dictory nature of reality, and it involves the ability to transcend uncertainty. Carol is not bitter as she speaks of the many disappointments in her life, although one might not be surprised if she was.

The journey of moving from external to internal regulation is one she has embarked on. She seems to rely little on the opinions of others. As well, she has developed a deep sense of 'interiority'. Faith is a part of her daily life. She has actively pursued knowledge of God and Christian meditation in recent years. Her belief system seems linked to her development of final meanings and wisdom. She said that she previously had a lot of unresolved grief but has worked through that with a counsellor. She demonstrated a high degree of self-understanding and perception of the needs of frail older adults:

> I only had about four weeks with her [counsellor], but I worked through a lot of losses with her; which I know, as one loss came up it reminded me of another, so, and there's been a lot of losses which have been a source of grief. And I think this is what's important for people to realise, people, when they get old, and they move into hostels and nursing homes, and they take with them a lot of unresolved grief, and they take with them a lot of pain, and they'd never been able to talk about it. People in their seventies and eighties and nineties have seen a lot of change and all these changes bring hurt with them, very often they do. And I think therefore it's very important that…some kind of pastoral care brings to the surface their pain and their loss. I think that's why I wanted to go into a place which had a church presence.

Carol shows wisdom in her ability to step outside the difficulties of her own life, and also to comment on the broader aspects of life. She is engaged with life, but also somewhat detached, and thus seems to be able to take an objective perspective on life in general. There is a sense in which she seems, in spite of her vulnerabilities, to be in control of her life, yet it is a control that is lightly held. She seems willing to let go of her life, to laugh at herself and, importantly, to face the uncertainties of the future. She neither dwells in the past nor is anxious about the future, even when she joked about possibly needing a 'pauper's funeral'.

At the same time, she is willing realistically to admit a possibility of needing assistance in living in the future. While she continues to grow and develop mentally and spiritually, she has a number of chronic physical conditions that even now make it difficult for her to live independently and alone. She is making plans for future care needs, investigating options open to her in hostel accommodation. Applying the definition for this study, it would seem that she demonstrates a highly developed level of wisdom. Yet wisdom is not something that she has actively sought; it has come as a gift, as grace in her life, an outcome of all that she is as a human being. It would appear that she is making a transition from doing to being, assisted by her transcendence of increasing frailty and her deep and growing faith.

In contrast, Betty does not believe in God, but lives by a philosophy of life. She sees her spiritual needs being met by 'being able to do what I think I ought to be doing'. Ill health of her husband and his increasing frailty have made her more conscious of the passing of life: 'It's all much more precarious because of our age and a feeling that you better make the best of it now, everybody else is falling down all around us.' Wisdom is a part of her living each day, being aware of her progress through life, and that of her husband, and being able to let go of the things that are no longer of value in her life. Betty has developed internal regulation and is quite self-reliant. A feature of this could be her independent professional career in later life. Betty seems to have embarked on an increased search for meaning in life at this point.

### Age and wisdom

It is possible that as people continue to age they may develop greater wisdom. This assumption is based on Erikson *et al.*'s (1986) final stage of psychosocial development, ego integrity versus despair, the successful outcome of which is wisdom. In this context wisdom can be linked to the spiritual definition being used here. Peck's (1968) stages of ageing are also useful in providing a frame for what is occurring here in the ageing process and the development of wisdom. Peck's second and third stages of psychosocial development, body transcendence versus body preoccupation and ego transcendence versus ego preoccupation, relate very much to that ability of the older person to come to new understandings of life in this final stage of earthly existence.

One may ask, is it time left to live that sparks this renewed search for final meanings? Is the turn to increased interiority seen in some older people stimulated by the search for God or the Ultimate in life, and how important are the life events that may present crises of meaning for that person in their journey? How important, for example, is a life-threatening illness or the loss of a loved one through death in sparking a search for meaning in life?

It is noted that informants Flora (67 years) and Sylvia (66 years) seem to have hardly started on the search for final meanings; Lisa (71 years) is another one who has done little conscious review of her life. These three women are younger. It is asked whether life review becomes more conscious and focused further along the lifespan; or whether it is perhaps accentuated by the person's perception of approaching death; or whether, indeed, there are other factors such as personality, stage of faith development or spiritual crises over the life journey that may influence the amount of life review undertaken by any particular individual. Perhaps it is as Coleman (1986) noted, that some people reminisce and others do not.

The connections seem far from obvious. For example, Flora was deeply affected by her husband's death from cancer, a number of years before: 'I had great faith until my husband was ill, he was only 49…and we knew…that he'd only live about five years, and I began to wonder then.' Flora is still young, at 67 years, so has possibly not begun to process final life meanings. It is interesting that her experience of losing her husband has had the effect of her choosing to reject God, or to at least, in her words, put 'God in the background'. She does not seem to be comfortable with uncertainty and spoke of the possibility of suicide should she be aware of becoming demented. She does not appear to be actively developing her spiritual dimension at this point, not in either a religious or secular sense.

Angela, at just 65, another of the younger women in the study, already shows signs of spiritual/psychological transcendence over a declining physical self. This may be connected to her 'awakening' in mid life:

> [it] was for me the Catechumenate [a course in Christian living] and that way, and that teaching that really did open up my eyes. It was like the blinkers had been taken off. As if I really heard for the first time… I started to believe, really believed… I guess (now) I'm more conscious of other people, I care more about other people, I'm not quite so selfish.

She is able to stand back. She said that there is more time to sit and think about life now. She evaluates where she has journeyed in that time, openly acknowledges her faults and can see how she had changed. Obviously, a lot of learning had taken place, and her conversion experience was perceived by her to be an important part of this. This informant recognises her changing self. However, she seems anxious about a number of aspects of her life.

Diane at 68 notes that as she grows older she realises that things that used to be a concern for her as a younger woman are now of little consequence. She already suffers from quite severe arthritis and this may be a factor in her beginning at this age to consider final meanings, as well as wider societal issues. She is currently concerned about changes in current government aged care policy, and expressed fear of insecurity for older people and their possible inability to afford health care in the future. She is vitally involved in public issues to do with ageing, and has an important contribution to make. She demonstrates a wisdom that allows her to see the whole perspective in what she is doing. Wisdom assists her in problem-solving exercises, such as what activities to retain and what to give up based on sound rationale.

Win, at 78, said she experiences lower energy levels these days, and she is resting more in God, with an acceptance that she can't do all she wants to. There may be disappointment in her declining energy levels and she endeavours to do all she can, but lets go of the things that are beyond her strength and/or ability. Win demonstrates the letting go that a number of authors have written of (Clements 1990; Fischer 1985). She has a deep faith; she is in a way shedding her former self and growing into a new identity with grace and humility.

This changing, in which she is taking an active part, listening to her own body, and prayerfully working through what God wants her to do, is almost sacramental. In all of this, she is, to use New Testament terminology, growing up into Christ. Overall there is a growing sense of wisdom apparent here, a complex interplay, continually testing between abilities and disabilities, checking 'is this OK?' Her working through this issue is demonstrated by the following explanation:

> Well I sometimes wonder as I get older, I find I can't do the same things that I wanted to do and then I find I get a bit stressed, you know I feel I can't cope sometimes... A thought came this morning that your memory would improve as you really live and and savour every moment and...do one thing at a time and savour every moment, it's awfully hard [laughs] but it is the thing.

It does not seem that there is a definite linear relationship between ageing and the development of wisdom. However this would need to be tested statistically. There do seem to be a number of factors influencing the development of wisdom in ageing, for example perceived vulnerability, age, faith, life experiences and crises encountered during life.

## Loss and wisdom

In some instances, transcendence was clearly visible in the interviews. This was particularly so for some who had experienced more of the losses associated with ageing, for instance Carol, Doris, Angela, Ann, Win, Edith, Mary, Sally and Helen. Such losses noted in this study include loss of role, spouse, physical health and mobility.

Yet some had not experienced so many apparent losses, but had still grown in wisdom, for example Betty. For others, ageing had not provided the answer to their searching, like Helga who still searches for a sense of peace in life. For most, the search for final meanings is evident and continues. A growing awareness of the paradoxical and contradictory nature of reality is a component of transcendence. The process of transcendence seems necessary to allow the move from external to internal regulation.

### Increased tolerance for uncertainty

Increased tolerance for uncertainty is one aspect of wisdom as defined in the study. Peck's (1968) stages of development in ageing again have relevance here. First, body transcendence versus body preoccupation. The older person experiencing the well-recognised decline of physical strength may be able to transcend the difficulties to find meaning in life in spite of their disabilities. Second, another likely event in ageing is the loss through death of people close to them. This may result in a greater focus on the person's own problems or may lead to their transcending these. Living with and accepting the paradoxical and contradictory is an important aspect of wisdom.

A number of the informants could fit this category. Carol lives alone and has multiple chronic conditions, and a deep faith. Eva lives alone at 83 and copes with a number of chronic conditions. She has a deep sense of the spiritual, but says, 'I'm not into religion'. She describes herself as a 'First World War baby boomer', a real survivor. Mary, who only mentioned her breast cancer in relation to assisting others, has had a very hard life and now lives life to the full, even though she has few material resources. She too has a deep spirituality, with no formal religious connections. These three women all demonstrate a high level of tolerance for uncertainty in their lives.

Yet another woman in the study, following a personal health crisis, turned to God. Edith (76 years) described how she believed she kept herself alive at the time she had a cardiac arrest. After her cardiac arrest, Edith said she thought she was back to all her miseries again, it took her a while to adjust to being back (alive).

> I really didn't want to come back. Everything seemed to be going wrong in my life. I was rowing with my daughter, I was rowing with my son. They couldn't understand, it just seemed I [was] going back years, blaming myself for my husband's death and everything just, caught up. And I hated people. And that was one of the things in my life that was very wrong... And when I had the cardiac arrest, and then when I had the bypass, the bypass mainly, I found I was looking at things differently... I wasn't angry anymore. And other things that had been upsetting me, I thought I was looking at them with an entirely different opinion. But I was looking at it and I wasn't condemning like I did... I feel that the purpose was I was going out hating, and I shouldn't be allowed to go out [that is, to die] hating. And I'd been brought back to show the reason for it and why I still have a purpose in life, even if it's only a short one.

This informant has recorded a marked change in her attitude towards life over the past few years. The medical crisis seemed to be an important factor in triggering this change. Her question, 'why was I brought back?', and her response to her own question were important in the search that has resulted in finding a new purpose and meaning in life. She too seems well able to live with uncertainty. Wisdom is necessarily an aspect of this change. She has grown in wisdom through her experiences and wisdom has helped her to see what is happening to herself. It is like a feedback loop, wisdom gets wisdom. Once the cycle has begun, it is suggested that it becomes easier to develop further in this direction.

Edith wrote a poem on fear as this was an important component of her journey. The poem illustrates some of the difficulties she has struggled with over the last years, and the working through and changing of her attitudes. I have obtained her permission to print it.

> 'Tis fear that I'm really afraid of,
> that I'll not be able to conceal it
> and I'll show my shame to all
> I would like to live a little longer,
> to see my grandsons grow taller
> please Lord, grant me courage to face it well
> let me laugh when I feel like screaming loud
> let me think of those who gave a helping hand
> and let me caste out the anger I had

at those who hurt me through the pages of my life
anger, fears, and contempt
why did I let these thoughts twist my mind?
they only destroy the good within us all
we can change these thoughts
for God is still there within our soul.

Her ability to stand back from her life and assess her effectiveness as a person, particularly in her relationships, is evidence of wisdom in her life. She is aware of her struggle to overcome hate and anger in her life, evidence that older people can and do change. She is able to manage well in the face of uncertainty, to let go of issues and, like Clements's (1990) model of stripping of roles, and the facing of losses in later life, she can be seen to be letting go and growing. Transcendence is also a feature of her life now. In recent times she has returned to her faith, and this has also provided comfort for her.

This study has provided an exploration of the spiritual nature of wisdom in a group of independently living older adults. Contrary to Blanchard-Fields and Norris's (1995) view, that a sizeable proportion of older adults may not exhibit signs of wisdom, this group of informants show evidence of wisdom, as defined for this study. This evidence is in the form of ability to tolerate uncertainty, to transcend present difficulties and to move from external to internal modes of control. Perhaps this group are a particular group, and untypical of the wider community. It is difficult to say. In the first place, it is not possible to obtain data of such an intimate nature from any person who is not really willing to share in such a sensitive area.

What this data does show is the degree of wisdom and faith stages of a group of older adults, living independently in the community, and who were willing to take part in this study. Are they atypical of the wider population in their age group? One cannot be certain, but it is worth noting the levels of wisdom demonstrated by these informants. This at least demonstrates the possibilities in the dimension of wisdom in ageing in the late twentieth century.

Some informants demonstrated an ability to step outside the difficulties of their lives, such as grief for loss of various kinds, disabilities and chronic illnesses. These informants were able to live comfortably with uncertainty, a feature of the spiritual aspect of wisdom, as defined in this study. The ability to face one's own mortality is an important factor of the development of wisdom in ageing.

## What is the value of the findings in the theme of wisdom?

The sample is too small to be able to do more than suggest further areas for study. However, wisdom is amply evident among the group of informants. This demonstrated wisdom is too valuable to waste. These people, and others like them, are a rich resource, both for improving their own well-being in ageing and for the whole community. These older adults show by their responses in the in-depth interviews the wealth of knowledge and understanding of life that they possess. Yet, in these times, wisdom seems not to be widely acknowledged and valued by society. There seems to be a desire to separate the present from the past, to live only in the present and the future. Well older people are quite often being made redundant from their work and at earlier ages, at a time in their lives when they have more to give because of their accumulated wisdom and levels of wellness, let alone their knowledge and skill levels.

As the demographic trend towards an ageing society continues, there will continue to be an accumulation of older people living in retirement who will see no meaning in life and no purpose for existence, while fewer younger people will be carrying the burden of supporting the retirees. This continued trend will lead to further sense of hopelessness for the older adults, while the younger ones will tend to become resentful of the burden they carry. Surely this society has to come to a realisation of the potential to overcome societal problems by rethinking the contribution of older adults in part-time work and new careers, of tapping into the resources of wisdom already present within the community.

A fundamental attitudinal shift is needed in the wider society to enable the changes necessary to be seen and then to be implemented. One major factor seems to prevent this attitudinal shift at present: ageism.

## Ageism and the relationship between the older person and the health care professional

Often when older adults require health care they find themselves treated in a paternalistic manner. Booth (1993) examined the comments of older adults on their experience of care and treatment in a large acute care hospital. Ageism was found to be common in the experiences of this group of former patients. Comments they made focused on often not having questions answered, being taken for investigations without proper explanation of procedures and being ignored by staff when they rang for attention. In fact the cognitive abilities of these patients were not acknowledged; nor was their need to be affirmed as meaning-making human beings, worthy of respect and real involvement in their care. Material such as that study produced cannot be ignored. In this study there is evidence of considerable wisdom and the ability to engage in complex problem solving related to personal well being. It is difficult to think that these older adults would not want to be involved in health-related decision making as well. In fact a previous study (MacKinlay 1989) found older adults in the main wanting to be vitally involved in health-related decisions.

The relationship between older adults and their health care professionals should be one of mutual partnership, not one-sided givers of care. Ministering to the human spirit includes treating the individual with dignity and developing relationships of mutual trust. This must include acknowledging the spiritual dimension in older people as well as the psychosocial and physical and working in relationship with older people in the provision of truly (w)holistic care.

## Summary

*Examining the spiritual context of wisdom in later life suggests an increased tolerance to ambiguity and awareness of the contradictory nature of reality, a deepening search for meaning and a move from external to internal regulation. It is noted that not all older people 'have' wisdom. A brief outline of a psychosocial perspective of wisdom in ageing is helpful in understanding the development of wisdom in later life but fails to provide the whole story.*

*The process of moving from provisional meanings to final meanings in later life is examined in relation to wisdom. A more conscious search for meaning is noted in these informants, along with a desire to deal with unfinished business. Regret, guilt, and the need for forgiveness and reconciliation are discussed in relation to the informants' backgrounds and spirituality.*

*Wisdom is amply evident among this group of informants. These older adults show by their responses in the in-depth interviews a wealth of knowledge and understanding of life. Healthy older people are often being made redundant from their work, at a time when they have more to give because of their accumulated wisdom, knowledge and skill levels. There is a need for rethinking the contribution of older adults in part time work and new careers in ageing; of tapping into the resources of wisdom already present within the community.*

CHAPTER 11

# *Hope, fear, despair and the last career*

## Hope and ageing

What is hope? Hope for the human being is essential for survival, it is what lights that spark at the core of our being. Hope is what energises an individual to keep on, it is what motivates. Paul wrote: 'Now hope that is seen is not hope. For who hopes for what is seen?' (Romans 8: 24). These words capture the sense of striving for something in the future, a goal to move towards. The opposite of hope is despair. It is such despair that Frankl (1984), writing of suicide, said intending suiciders experience, believing they have nothing more to expect from life. This attitude, turned around, can engender hope: it is *not what they (or we) can expect from life, rather, life still has more to expect from them*, no person can be replaced, each is an individual. As Frankl looked back over those prisoner of war experiences he said: 'Whoever was still alive had reason for hope' (p.103). There was still a sense of something in the future, a reason for living. Kimble (1990) took up this theme, writing:

> The awareness of possibilities and the understanding that an individual is a deciding being conveys hope. Hope must be seen in relation to freedom. To be free is to stand before possibilities. It is to transcend the present situation and see one's capacity to alter the status quo, even if limited to one's attitude towards unavoidable suffering. Without such a concept of freedom, there can be no hope. (p.118)

In this understanding of hope, even suffering, that is, unavoidable suffering (because avoidable suffering can never be justified), is a situation in which hope can exist. Frankl (1984) wrote that the concept of the 'courage to suffer' is the greatest courage (p.100).

In ageing, the hope that was present in mid life through meaning in roles or work, parenting and other achievements may seem to all but disappear. Hope in ageing must draw on new avenues. A growing sense of wisdom and transcendence, a deepening sense of interiority, the transition from doing to being allow new meaning to emerge after the middle years.

How can hope be identified among the group of informants in this study? It is suggested that there are two ways that the in-depth interviews can be used. The first is to acknowledge the instances where informants used the word 'hope'. It is noted that at no point during the interviews were they asked specifically about hope, although there was one question that asked: 'As you get closer to the end of your life, what do you look forward to?' This question obviously was implicitly about hope, but not all responded to the question in terms of hope. The second way in which 'hope' is identified is more oblique; by studying informants' conversations in the transcripts to identify examples of a general attitude of hope and evidence of 'spiritual integrity'.

However, it should be noted that not all older people may effectively negotiate this stage of life finding hope, and some may instead experience a sense of fear or despair, or perhaps tend to deny the reality of their life journey.

## Remarks from informants related to hope

I have tried to include all informant statements where they have used the word 'hope'. Like 'faith', hope too may mean different things to different people, therefore I have used it here in the sense of future things that are looked forward to, things 'not yet seen' that are of an important nature to the informants.

A number of the informants spoke of the hope they held for their families, of seeing their children well established in adult life, of having grandchildren. Some spoke of the hope for family reconciliation.

When I asked Carol what she looked forward to she said, 'Peace! I look forward to having people looking after me... I hope one day I'll go into a hostel and I'll have peace... I look forward to having a bit of care.' This woman had never married and is socially isolated now, although she is not spiritually isolated. She lives with a number of disabilities.

George spoke of his hopes for the future: 'So I simply, selfishly, wish that my health will hold as long as it can, I hope that when the time comes I'm taken quickly and not linger, I hope that my sister manages to be well provided for.' George, like a number of others discussed in the section on vulnerability hoped not to have to suffer. George was one of a few who spoke of an afterlife:

Now that's all very simple, what one looks for ahead, I just do not know; I choose to believe in Heaven whatever it may be. Goodness knows what it may be like and who would be there. Now if there's no Hell, I don't know that there's a Heaven. Now I say this seriously, I'd be there stirring the pot for these villains and these people in Bosnia and Rwanda and all those, so if you believe in Heaven, you must believe in Hell. And so I would like to believe there's a Heaven where certainly some good people will go and other people in due course will go directly or go through a state of purgatory or whatever ultimately will get there. What they will find I would not know. But I'd like to believe there is something. And on my good days I do believe it and on my bad days I don't.

Sylvia holds hope for her children, that particularly her son, will choose to live responsibly; he has broken contact with the family. Her main hope now, she said, is that neither she nor her husband will have to live long without the other. At present she is becoming more physically dependent, so this is a real concern.

Angela said: 'I can get over it really now, it's having hope I guess, hope.' She said this on looking back over all the difficulties in her life, and in light of her new sense of being able to manage effectively now. (She had a conversion experience in mid life.)

A couple of the men spoke of financial concerns. Stan remarked, 'I just hope I can manage financially.' This man expressed a very simple acceptance of life and faith. He did not enlarge on this statement, so whether his hope is realistic or not is not known.

Ann spoke of past actions for which she felt guilt but said, 'I just sort of hope that I do better…'. There was a realisation that she could not go back to 'fix' the past. In her case it was hope that enabled her to put the past behind, having learnt from her experiences, and face new challenges in the present and future.

Ben says his faith is the only source of help for him in life. It has given him hope when he was divorced, also when a prisoner of war in the Second World War, it was prayer and hope that brought him through. For Ben his memories of difficulties in earlier life, and his support then from prayer and faith, gave him hope for the present.

Edith has expressed her sense of hope in the poem she wrote on fear. For a number of informants their hopes were expressed in what they feared, their hope was what they wished for, perhaps longed for, but feared they would not have. For this woman, the words of her poem had been fulfilled. She had cast out her anger, she wasn't hating any more, she had another chance in life and she was living it in a new way, with a new sense of freedom.

Betty looks forward to 'being able to go on doing the sort of thing I enjoy doing now'. This woman does not believe in an afterlife and wishes her life to continue as it is. Both she and her husband have had health problems recently, which, as she remarked, has made their lives more 'precarious'.

Another woman, Mary, also expressed similar hopes. As she said: 'I'm just hoping to keep well and be able to keep on doing what I'm doing...and whatever comes afterwards well, I have to just, you know, because, I s'pose I'm as religious as most people are, in my way.' This woman has never been part of a church-going family. She is involved in a wide range of community interests. As an older woman she has developed a deep spirituality through life experience and reading.

## Spiritual integrity

For the purpose of this study spiritual integrity is:

> a state where an individual shows by their life example and attitudes, a sense of peace with themselves and others, and development of wholeness of being. The search for meaning and a degree of transcendence is evident.

True wholeness and integrity is probably only possible at the point of death, however many may approach it in the latter stages of life. There is a sense in which it seems spiritual integrity is what Fowler (1981) is describing in his final stage of faith development. Spiritual integrity must also be closely related to wisdom, and Erikson *et al.* (1986) would say that wisdom is an outcome of ego integrity in ageing. In practice, it is very difficult to tease apart the components of spirituality, and it has been attempted here only in an endeavour to gain a better understanding of the whole; that it may assist in the development of more effective strategies for providing for the needs of spiritual care, by all levels of health and pastoral carers.

### Three examples of the journey towards spiritual integrity

Three examples of informants moving towards spiritual integrity are presented as a way of viewing the general attitudes of hope. The first woman is married and experienced conversion in mid life, she is now actively involved in a faith community. The second woman has never married and developed a strong faith from her teenage years onwards. The third lives alone, is 83 years of age, has been widowed for most of her adult life and has had no contact with a church community for many years.

## A mid life conversion

Angela said that life opened up after she had surgery at age 55 (hysterectomy). Prior to this she had been a 'habitual' church attender. Then she began searching and began a course of study in Christianity. She remarked that it was like having the blinkers taken off; as if she heard things for the first time. She says she is grateful for her 'awakening...everything had a new meaning'. She said: 'I don't understand it, but I'm grateful for that.' She sees no hope in dwelling on problems and says 'there must be hope'. She argues against the physical evidence of decline and accepts that hope is there, in spite of what she sees happening in the physical ageing process. She said that there is more time to sit and think about life now.

This woman has changed over the last few years to a sense of deepening spirituality. She is working actively in this area of her life, shows a real awareness of her past faults and is developing skills to deal more effectively with them. She is open to spiritual growth and to relating in new ways to others.

## A deepening spiritual integrity

Win appears to have reached a sense of integrity in her ageing. At the same time she is conscious of her own continuing spiritual journey, but with a sense of peace and contentment, and a deep appreciation of life: 'Joy, and you know I can think, I should take more note of these little things. As one of my neighbours said, "I look for the little miracles every day".'

She said she had learnt the importance of listening to God. She spoke of her spiritual journey: 'We need to accept our life as a journey, a spiritual journey, constant development. Don't stand still.' She constantly reminds herself that God is there even if she doesn't feel anything. As she quoted: 'O Lord, help my unbelief' (Mark 9: 24). In mid and later life she has gone back to study and achieved in subjects she had never been able to succeed in before. She found herself gaining in confidence to take on new things. This was a common finding of mid-life psychosocial development identified by Neugarten (1968).

Win said that she used to be very conscious of what other people thought of her, but now she realised her life didn't depend on what others thought, and what she thought she could do, that wasn't the important thing, 'it's what God wanted me to do'. She shared an anecdote of how she started doing things in small ways, assisting with tasks, and grew in confidence: 'In one way it's given me self-confidence but also I felt well, most of it, I have to…pray about it and…I sort of let God show me.' She went on to explain her life meaning and centre now:

> You know the other day I had the thought, to really live, that life is for living not for just doing things automatically, and to seek God in everything, you know that verse, do all to the glory of God, everything that you do, and I thought, well does that mean if I should rest more, can I do that to the glory of God?

### A First World War baby boomer

Eva, at 83 years, lives alone and has a wonderful and deep spirituality and philosophy of life. She spoke of her joys: these come for her through contentment in life, having her own house, reading, going out once or twice a week. She had to carry the responsibility of being mother and father to her children, as she was widowed early in life. Her husband died while she was pregnant with their youngest child.

She said that for her, meaning in life was 'being content with what you've got … what's the use of possessions?…they're only an encumbrance'. Eva said that she has always questioned life, as she said: 'But you must remember we were the *baby boomers of the First World War.*' This, she said, set her group apart as special at a particular time in history. She is a very resilient person, gifted in a number of ways, still with a lot to give to others, including her adult children.

Eva appeared to have ample spiritual resources to maintain herself in her living situation. It would be reasonable to say that she had achieved a high degree of spiritual integrity, and was continuing to grow spiritually.

### Contentment, acceptance, peace and joy

#### 'I'm contented, I'm just contented.'

A number of informants reported a sense of joy or contentment in their lives. It is uncertain just where these comments should best be placed. However, there is a sense in which it is not really possible to experience a truly deep joy, or peace, or real contentment – contentment in this case being differentiated from resignation or apathy – without hope and without being able to transcend difficulties of everyday life.

Vera finds joy in many things, currently through working with a group of older people doing Shakespeare. She said her husband was 'a great source of joy'. There was joy from seeing her adult son establish himself in life, and "joy was taking a university degree... I was 60 before I graduated'. And she enjoys walking.

For Diane one of her greatest joys was putting her feet on the Antarctic for the first time, which she described as an incredible emotional/spiritual experience.

Daisy finds meaning in life from her husband, family and friends; from general interests and 'definitely my own faith because otherwise life doesn't have much meaning, actually and something to lean on, draw on...every day'. She said: 'I [have] lots of joys. Well every day's a joy because there's something new and, I think your family's constantly a joy... I still find life very good, enjoy it.' She has many special memories. She says she's 'a fairly contented person' and 'I think as you get older you, you really do have to live day to day.'

These informants were all continuing to live independently in the community and they were still in control of their lives. They showed evidence of growing towards spiritual integrity. But they had not yet come to the last career, the preparation for dying. What differences would realisation of immanent death make for these people? How would they face death in a death-denying society?

## Facing death

During the twentieth century in Western countries death became both more medicalised, and it has become the norm for people to die in hospitals. Further, death (mostly violent) has become an increasing part of the nightly television news. In the early 1990s, when I first suggested registered nurses ask residents of nursing homes if they had any fears, for example fear of dying or death, I was met with a variety of responses, including: 'The residents don't want to talk about death'. It seems that a great deal of activity in nursing homes goes on to escape the inevitable fact that death comes to all of us.

When we surveyed elderly residents of nursing homes (1992) we found that many of them did want to speak of their fears surrounding death. As one of the registered nurses remarked at the time, 'It was like opening the flood gates'. It seemed that certain subjects were not really on the agenda, and unless staff working with elderly people affirm the possibility of raising such sensitive issues, then the questions may go unasked and, of course, un-answered.

## The last career

Heinz (1994) has described the time of coming to the end of life as the last career of the human being. He urges us to take up the last career which he sees as 'the great imaginal task of aging, laden with spiritual possibility. This is the time for the successful negotiation of a final identity that gives retrospective meaning to life and prospective meaning to death' (p.5). Heinz suggests that in our society, through the development of technology and the medicalising of death, we have lost the ability and the framework to really develop the last career, to the detriment of succeeding generations.

Heinz sees the last career as a means of passing on to the next generation the meaning of our culture, as well as making individual sense of our lives as we have lived them. The loss of last careers, he says, is a loss of the opportunity for individuals and societies to collaborate in forging last careers. If this challenge to develop the last career is taken up, the possi-bilities for both individuals and the community could be to produce over time: 'a culture of aging, last career, and death, a network of symbols, rituals, and meanings through which to mediate and express life and death, youth and age within a larger system of meaning' (p.7).

This final stage of life is a time when we must be willing to allow ourselves to be called into question. Heinz (1994) asks a vital question of our ageing: 'Will our dying be clothed in the metaphor of self-transcendence or of the ultimate protest of complete autonomy?' (p.16). What will our spiritual work, our spiritual autobiographies, reveal? We are only now beginning to re-recognise the importance of this spiritual lifelong journey in our sophisticated society. We need to re-learn the ways of bringing this last career to fulfilment in appropriate ways for the people preparing for the next millennium. In part Heinz is saying that we need to grasp the nettle of dying, to stop denying its place in life, and to take up the challenge of the last career.

Heinz (1994) ends by saying that this is work no culture can afford to leave undone. It is important to visualise the meaning making of ageing, or the last career, as being real work, and not to reduce it to simply a sentimental journey of nostalgia (as can be done in activity groups using reminiscence). The importance to at least some frail older people of discussing religion is highlighted by the fact that religion was the preferred topic of geriatric patients in group therapy sessions at a state hospital in the

USA, (Moberg 1968, p.504). Has this changed in the intervening decades? The wish to come to final life meanings, which includes the perception of approaching death, was also evident in the study of frail older people in nursing homes by MacKinlay (1992).

### Facing death

Informants in this study were asked whether they had any fears as they grew older. They were not specifically asked about death, but if they mentioned death, any comments they made were clarified. A number did not mention death. As preparedness for our own dying is becoming a more readily recognised need, it would have been useful to ask the informants about death and dying. Vera spoke of her mother's death, saying it had been a relief, as she had cared for her mother who had dementia.

### Fear of dying

A number of informants spoke of a fear of the possibility of prolonged suffering that may precede death. None seemed to fear 'being dead'. Only Beryl said that she did not like talking about death. In one respect this group of older people is one step back from the process of dying. It will be important to follow this theme in a further study with those for whom death is closer and thus more urgent: the frail elderly residents of nursing homes.

### Belief in God and fear of dying

Wisdom is evident in Doris's life in her ability to reconstruct past experiences and to learn and grow through them; it is also evident in her ability to deal openly and effectively with past disappointments. She says she doesn't want to die because she enjoys living. However, she does say she might be fearful of pain in the process of dying. She made a clear distinction of not fearing being dead: says she is 'perfectly sure the Lord looks after everybody'. Speaking of her husband's death she said:

> I think, the grief, when one loses one's husband, is something that, once again, rocks your life to its very foundations, doesn't it, because it's something that you sort of foresee it a little, but you don't anything like foresee the way that grief's going to affect you, in all the different ways it's going to affect you, I don't think. Don't know of any other big griefs like that.

Her husband died about nine years before. The memory of the loss was still very evident for her, although she had worked through her grief and is now living effectively in the present.

Ann spoke of her grief when her brother died about three years ago. 'Oh, I lost my brother, my younger brother with cancer and he was the youngest of the family, we all found that very hard…you expect these things as you get older.' Her grief was tinged with the acceptance of expected loss of relationship with increasing age. Any yet, there was an added sadness, he was after all her 'younger brother' and thus in a way should not have been expected to die before her. She spoke openly about death, reflecting that a number of her friends did not want to talk on that topic. Ann seems to have no fears of death, although she expressed some uncertainty about 'what happens afterwards'.

> I am surprised quite often at the number of my friends, and I'm 71, who don't think about death, ah probably don't want to think about death, don't want to think about what happens afterward, that's something that does surprise me…it's going to happen, getting closer every day and what happens afterward, and that's something that I really can't understand, you know that they just don't think about.

At this point, I wanted to follow through further on her attitudes towards dying, so I said: 'I'd just like to explore a little further on talking about dying and I'm wondering, do you have any fears about the process of dying or death from your own perspective?' She responded:

> I don't know that I have any fears because nobody knows, we've never had any information back, have we, and nobody knows really what is at the other side, still it's part of life, and we'll just see when it happens, but it's not something that can be avoided.

This woman spoke openly about death, but did not specifically speak about the process of dying. From her earlier comments about family situations and death she had obviously been close to the grief of others and had no difficulty in talking about those situations or death itself. Earlier she had remarked: 'I have the fear of most old people that I'll lose my independence and that I'll become immobilised, I'll lose my sight or you know, mainly physical things.' These comments come nearer to dealing with the process of dying. When I asked the direct question about dying and death, she responded only to the death part.

Sally said: 'Of course I'm an old lady now, you know.' There was an air of acceptance of ageing in that. She noted: 'You see so I just go back and I live in my memories a lot too.' Speaking on dying, she said:

> Am I scared to die? I don't know, but where I'm concerned sometimes I'm a wee bit frightened and then I just hope I just slip away...but I just, I just, gee there I come back to God again, God's looking after me and if He thinks I should do that He'll show me the way. That's how I live...I mean we don't know, we just have the faith that we're going to go to heaven.

She appears to have changed little in her faith over the years, except that she attends church very infrequently now.

Helen, who had constructed her own belief system, said that drawing on her life experience she thinks people handle grief 'in a different way' as they grow older, depending on their understanding. 'It's part of maturity and part of learning to love to be able to let go, and you must be able to let people go, they don't belong to you, they are their own individual souls and they've got their own path to walk and work.'

She expressed an understanding that there's nothing to fear in death: 'I have no fear whatever of death... I think there's an appointed [time] which my soul knows, and I'll probably know, when that time comes.'

She noted: 'As people get older they start to remember things that happened long ago, they hadn't thought of for fifty, sixty years and it's amazing.' Helen was very conscious of the process of reminiscence in ageing. Looking back through her life she says there have been a 'lot of stressful sorrowful things, that caused me grief and sorrow, but they were times of awakening'. She says she sees the search now as being 'for wisdom, which is more than spirituality'. Helen was recognising points of crisis that became growth opportunities in her spiritual journey; she demonstrated a deep self-awareness of her own journey.

Eva fears being alone when she dies, and not being found. This woman shared how a friend of hers, living alone, had died and had not been found for about a week. She joked about what might happen to her. Eva has no family anywhere near, the nearest probably about four hours drive away. While she expressed a sense of contentment at living alone, there was also this fear of dying alone and not being found. This is a fear other people have also expressed to me, even some who have been residents of nursing homes, fear that this may be their lot. Dying alone is a fearsome thing. The litany in the Anglican prayer book (1978) recognises this in the words, 'from dying suddenly and unprepared, good Lord deliver us'.

## No belief in God and fear of dying

Helga said that after her father and sister died she had changed; turning away from any beliefs she had before.

> But then, see, I don't even believe in heaven or hell, I believe it's here on earth. Not much heaven... That's what I say, because, maybe I'm not a Christian, and I wish I could...but...it only just made me bitter, that people would have to suffer, when there was so much emphasis put on Jesus suffering on the Cross. And I felt my sister had gone through suffering, and other people had gone through suffering, just as bad, you know, during the war.

Helga continued to search for a sense of peace in her life. There was little in her life that gave her cause for hope.

It is apparent that Beryl has not come to terms with her own mortality at this stage. Even though she raised the topic, she was the only one in the study who did not seem comfortable talking about death.

> I was just listening to a talk on death on the radio, one of these answer-back things a little while ago and the contention there was that we deny death...and I was thinking yes we probably do, but I don't see why one should think too much about it when it's not happening, I'm, I'm very much living in the present, not in the future.

Beryl described the experience of losing people through death as 'violent when you lose them and you still miss them, grief for lost opportunities'. Of what happens when we die she said: 'The light's switched off in the literal sense, it's stopped; I think it's just the energy or whatever it is, just, I mean this is my provisional [laughs] my provisional definition [laughs] I mean it could be anything, I mean who knows but as far as I'm concerned that's it.' But she noted that you have to cope: 'I suppose stoicism is nearest to describing [it].' Of fears, she says she does not allow them to surface: 'If there were a real crisis...you don't have any power over that.' She has no concept of an afterlife. She remarked that she has been to two funerals, and did not like being there. She does not believe in God. Beryl was the only one to voice such strong feelings about death.

Eva is not afraid of death, but uncertain of what lies after death, voicing some sense of reincarnation. She said: 'your soul may go to do other things or if you've been very wicked I do think you come back to try and improve yourself to get to the Ultimate. I don't know.' She does not have a belief system at present.

## Hope at the end of life

Most of the informants focused on the here and now. I did not ask them specifically about their hopes for an afterlife, although some mentioned it, more saying that they were not sure about what would happen after they die than anything else. None of the informants said they hoped for eternal life; some did say they wondered what heaven would be like, and some looked forward to meeting their husbands again. A couple of informants expressed a concept of reincarnation. One of these was the woman who had constructed her own religion. None of them expressed any fear of being dead, only fear of the process of getting to be dead.

Hope, for older adults, may be more precarious in our society now, with some informants talking of suicide or euthanasia as an option if they come to a stage of losing control of their lives. Setting this present scene against Frankl's (1984) writings from a time of great devastation of families and life during the Second World War, where many people, including prisoners of war, were able to retain their hope, it is asked, what has changed? It almost seems that there is less hope in society now than in the middle of a world war.

One possible answer could be the tremendous emphasis on individualism since the 1960s. The sense of community and care for each other seems to be dissolving in the face of economic rationalism, a particularly grim prospect for these older adults who have lived and struggled, the older ones, at least, through two world wars and a depression, and have struggled to make ends meet. These older people now find themselves living in a world which seems to have lost its sense of direction. Meaning in life may be threatened as they see values and morals, as they knew them, eroded, while they live out their lives with an increasing sense of vulnerability.

## Belief in eternal life

Few of the informants, including those who acknowledged membership of a Christian denomination, spoke of either the possibility or certainty of eternal life. It would perhaps have been easier to use a questionnaire and simply ask, 'Do you believe in eternal life?' than to use in-depth interviewing, as has been done here. However, it seemed more appropriate to allow the informants to speak of what they deemed relevant to the topic of spirituality and meaning in later life rather than to confine them to answers to specific questions.

So the question remains, do the adherents of the various denominations believe in an afterlife, or not? For these informants, and others like them, it may be important to provide learning opportunities to enable them to explore the content of their faith. It may also be that questions about an afterlife are not generally foremost in the thoughts of independent older adults; it may be the frail older adults whose thoughts turn more to questions of life after death.

### Summary

*This chapter examined hope, fear and despair in the informants' lives. It also explored their attitudes towards the last career, that is, preparing to die. Hope was evident in the stories of the informants. Often it was identified in their relationships with children and most particularly with grandchildren. It is noted that only a few of the Christians in the study spoke of the hope of eternal life.*

*As Erikson had described the final stage of psychosocial development as integrity versus despair, so a spiritual developmental stage of integrity was described in this study. This was described as the person having a sense of peace with themselves and others, while moving towards transcendence and wholeness.*

*Preparing for death as a last career became increasingly difficult during the twentieth century, in death-denying western societies. While most informants spontaneously expressed fears of facing a prolonged dying process and possible suffering, none expressed a fear of 'being dead.' One fear noted by a few of those in this study was dying alone; this may be a tragic reality for some. All these informants had already faced a number of significant losses in life, such as death of spouse and loss of mid-life role identity. They spoke openly about death, when given the opportunity.*

# CHAPTER 12

# Humour, laughter, spirituality and ageing

## Humour and spirituality

Is there a spiritual component in humour? Is laughter part of the spiritual dimension? Humour and laughter occurred at times during a number of the interviews. Although this was not an aim of the study, I decided to explore how humour had been used in these instances.

Humour and laughter are closely linked; however, laughter and humour can each occur separately (Lefcourt and Martin 1986). Commonly, they say, humour is understood as the functioning of rather complex higher-order cognitive-emotional processes, while laughter is understood as a reflex-like physiological-behavioural response. Like crying, humour and laughter may have a number of meanings and functions. While humour can be used to mock, ridicule or coerce, it may also be a means of reducing interpersonal tensions and 'expressing a feeling of oneness with others and the universe'(Lefcourt and Martin 1986, p.4).

Frankl (1984, p.63) writes that humour is one of the 'soul's weapons in the fight for self-preservation'. Frankl writes out of some of the experiences of humour in the most difficult of Second World War prison camp settings.

Humour which occurs in situations that would normally elicit a negative response, such as sadness or fear, was one of three categories of humour referred to by Freud, in Lefcourt and Martin (1986). It is suggested that the release of laughter allows an altered perspective of the situation, and results in avoiding the negative consequences of the situation. 'The laughter of humour arises from the release of energy that would have been associated with this painful emotion but has now become redundant' (p.6). In a way, this can be referred to as a defence mechanism, enabling a person to avoid negative consequences of a situation. Freud's work is seen as one of the arousal theories of humour, focusing on affective or arousal-related aspects while acknowledging the place of appropriate cognitive elements such as jokes.

Another group of theories of humour are the incongruity theories. These focus on the way in which humour alters the person's perception of the situation, making it less stressful and therefore less arousing – in other words, the situation is defused (Lefcourt and Martin 1986), producing a healthy response to tension-raising situations. A final group of theories of humour, the superiority theories, claim we laugh at others less able than ourselves, or at other people's misfortunes. It may also be considered that humour of this type can be directed at one's self. It is possible to laugh at one's own misfortunes, resulting in enhanced feelings of self-esteem and mastery, thus threats to the self can lose their power and be dismissed. Lefcourt and Martin (1986) found in their study that humour touches on matters of great profundity in the human condition. Most relevant to their findings was the 'value of acceptance and forgiveness of one's self and others that is inherent in humour' (p.124).

> To laugh with someone about what would seem to be an alien anguish is to know that anguish as a surrogate for one's own familiar pains; and the humour that results is perceivable as one shared 'victimhood' – the state of our species all too aware of its own mortality. (Lefcourt and Martin 1986, p.126)

Humour was considered as an expression of spiritual maturity by McFadden (1990). Perhaps a sense of humour is really needed to enable older people to deal with some of the difficulties they encounter in ageing. McFadden states that Freud's approach to humour gives the best understanding of its use by older individuals. Humour is used by older people in a variety of situations, for example when referring to problems with an ageing body. She says:

> The individual who makes a humorous remark about the ageing body economises on the affect of self-pity but at the same time does not avoid recognition of physical difficulties by denying, rationalising or even repressing their existence. (p.137)

McFadden says that, according to Freud, humour was seen to possess some kind of grandeur, describing it as being like 'triumph' and 'victory'. He also said that the pleasure of humour was 'liberating and elevating'.

So what is it about humour that allows people to transcend life's difficulties? McFadden (1990) suggests that this perspective of humour is in itself paradoxical. It is seen as requiring a kind of detachment from the immediate situation, the ability to self-transcend, while at the same time requiring an intimacy with events, other people and the self. To be able to laugh at or smile at a given situation requires both being able to stand back from the situation and being 'utterly immersed' in the experience.

McFadden suggests the ability to do this may well be an expression of spiritual maturity.

Authentic humour should be separated from humour that is morally inappropriate. Authentic humour takes the moral responsibility of its freedom seriously. McFadden (1990) says that authentic humour is able to triumph over suffering, that is, when suffering has been consciously acknowledged. The ethical dimension of humour is that it does not cause suffering. Further, authentic humour of the spiritually mature person is acknowledged as conveying a deep sense of trust and hope.

It may be possible to devalue authentic humour, not recognising that it is a sign of the spiritual dimension. It is important for carers working with older adults to be able to recognise authentic humour in those they work with, and to also learn to use humour appropriately in their own work. It is just as important for carers not to use humour inappropriately, in a way of being condescending, demeaning or 'putting down' the older person.

## Humour and the spiritual dimension in ageing

On a number of occasions, in different in-depth interviews, the informant would spontaneously laugh. I also found that quite often both informant and I, as the interviewer, would laugh together, spontaneously. It seemed to be a kind of empathetic response, and not always in the context of funny situations. A number of the instances of laughter were quite sensitive episodes, involving dying, or other situations where something had gone very wrong. There were a number of instances of laughter where the informant was recounting an anecdote and laughing at the memory, particularly of things they had done as children. I have only included examples of humour and laughter where it could be said that the situation touched on the spiritual, or at least a very deep level.

What was the effect of laughter in these situations? In almost all examples, there was a raised consciousness of us both being in this situation together; a sharing of something very deep, a privileged moment. The laughter was accompanied by smiling, quite often eye contact and, afterwards, a sense of release; certainly on my part and, I suspect, on the part of the informant. The informant would always proceed to share further, and perhaps even more deeply, following such an episode.

Flora seemed initially to be testing; was it all right to do what she was sharing? She said:

> If something upsets me I talk to his photograph, [laughs] you know, so I think, well I must have faith in something, I mean, you don't just talk to a photograph, do you? I mean you know I really think I'm talking to him.

This informant was speaking of something very personal and intimate for her. She laughed as she shared with me. The incident centred on her reflection of a habit of talking to her husband's photo. I sensed she was unsure how I would respond to her behaviour, and the laughter seemed almost to ask for affirmation from me, would I laugh too? In this instance it didn't seem appropriate for me to laugh, it was too sensitive. She paused for a long time after sharing that with me. She seemed to be comfortable with what she had shared and then went on to share more about her faith.

Flora joked about her fear of developing dementia:

> Now talking to friends of my own age I think we all end up, we have a dread, you know when we can't think of something, either somebody's name or a word you can't think of, we say, Oh the old 'alkaselzer's' coming on, we all dread it.

In this situation the joke is a way of dealing with something that is feared. It allows the people to talk about it, but eases the tension, in that they may laugh together about something they hope will never happen to any of them. This time we both laughed.

Carol was one of the informants who lived with a number of chronic physical conditions. She was not well off financially, but she had a wonderful sense of humour. She told an anecdote of her problems about worrying that she would not have enough money to pay for her funeral:

> So she [social worker] explained to me that I could have what used to be called a 'pauper's' funeral [laughs]. Oh I laughed, and I wrote a story and it starts off, 'Well I'm heading for the pauper's grave' and I put all the reasons why I was heading for a pauper's grave. So I sort of likened myself to Forest Gump, I'd been an idiot all my life, that's why I was heading for a pauper's grave. So I have to make it clear to my son or somebody, that when I die, if there isn't enough money, they can go, they get I think two weeks pension, and what I have, and they can, if that isn't enough, I can have a pauper's funeral. Oh dear, it's laughable really.

In the midst of her disabilities and other difficulties, Carol is still able to laugh at herself. She laughed a lot during the interview (we both laughed) and yet it seemed almost incongruent that she should seem so happy and so much at peace when speaking of the difficulties she was living with. There is a sense in which it is only because Carol has been able to transcend her difficulties that she is able to laugh about her difficulties. She seems to have a way of distancing herself from her difficulties. This is a real strength within herself.

Ann was another who laughed when remembering sad times:

> Oh I lost my brother, my younger brother with cancer [about three years ago, they had been close to one another] and he was the youngest of the family. We all found that very hard and I went to see him in hospital; just like my father, praying out loud all over the ward [both laugh], but I mean these things, you expect these things as you get older.

In this example, both informant and interviewer laughed together at the mention of the informant's brother praying aloud in a hospital ward while he was dying. This seems to be a case of cognitive dissonance. The situation was certainly not humorous. Perhaps it was to lighten the moment; perhaps the event of both laughing together was a kind of empathy in a sensitive situation. There was a sense with this woman too that she was able to transcend her difficult issues.

Were these examples of a spiritual nature? Yes, I believe so. It was a way of connecting with another human being in a deep way, in a situation that often was too deep for words. It was spontaneous, never contrived, I believe, by either of the parties. It was a way of 'being with' or 'being present' to one another.

Laughter in such circumstances is I believe an important way of connecting with the other person. It can be used very effectively in a therapeutic situation. However, it is a strategy that cannot be forced. Laughter used inappropriately would be disastrous to a relationship. It is only when a sense of trust exists between the parties that it is possible to use humour in such a way. And yet, it must be remembered that in each case, as researcher, I had only met the informant on one previous occasion. So it would appear that it is possible to develop communication to such a deep level of connection and sharing in a relatively short period of time.

## Death, dying and laughter

The topic of death provided an instance of the use of humour for Eva. She fears being alone when she dies, and not being found. This woman shared how a friend of hers, living alone, had died and had not been found for about a week. She joked about what might happen to her. She said: 'and she'd been dead a week. Now that shocked me and I thought [if she died alone] oh and the two cats, you know, they'd eat me.' In this instance Eva was sharing a very real fear, but she laughed as she joked about the most unlikely and horrible outcome of dying alone. Again, this was evidence of transcendence.

It is worth noting that most of these examples were in some way connected with death, with the possible exception of Flora, who appeared to be seeking affirmation for her sharing. Each of these informants appeared to be using laughter and humour as a way of connecting deeply when speaking of death and dying. In each case there was a sense of the meaning of the conversation that transcended the mere words. Body language was also a part of this, with smiling and relaxed attitude. It would seem that laughter was used in a therapeutic manner in these examples.

These instances of the use of humour link with the findings of Lefcourt and Martin (1986) who found that humour was related to matters of great 'profundity' regarding the human condition. As well, McFadden (1990) suggested that humour was needed by older people to enable them to deal with some of the difficulties they encountered in life. The ability to laugh at themselves certainly was illustrated in the examples in this study. However, it is unclear whether the ability to laugh at oneself helps the individual to cope with a situation, or whether having to cope with difficult situations may help the individual to transcend the difficulties and in turn develop skills to be able to laugh at themselves. McFadden also noted that humour could be considered a sign of spiritual maturity. If this is so, then perhaps the laughter used as a means of connecting and transcending may be a sign of spiritual maturity. The findings here suggest that further study could be fruitful.

## Gender differences and the use of laughter

Another point of interest regarding the use of laughter in the interviews is the apparent differences between the women and men in the sample. The only examples of laughter used as a means of deeply connecting from the informants were from the females. The men in the study seemed to be using laughter differently; mostly it was used in the context of content rather than as a means of deepening the connection between informant and interviewer. Stan actually seemed to use laughter to avoid going deeper into conversation. Particularly this was noticeable when he was asked a question that he did not want to answer. He would laugh and then brush off the topic at a superficial level.

It would be valuable to explore further the use of humour and laughter and its connection with spirituality. Of particular interest are the ways laughter was used by women in this study as a means of connecting more deeply (noted in the examples related to the topics of dying and death). The differences noticed between the females and males in the way that laughter was used is also interesting. This may be a factor of gender-based differences in communication styles or even a difference in expressing spirituality between the genders.

It could also be that the differences may be an effect of the gender of the researcher. Female interviewing female may elicit the use of laughter to deepen the connection of the interchange in the relationship of the interview, while female interviewing male in a sensitive area of spirituality may elicit the use of humour at a more superficial level, that is, related to content rather than connection.

Although a study of laughter and spirituality in ageing had not been planned, it seemed appropriate to explore the instances of laughter and humour contained in the transcripts as these were related to spirituality. The findings here indicate that it may be fruitful to study the area further to gain a better picture of what is happening in these interchanges between informant and researcher. It is possible that there may be ways in which humour may be used therapeutically.

## Summary

*Although a study of laughter and spirituality in ageing had not been planned, it seemed appropriate to explore the instances of laughter and humour contained in the transcripts as these were related to spirituality. Humour was used on a number of occasions when deep issues were being explored. Laughter also occurred while sharing some particularly sensitive memories. For the women in the study, laughter and humour was often used as an entry to sharing more deeply; on the other hand, the men in the study seemed more likely to use humour as a deflector when the conversation became too sensitive.*

*The findings here indicate that it may be fruitful to study the area further to gain a better picture of what is happening in these interchanges between informant and researcher. It is possible that there may be ways in which humour may be used therapeutically.*

# CHAPTER 13

# Spirituality, relationship and issues of isolation in ageing

## Relationship and the spiritual dimension

It is important to define the context of relationship used in this study. The study of human relationship may be pursued from the perspective of various of the behavioural sciences. When the focus of relationship is placed on meaning within human relationship, then it is most appropriate to study it within the perspective of the spiritual. The spiritual dimension acknowledges the two dimensions of relationship, the perpendicular, that is, with God, or some sense of 'other' and the horizontal, that is, relationship with other people. As well, a critical aspect of the spiritual is related to where each individual finds ultimate or core meaning in their lives. For many, perhaps most people, the meaning derived from human relationship is an important and, in some cases, the most important part of their lives.

## What do older people seek in relationship?

Is it satisfying sexual relationship, is it companionship, is it someone to listen and to share with, maybe to be a part of their life review? Probably relationship for older people is all of these things. It has been said that a close relationship exists between spirituality and sexuality. How does this relate to intimacy?

## What is intimacy and how is it important for older people?

Carroll and Dyckman (1986, p.123) describe intimacy as 'the ability to let myself be known by another and to be comfortable in that revelation'. They go on to say: 'At the deepest core of my being I need to be known and loved as I am.' They acknowledge this need as a reciprocal one. Intimacy is a deep and safe place to be, to simply 'be' with another, without the masks, the facades, the inhibitions. It is touching deeply into another human being, connecting at a deep level. This is an expression of the so-called horizontal dimension of spirituality.

Meaning in life ultimately is that search for oneness with God. And yet, human relationship is a critical part of this too. Carroll and Dyckman (1986) suggest that human relationship with God tends to mirror and be mirrored by our relationships with others. However, people differ in the way this is worked out in their lives, for some, they say, 'an intense deep relationship with God, developed through personal or liturgical prayer, leads to more freedom in human relationships and a heightened capacity for human intimacy' (p.129). For other people, Carroll and Dyckman say, relationship with others is the prior position, and from effective human relationships there may be an opening to and availability to the love of God.

### Relationship: individuation or connection?

Vogel (1995) wrote that, particularly for older women, basic socialisation included a world view that 'devalued women and connectedness and that valued independence and power with a white, male base' (p.80). Argued on this basis, that world view affects that whole age cohort, both men and women, who are currently over 65 years. The implications for those older people, then, would limit roles available to them and their sense of who they are as individuals. Vogel says that 'When human vocation is viewed as a partnership with God who invites persons to fashion a community even as they are fashioned by God, then understanding of what it means to grow and to be transformed takes on new meaning' (p.80). Using this approach, it is no longer possible to regard people simply from an individualistic perspective.

Relationship forms an important part of being human and of finding meaning. These remarks are equally true for both men and women living in a society that emphasises individuality above the well-being of the community. Yet, even in community and through community, 'soul nourishment' is necessary, as in older age the physical, psychosocial and spiritual dimensions are 'inexorably connected' (Vogel 1995) and concerned with health and role changes.

### Ageing, social isolation and loneliness

Current government policies in aged care in Australia support older people remaining at home and receiving community services. This has been thought to provide more appropriate care and is also economically attractive. However, Sax (1990) has been critical of the lack of consistency of goals in aged care policy.

McCallum (1990) notes two trends in aged care policy in the Australian scene: first, integration of elderly people with the rest of the population and, second, an emphasis on using 'need as the criterion for public support rather than the status of being aged'. These trends continue and there are both advantages and disadvantages to these trends. First, it is important to maintain links across the generations, effective relationships between young and old are a vital aspect of maintaining a functioning society. Second, need is an important criterion in policy, but to focus only on need is to neglect the quality of life issues that are characteristic of being aged. To give just one example, for increasing numbers of older people, particularly women, living alone becomes a fact of life; loneliness and finding intimacy become issues for many of these people, particularly those who are more frail.

### Living alone in older adulthood: is there a real choice?

Older women in particular are more likely to be widowed and living alone. What are the benefits and the problems for older people living alone? A high value in Australian society is to be in control of one's living arrangements. A sense of freedom is prized by many older adults, and this freedom is judged to include the ability to make life choices.

Rubinstein, Kilbride and Nagy (1992) found in a study of frail older adults living alone in the USA that even though they all experienced severe health problems, generally had low incomes, were socially marginalised and had few social supports, 86 per cent reported they lived alone by choice. Of those choosing to live alone, 40 per cent did so because they wanted to be independent, 22 per cent because they 'simply enjoy living alone' and the remainder because they wanted to be both independent and to live alone. The authors note that their informants exhibit a strong sense of personal responsibility for their own fate in life. Further, they note that these may not be expected responses in a group of older people who may well feel helpless and victimised by their circumstances. The researchers' qualitative data revealed the reasons for the desire for independence to be: 'not becoming a burden on family or friends; privacy when one wants to rest to alleviate pain or exhaustion; being one's own boss; and not having to adjust to the needs of others' (p.54). It is noted, however, that the social background of these informants may have meant that a real choice for them in living conditions did not exist, considering their low socioeconomic status. This may or may not have influenced their real choices in relation to expressing loneliness.

Rubinstein *et al.* (1992), in their study of frail older adults living alone, made the important point that, on a loneliness scale, 50 per cent said that being alone made them feel lonely often or sometimes and 50 per cent said it did rarely or never (1992). Thus, in that study, simply living alone did not appear to be the cause of loneliness. The question of loneliness would seem to be much more complex.

Further, Lowenthal (1968), in a study of social isolation and mental illness in older adults, concluded that isolation 'may be more of a consequence than a cause of mental illness in old age' (p.233).

A study conducted by Keith (1989) explored the relationship between patterns of isolation/satisfaction among unmarried people. They tested four patterns of relationship: satisfied affiliated (not isolated; satisfied); dissatisfied affiliated (not isolated; dissatisfied); satiated isolates (isolated; satisfied); and desolate isolates (isolated; dissatisfied). In their findings they reported the majority of the unmarried were satisfied affiliated, while there were 20 per cent dissatisfied affiliated, wanting even more affiliates than they had.

They found men more often to be desolate or satiated isolates than women. They found 71 per cent of women to be satisfied and affiliated, while for men this was 62 per cent. Those who had never married and widows were twice as likely to be contented and isolated. Keith (1989) reported that: 'Isolation per se was not a critical determinant of happiness because satiated isolates were happier than desolate isolates and the dissatisfied affiliated and enjoyed happiness comparable to that of the satisfied affiliated' (p.159). (Income and education were not significantly related in the study.) These results, from one study, may indicate the complexity of the relationship between isolation and loneliness and life satisfaction. Again, meaning in life and the personal spiritual development of the individual may be important factors in the level of spiritual well-being in older adults who live alone.

While individuation is seen as a strong component of human psychological development, relationship and community are essential components both of psychological development and spiritual development. It is within the arena of human relationship and the spiritual that this study is concerned.

# Types of relationships from the study

There were a variety of types of relationships of the informants in this study. First, whether the individual had satisfying relationships or not; marital status was an important aspect of this. Second, whether the person lived alone and was isolated or not isolated.

## Types of relationship

The following types of relationship were identified within this group of informants:

1. married, never married, separated, divorced

2. types of relationship with children, grandchildren

3. being a single mother

4. widowhood

5. being alone and being lonely, recognised as being different by some

6. friends

7. belonging to a group.

# Living alone and isolation

There may be a tendency to consider all who live alone in ageing in the same way. However, it can be a mistake to do so. Relationships for single, never-married people and their social status may well differ, presenting different issues for them in ageing. After all, widows do have an identity and socially perceived role in most Western societies. On the other hand, single people who have lived alone may have been more used to developing their interiority, even during mid life, than their married counterparts, and thus the experience of living alone is a different one.

Intimacy is as important in ageing as at any other point of the life cycle. For any single older adults, whether never married, widowed, separated or divorced, the question of access to confidantes and intimates arises. For older women, sexual partners may be difficult to find. Relationships that are based on the comfort of companionship may also be difficult to establish, particularly for those older adults who are dislocated from their known and familiar environments in old age.

## Table 13.1 Relationships of informants (in-depth interviews)

| Married | 9 |
|---|---|
| Separated | nil |
| Divorced | 3 |
| Widowed | 8 |
| Never married | 4 |
| Total | 24 |

Table 13.1 shows that 15 could possibly be living alone, (those divorced, widowed and never married). In fact, one of those divorced had another long-term relationship. It is also noted that, among this group of informants, living alone did not necessarily result in the individual feeling isolated.

### Loneliness and spiritual isolation

It must be asked, what is the relationship, if any, between loneliness and spiritual isolation? And the question of spiritual well-being when living alone returns to the question of the individual spiritual journey, the way in which the individual has been able to grow into greater interiority as they age, and the resources they have to draw on and assist them to develop.

Spiritual and social isolation may be present together or not. It is also possible to be socially isolated but not spiritually isolated. Where the individual had a deep sense of spirituality, social isolation did not seem to have the same impact. Thus in this group of informants, it could be said that spiritual resources could be a means of protection against isolation.

### Meaning in life through relationship

Meaning expressed through human relationship involves support and the need for connection with others. Meaning through family was important in some way for all informants; for some it gave the greatest meaning to their lives. A number of the informants derived greatest meaning in their lives through other human relationship, outside the family. Still some others seemed satisfied with few social interactions with other people. Quality of relationship is an important component of finding meaning through relationship. That quality of relationship can best be described as the need for intimacy, important at any time during the life cycle and no less so in ageing.

The need for intimacy was clearly expressed by some of the informants in this study.

A critical component of relationship for those informants in this study who were married or widowed was the importance of the marriage relationship. Most of those married said their relationship with their spouse was what gave greatest meaning to their lives. Most of those widowed acknowledged the loss of the most significant relationship in their lives. This, among a sample of older adults who had mostly been married for thirty or more years, and all to the one partner. The ultimate human spiritual relationship is that of a husband and wife.[1] That is not to say that all people ought to be married; rather it is simply to acknowledge the specialness of the marriage union.

This study of 24 independently living older people raises the question of a possible difference from community norms in regard to the importance of the marriage relationship in this cohort of older people, in comparison with community expectations of older people and current societal attitudes shown in high levels of marriage breakdown. It is worth commenting on the fact that for some of these older adults, their life's meaning and spiritual needs were focused in their partner. This seemed to be so, even for those widowed for a number of years; they still acknowledged the importance of that relationship to them not only before but after their spouse had died.

Their sense of loss does not seem to diminish over the years. If this kind of finding exists more widely among this cohort of older people, then there are implications for the way aged care is provided, so often without regard to the feelings and needs, or the meaning, in the older person's life of intimate relationships. Indeed, some who provide long-term care for frail aged people may have little understanding of the types of long-term relationships of these people, and their level of commitment to each other, even in adversity. As well, one of the myths of ageing is that sexual needs are either not important or non-existent after fifty or sixty years of age. The longings for a sexual relationship among this group of older adults cannot be dismissed. Two of the informants in this study expressed this very clearly, and other studies have also noted this need (Masters and Johnson 1968). Often when one partner of an older couple needs institutional care, there is little recognition of the needs of the other partner.[2]

## Widowhood

There were seven widows in the sample and one widower. Loss of one's spouse through death was a devastating experience for most. Only one of the informants had lost his spouse during the last two years. That was the only male to have become a widower in the study. He had lost his wife about two years before the interview. Most had worked through their grief and to varying degrees had picked up their lives again. Most had support systems that enabled them to function effectively in some kind of relationship. Adult children and/or grandchildren were important for a number of informants.

Flora has been a widow for more than fifteen years. Her husband died from cancer. Meaning now is found through her children and grandchildren. The birth of her children and grandchildren were special events in her life. The support she experiences from one of her daughters is very important. Flora remarked: 'I never want to get married again, I had such a wonderful marriage the first time. He's part of me and part of our family.' Although it is a long time since her husband died, she still feels very close to him, playing music they had both loved and shared. She says that she feels distant from God. Maybe she has replaced God with her husband.

Doris, a widow, said, 'the grief…when one loses one's husband, is something that rocks your life to its very foundations'; her husband died nine years ago. She also described an experience related to her son entering the priesthood that affected her whole life. At the time she had believed: 'it's the greatest thing a…Catholic boy could do, so I suppose, in lots of ways I put that before him'. Later, she found it very difficult to accept his leaving the priesthood, 'so it was really, I suppose, for myself more than the Church, that I was angry'. The decision of her son to leave the priesthood triggered major changes for her:

> I just know that I have to completely rethink my whole theology of my whole idea about the Church…and what true spirituality is. So that was a time of great questioning for me. And I've continued to question, ever since that.

Doris's spiritual needs seemed in a way to be focused on the vocation of her son in the priesthood. When he left the priesthood she experienced a type of spiritual crisis: where did meaning now exist for her, if not through his vocation? In the end she thanked God for that experience that had forced her to focus on her own spiritual journey:

I had to rethink my whole spiritual life like that, and it was a real trauma for me, but I came out on the other end of it, you know, just thanking God that it happened. Really because I think it gave me a spiritual life that I wouldn't have had if I'd just gone on [without being challenged].

This was identified by Doris as a life-changing experience, triggered by a challenge to her whole belief system. She was assisted in coming to terms with the experience by another priest. She had to make a cognitive shift before she could be open to spiritual growth. Part of this was to 'let go' of her son and accept his decision. As she acknowledges, this experience was a stimulus to the beginning of real spiritual growth within her. She is now reconciled with her son.

Her story of the working through of her great disappointment of her son leaving the priesthood was obviously not an easy time. She said she was 'bitterly sorry' for her part in it; and yet she is able now to thank God for the experience, and to recognise how she has grown through that. Rice (1990) has written that some of the greatest difficulties that priests who leave the Catholic Church face is the reaction from their families. Among the most poignant of his anecdotes are those about the difficulties of mother–son relationships.

Doris enjoys close relationships with children and grandchildren; she loves her family dearly, and thinks this is reciprocal. She talked of the joy and importance to her now of intimacy in family relationships. The relationship she has with her two brothers is also 'precious' to her. She also finds great support for living, through a small group of people (from her community of faith) who have been meeting weekly for a number of years. She has experienced deep relationships within this group, with a sense of caring, accepting, and sharing their deepest needs:

but, you know, above and beyond all that we actually do in this group…there's that closeness, that caring for one another, and sharing our really deepest feeling, our deepest needs. And that's where we go or come to, when we're in need.

This group forms a very important aspect of relationship for Doris. She enjoys meaningful and close relationships with group members; they have become almost an extended family. Her long-term group is of special importance to her; it would seem to be a place of free, open and trusting relationship, as is the relationship she has with her other confidante. As well, she remains active in her faith (church) community, taking communion to the sick.

So do her relationships provide for her spiritual needs for meaning, for the so-called horizontal dimension of spirituality? Although the death of her husband was a major loss in her life, she has rebuilt her life and relationships. This woman expressed a high level of satisfaction concerning her relationships, particularly those that enabled her to share at an intimate level. Doris has a deep self-understanding and recognises her need for someone to share with on a spiritual base; and she acknowledges she has such a relationship.

Stan, on the other hand, is much more isolated, although he may not agree with that assessment. He is a very 'self-contained' man. He is a widower and lives alone. He is restricted in his ability to travel since his stroke, about a year before the interview. He spoke briefly about how his wife had died:

> Oh well, my wife died a couple of years ago, and that was a bit of a shock… Well, she's not here, you know, and that's part of it. I mean, I was expecting her t' kick along with me, you know.

He did not want to talk further about his grief. He receives support from his son and daughter who visit. He tries to support them materially; he expressed a strong sense of responsibility to his adult children, and a concern to provide for them what he could. He attends a community contact centre one day a week; one of the volunteers takes him there and back. He seems to enjoy the company there. He has no other social contacts, apart from his children and the contact centre, and it would appear, no close social and emotional supports. This man did not have the extended network of friends that most of the widows had. This is consistent with other studies of social contacts of older adults (Kendig 1986).

It is difficult to estimate the degree of emotional and spiritual support Stan gains from his relationships with others. He did not seem to wish to share at this level. Perhaps his age, gender and cultural background may have been factors here. His socialisation and sex role development may also have been factors in his seeming lack of desire to communicate at a deep level.

Edith's husband died about eleven years ago. She reported being devastated by his death. She blamed herself for her attitudes towards her husband before his death. She said she had hated people, and that she was the subject of 'bitter gossip', and in this she had blamed her husband for not standing up for her. She has felt ostracised by women in the church at times.

She described how she used to row with her daughter and son, 'everything seemed to be going wrong'.

Since then she has had a cardiac arrest, and now, she notes, things are very different. In this section from her interview she shows deep discernment of the meaning of her post cardiac arrest life:

> I think, why I changed, [is] because I was meant to change; there was something for me to do... [now] I'm more tolerant to my son and daughter, where I'd flare up, I just calm things down, and no, that would be it. I don't even have to assume it, I know.

She reports many important changes in her life now. Meaning in life now is through her family; her energy now comes from her meaningful relationship with her grandchildren. Edith acknowledges the importance of relationships within her life, and the meaning she gains through these. She has an effective support system consisting of family and friends while continuing to live alone.

Eva was widowed as a young woman. She was pregnant when her husband died, probably about forty to fifty years ago. She said: 'When my husband died I felt like dying too.' Being mother and father to her children was an important and big role for her. She had support through Legacy: 'Couple of times the eldest daughter, I had a bit of trouble with, but of course Legacy helped me there marvellously, and on the man's point of view.' Meaning now comes through her grandchildren.

She sees being able to do things as being important for her, remarking that some people have little to do, and are not proactive in developing their own interests: 'They're not good companions for themselves.' Eva demonstrated a wonderful balance between the need for emotional and spiritual support and being content with her own company. Eva explained that being alone was not a problem: 'I'm quite content with my own company, I haven't gotta go out seeking people.' This is consistent with the study of frail older adults living alone (Rubinstein *et al.* 1992) where 50 per cent said living alone rarely or never resulted in them feeling lonely.

Sally said: 'Of course I miss [husband] very, very much.' (This was thirteen and a half years after his death.) She shared how she had difficulty expressing her sadness when her husband died. And now, she said: 'My saddest thing is not having [husband], that's my sadness, but then [God] called him home and I say he's needed.' Both she and her husband worked in entertainment for many years, and she continues to give of herself, singing at community functions. She remarked she is 'contented and happy in my home and with my friends and my interests in life, such as a social group for retired people and a contact centre, music and legacy widows'. She goes out two to three days a week: 'I need something 'cause it's too lonely to be on my own when I had a full life.' She expressed acceptance that her children need to live their own lives. She needs to rely on others to drive her where she needs to go.

### Talking to husband and/or husband's photograph

Two of the widows in the study reported talking to their dead husband's photograph. How can the talking and perhaps praying to a dead husband's photo be explained? Flora talks and possibly prays to her husband's photo. 'If something upsets me I talk to his photograph, so I think, well I must have faith in something, I mean, you don't just talk to a photograph, do you? I mean you know I really think I'm talking to him.'

I returned to visit Flora to ask her more about her husband's photograph. She said that when she has problems, she looks at his photo and talks about the problem, looking for guidance. She said that when he was alive, she used to talk things through with her husband. She finds talking to the photograph a comfort. She says she is not sure why, but maybe, she suggested, there is a link with a higher being.

Edith also reported talking to her husband's photograph when she has problems: 'I've got my husband's photos in there, my daughter had them enlarged. And I go in there and have a talk to him when I say: I'm afraid I've made a right bloody mess.'

For these two women their actions seemed to provide a sense of comfort, a connection with their deceased husbands. It was an important connection, but it is difficult to say quite how this functioned. One could speculate that the photo became a symbol of the woman's past life, and a memory aid to her role as wife. Probably it was connected with a longing for the deceased person. It is also asked if it could be a way of praying to the person they believed was already with God, and who could intercede for them.

Sally, like a few of the others, maintains a relationship with her husband, even though he is dead. She certainly recognises his death as only too real, but at the same time she continues to speak to him. It may even be a form of prayer. After the grief has been worked through, the loss is still real, and it seems that talking to him gives her a degree of comfort. She also seems to process some of her problems in life through these conversations.

None of these widows had remarried and all three had long marriages. In some ways it appears that they are continuing the habits of a lifetime, discussing problems and talking to their former husbands. The photos were certainly important to the two women who mentioned them. It is noted that in other cultures, for example Asian cultures, photos or other symbols of dead parents and spouses are often a focus for regular, or even daily remembrance rituals. In nursing homes it is common practice to have some of the resident's memorabilia in their room or bed space; photos are a common part of this and, it would seem, important.

It is asked here, when can such behaviours be considered appropriate and when a sign of mental illness? In each of these cases the women do not seem to dwell on their relationship with their former husbands to the degree that they are living in the past, nor are they in denial of the husband's death. Rather, it seems to be a means of comfort, and perhaps in a way another dimension of relationship, that provides a degree of intimacy that they need. In this context it would seem to be a healthy behaviour, taken with other interpersonal behaviours they have in their repertoires of relationships.

## Never married

Four informants had never married, three women and one man. Two of the women in this group seemed to experience particular types of rejection from others who are married, and even described themselves as being treated differently from those who were widowed and lived alone. The third woman had accepted that it was God's will that she would not marry. This woman did not appear either socially or spiritually isolated.

It is possible that the first two informants were unable to accept their situation and carried a sense of failure, based on societal expectations (probably more strongly held in that cohort of women), that women should marry. Isolation within church communities of those who are single was another factor to be negotiated for these never-married women. For these women the church community was perhaps more truly their family than for other members of the church. If they felt rejection here, then there seemed to be no other place to go. The never-married male did not seem to experience the same kind of discrimination. He spoke of consciously making the decision not to enter into a lifelong intimate relationship with another person – a decision he has never regretted.

Two women who had never married had few close contacts. The first one was limited in her contacts now particularly because of her increasing frailty and lack of access to transport of her own. This woman was socially isolated, but had developed a deep interiority and was not spiritually isolated. The other woman who had never married had few social contacts she felt comfortable with. These two women acutely felt their status as single, never-married women, and this not least in church circles. They both spoke of this spontaneously. I asked the second woman if she perceived any difference between her status and the status of widows within the church. She felt sure there was. She said that she felt she was treated at a lesser level than the widows.

The feelings of these two never-married women may have been unrepresentative of never-married women in general. There were, after all, only two of them. However, it is worth considering their predicament when considering the great emphasis put on family both within church circles and in the wider community. It was a socially isolating issue for these two women, in this particular cohort of women. Is it so for others too? The other never-married woman in this study had accepted her situation and her choice. She did not seem to experience difficulties to the same degree.

On the whole, the never-married man did not seem to want for support. He made the clear distinction to me of the difference between being alone and loneliness.

### Social isolation, but not spiritual isolation, in ageing, never-married

Relationships have not been easy for the most part for Carol, who was brought up by her grandparents. She did not mention her mother at all during the interview. She has identified many difficulties in her life, including having an illegitimate child and never marrying. She experienced rejection by a number of church members because she was a single mother. After the birth of her baby, as a single mother she felt she was cut off from God through actions of people working in the church.

In the last decade she has found that the only way she could have a relationship with God was through a person's caring. She said of this experience that, for the first time, 'I felt I had a mother'. This 'mother' was Mary MacKillop, the founder of the Sisters of Saint Joseph (O'Brien 1994). It seems that she perceived finding Mary MacKillop to be a really significant event in her life.

Carol has little supportive contact with her son now, and no other family or other intimate contacts. A counsellor helped her to find meaning in her life. She said: 'The only support I have now comes from the people in the church I attend.' But, she added, most of the people who attend that church are in the 40–50 age group and are very busy with stressful work; therefore she is reluctant to ask them for help. Physical disabilities also make it hard for her to go out. As well, she fears intrusion into her life by others, so she is socially isolated.

Carol has no friend with whom she can confide and share an intimate relationship, and is very aware of her needs in this area. She expressed a wish that she could have a regular visitor she could talk with at home. But at the same time she has been working on her relationship with God. She has developed her spiritual dimension to a high degree, and seemed able to transcend her life problems.

When I visited her a year later to clarify some comments in the transcript, I had expected that she would have been even more frail than on my first visit; in fact I had wondered if she might even have moved into a hostel. But she was still managing just as well as the year before. She said that adequate social support was becoming a real issue. She said she can't rely on human contacts, 'people die and children move away'. I asked her how she feels about this. She replied 'It's scary', and went on to say, 'but it throws you back on yourself, and a need to explore your own depth'. This is something she has continued to do; she is still growing spiritually.

### Never married, not socially isolated

George has never married, and says he never has regrets for choosing not to. He is definitely not socially isolated, in fact he draws a real distinction between being lonely and being alone. He did say that he was too self-centred to marry. He has good, if fairly distant, support from a couple of Christian families. He is not critical of this, it seems to be as he wants it. His sister lives in the same house but, as he stressed, they live separately.

This man does not seem to need the company of others. He appears to have sufficient resources within himself, perhaps one could say he has achieved a high level of individuation. He has contact with members of religious orders and his contemplation of their lifestyle may be a factor here. His obvious interest in reading and writing are factors in his life satisfaction.

Win accepts that it is God's purpose in her life that she would never marry. Once having decided that, she accepted the decision and appears comfortable with it. It is interesting that she did not report the same kind of perceived rejection from other church members as the other never-married women. This may be related to her sense of satisfaction with her decision not to marry.

She expressed regrets for not doing more for her father when he had a stroke. Her emotional and spiritual supports are from sharing deeply with a woman whose husband is a resident in a nursing home and has Alzheimer's disease. 'Also my neighbour and the church people I can share with, some of them sometimes don't understand a lot of what I'm meaning.' She recognises that her understanding of the spiritual has moved to a different level, a level at which she cannot share with some of the others. She also has other people she can share and pray with. She told an anecdote of visiting a former resident of her village, who was now quite frail and in a nursing home. This anecdote illustrates some of the deepness of this woman's spirituality, her understanding, her acceptance of life, ability for relationship and compassion.

> I'd had the thought to go over and see her that afternoon, and oh I thought, oh dear it's too hot, don't know whether I'll bother, and then I thought, no I will [go and visit her] I'm halfway there. I'll go up and see her. And so we had a wonderful talk about death and dying and she said, 'I don't think I'll see my 95th birthday' or something like that, she said and I could tell she was… [she paused]. She said her legs were aching so I said 'Well shall I rub your legs?' so I rubbed her legs and the next day I heard that she'd died, and I thought well you know, obey, obeying the whisper of guidance really was the thing that you know. I felt sad that she had died but I felt so grateful that I'd had that time with her before she died.

This woman, referred to the 'whisper of guidance' that she followed, in her words, 'obeyed' in going to visit her friend that day. From other parts of the taped interview it was obvious she regarded the source of this guidance to be the Holy Spirit. The time the two friends shared was obviously an important time of deep and open communication, and a seeming mutual recognition of the approaching death of the informant's friend. There is a sense of the specialness of that last physical act she rendered to her friend, of rubbing her legs. Then the next day, when she heard of her friend's death, there was acceptance of the end of a life, and sadness, but also a sense of the grace present in the situation of the previous day; she was grateful that she had been and spent time with her friend so soon before she died.

## Never married, socially isolated

Dawn regrets she didn't marry and have children. She said that as a young woman she had said she would not marry, but later that she had not really understood the implications of that decision. It seemed there were some regrets, and she felt unequal with other women who were married. She spoke of the importance of family to her, particularly a continuing close relationship with her brother. She believes she has nothing in common with her sisters. Her father was in the First World War. She spoke of the influence of her mother on her development, and she reported having a sense of distance between herself and her parents. She said she had always been rather strong willed, but at the same time didn't have 'the confidence to capitalise on opportunities' in life. She spoke of the tensions in being single and wanting to be independent of her family, but still be a part of the family.

She later went into the airforce, and feels that being in the forces had an influence on her life that 'changed me terribly and it isolated me from my family and it still does isolate me from a lot of women'. Life 'took a different turn'. She thought this may have been through living alone – she had plenty of time to think about things. After the war she worked hard and bought a house. 'But of course in spite of that, you know you've proved yourself as a person to society, you're still not a person unless you're married.' Then she went on to make this comment: 'And I'm very sad to say this, you are not [a person] in the church 'cause the church is, a male hierarchy... Up 'til now, maybe it's changing.'

This woman showed her concern for her difficulties in relationships with other women, particularly married women.

> I do resent the fact that I get so much animosity from women of my age, but I realise why; because the women of my age were married in a different era. When they married when they hadn't thought...their mental urges did they, you see, they gave up their chances to be business women and they look at me now as though I've had that chance and they resent it.

She spoke of her realisation later in life of the need for self-responsibility:

> No one owes you anything, your life's in your hands, I mean, if I'd realised that when I was younger, I'd have had a much better life of course but I didn't. I think that's the thing I regret that I wasn't taught to realise that I was an important person, you cope with other people and they try to put you down which they, they do all the time you know...

She acknowledged that her family is becoming increasingly important as she grows older, particularly her brother. Her independence has been important throughout her life, yet there seemed to be an unmet need for relationship too. There is a certain sadness about Dawn's life story, she regrets never having married, she regrets not having taken the opportunities that presented themselves to her, and she regrets being dependent on others. The decisions were hard ones.

## Married

There were nine married informants. Apart from Beryl, the married informants all seemed to acknowledge the importance and depth of meaning that they experienced through their marriage relationship. Beryl did not mention her husband, except in the context of marriage setting back her prospects of a career. In this group, the informant's marriage was mostly regarded as being the main source of meaning in their lives.

Vera affirmed the importance of marriage to her, her relationship with her husband and respect for her husband's lack of belief, taking care not to offend him in her worshipping habits. She expressed joy currently through working with a group of older people doing Shakespeare and from seeing her adult son establish himself in life.

Sylvia said meaning in her life is through her husband and she regards their relationship as being very important in her life. She is concerned over the homosexuality of her son-in-law; this has been a grief for her that she finds difficult to accept. She expressed anger over the 'lost marriage' of her daughter. She seemed to find it hard to accept changing community acceptance for homosexuality.

She has good support from friends; this has been of mutual support over the years. She expressed concern for her adult children, one of whom has cut contact with the family and has been taking drugs. She asks what more she could have done to help them grow into 'good' adults. She also expressed concern for her mother, who has Alzheimer's disease, and who she sees now as a 'non-person'. She would have no spiritual problems with euthanasia.

Lisa stated that as well as the importance of her marriage relationship she has been influenced by the example of a few exceptional people who lived their faith 'in terms of the idea of love, which is for me, what it's really about'. Meaning in life for her is associated with other people. She said she thought mostly about relationships with others, rather than with God.

Angela has taken a course of study [Christian] recently. Through this she can now accept her husband better, and she reports that this course has helped with her marriage.

Several informants spoke of the difficulties and responsibilities of bringing up their children, while Angela spoke of the spiritual support from her older daughter and joy from her son. She said of the support she has from her daughter, 'she has actually prayed over the phone for me, on one occasion'. She was pleased to have this closeness of relationship with her adult daughter. She also spoke of the joy of being a grandmother. She is a member of a long-term study group through which she receives good support.

Betty is re-evaluating meaning in her life at present; since her husband has been ill she seems to have a new urgency regarding family contact. As she says, 'It's all much more precarious because of our age and a feeling that you better make the best of it now'.

For her, support comes from 'some very close friends' and family, 'but one doesn't expect them [family] to understand in the same sort of way', and 'my family love me and my friends understand me'. She made little mention of her marriage, apart from the comments about it retarding her career. She regards her doctor as both doctor and friend. Her energy comes from being healthy, and friends, family and activities she is 'immersed' in.

Daisy says her main worry is how her husband would cope [without her]. 'He's not really good at it [laughs].' She remarked that younger family members don't always understand the needs of older people. 'I think the biggest problem [as you age] is, you lose your friends, they pass on and I really do think that that is a problem…'cause you, you sort of feel, well where do I go from here?'

## Divorced

Three of the informants were divorced. Divorced informants varied in their social and emotional supports. One woman was desperately lonely for relationship with a man. She said she missed the comfort and sexual relationship very much. One other woman had filled her life with other relationships, bringing up children and being actively involved in the wider community.

The one man who was divorced still felt the hurt of that after many years. He is in a stable and caring relationship now. Ben was divorced about thirty years ago and his wife took the children with her. All but one son have kept contact with him. In recent years he has found joy and trust through a stable relationship. His main support now is through this friendship and the church. He says he has something to do all the time, with gardening and working at an aged care centre where he helps others.

Helga's marriage broke down and her former husband took the children and married again. He died not long after. She was concerned as a young woman that she didn't appeal physically to men, and worried about what other people thought about her. She said that she had married 'for the sake of marrying', because she 'wanted kids'. She had four children in five years, and found it hard to discipline children. She was afraid of having more children, and her sexual relationship with her husband suffered.

She and her husband had lived in the bush while married, and she admitted missing her former social life and feeling guilty. This woman reported: 'Basically, I'm a home maker, very much, I was quite happy to be a married woman, mother, housekeeper.' She still carries a burden of care for her adult children, who apparently experience a lot of problems. She now lives alone but would love to have a relationship with a man. She says she is very lonely, 'sex is good and healthy', that she misses intimacy and the financial support of a relationship, and she expressed the desire to be cared for.

She says she has social support from a number of friends, but none really close at present, but then confided: 'I still get hopelessly lonely, when I come into an empty flat in the evenings, and in the morning, because I haven't got many really close friends, just round here.' In fact, she seems to have few inner resources to assist her overcome the loneliness that seems to characterise her life.

Mary, divorced and a single parent, remarked: 'There's more to life than this' [bringing up children]. She brought up the children largely by herself. She finds meaning in life now with her family. She had five children two of whom have been killed in recent years.

Her main regret is that she was always shy and didn't have confidence in herself until she was nearly 50. Now she likes to be with people, and 'I like to think that even my painting gives people encouragement'. She sees things differently now. Asked what she thought had made a difference to her self-confidence, she replied that she thinks it was when she had a few pictures accepted. As for emotional and spiritual supports, she spoke of how she likes to help others. She is involved in community activities.

Helen is divorced and has worked for a number of years. She lives alone and owns her home. She finds meaning now in serving others. She writes, and her books written with others have raised money for an aged care centre. Her life is full, but she also loves solitude, silence, and time, 'quality time to myself, and at last I have that'. She is close to her sister. They lend each other books on things like yoga. She remembers childhood Christian stories, and her readings have led her to various faith views. She says she has always believed in being independent. She reported that there were very few people she could talk to in a confidential way.

## The importance of children and grandchildren

Adult children were in most cases important to the informants. The closeness of relationship varied, mostly, it seemed, due to geographical dispersion of family members. All those who were grandparents spoke of the joy of their grandchildren. One woman who had no grandchildren told how she listened to her friends talking about their grandchildren, and wished she could have this joy too.

## Social and spiritual isolation in an ageing society

Human relationship provided an important source of meaning in some way for all the informants, except perhaps one male. Lack of intimate relationship was a source of sadness for one divorced woman. Attention is drawn to the importance attached to the marriage relationship for most of those interviewed, a value that may not be reflected by some young carers of older people. This possible difference highlights the need for those working with frail older people to learn something of the values, beliefs and background of this cohort of older adults.

With the current trends in society to encourage and facilitate living at home for more older people, and with the increase in numbers of older people in the population, it is likely that there will be even more people living alone. The issues of both social and spiritual isolation will become increasingly important. The issues may need to be addressed at multiple levels: of appropriate housing for older people, better community-based services and, just as important, dealing with the issue of spiritual isolation and meaning in life.

The stories of these independent older people emphasise the need to provide for both social and spiritual needs of these older people. The need for quality time and intimacy with others is obvious. What is not so obvious is how we might do this. It is an enormous challenge for the twenty-first century. Another challenge is to assist these older people to develop effective strategies for deepening their own spirituality and finding meaning in their later years.

## *Summary*

*Two dimensions of spirituality and relationship are acknowledged: first is relationship with God or some sense of 'other' and second is relationship with other people. For many, perhaps most people, the meaning derived from human relationship is an important and may be the most important part of their lives. The need for intimacy, that is connecting deeply with another human being, is no less important in later life than at any other point of the life span.*

*There were a great variety of types of relationship among this group of informants. Those never-married informants faced different issues for relationship from the widows. Two of those never married found it hard to feel accepted in their church communities. Both of these women were socially isolated.*

*Most widows expressed profound grief over the loss of their spouse, even many years later. Some still talked to their deceased spouse, and some asked their dead spouse to intercede with God for them. The marriage relationship was the main source of life meaning for most of those still married and one divorced woman longed for intimate relationship years later.*

*For some older people having a portfolio of spiritual strategies seemed to offer protection against spiritual and perhaps social isolation too. Issues of social and spiritual isolation are likely to become even more critical in the future as more older people live alone. There are enormous challenges to families, the church and aged care services in finding ways to meet these needs for intimacy in later life.*

## Notes

1   In the Christian faith, this relationship is one of a deep intimate physical, emotional and spiritual union, 'the two shall become one flesh' (Gen.). As male and female are made in the image of God, so each needs the other for human completeness.

2   Few long-term aged care facilities provide accommodation for couples; some of the newer retirement complexes are now considering providing accommodation for married couples. There were no gay or lesbian couples interviewed in this study. The needs for intimacy of all groups of older people require a sensitive and compassionate approach.

# CHAPTER 14

# A picture of spirituality and ageing

## Continued spiritual development

A spiritual journey and continued spiritual development in the later years certainly seems to be a reality for some older people. The spiritual growth (or spiritual integrity, or could it even be called spiritual maturity?) that seems to be a characteristic of some of these informants appears to be an important aspect of growing into integrity and wisdom in ageing. Listening to the informants gives a window into what has been effective for some older people in their life journey.

## Characteristics of those who appear to be moving towards spiritual maturity

All or most of the following characteristics have been reported by, and are evident in, informants, who appear to be progressing along the way to spiritual growth and maturity. Spiritual development and growth as a process towards achieving spiritual integrity has been identified as a developmental task of ageing.

These characteristics include: an openness to change and learning; an attitude of searching for the ultimate meaning in their lives; relationship with a confidante and/or membership of a long-term small group. It also included transcendence of disabilities and losses encountered in ageing; acceptance of their past life and a readiness to face the future, including the ability to live with uncertainty, and, finally, a sense of freedom and a move to a greater degree of interiority.

These characteristics are those that mark the older person as 'a delight to be with'. They are contrasted with the characteristics of older people who seem to have a sense of fear, and perhaps despair, as they approach the end of their lives. Can these characteristics of spiritual maturity be learned?

## Growing towards spiritual maturity

The greatest factor among these informants that seemed to be influential in shaping their lives and stimulating them to move to greater spiritual maturity was the life experience and the losses they had encountered along the way. Now it is not possible to replicate the life experience of another; for instance, no one can experience the losses of another in quite the same way. However, it is possible to acknowledge the passing of time for each individual in this life. That is, it is possible to mark the developmental crises that accompany events such as age-set retirement from work, moving from the family home to perhaps a retirement village, hostel or nursing home. The same is possible for significant birthdays and anniversaries. Older people may be enabled to celebrate these events and to process the meaning of these into the whole journey of ageing.

What is the meaning of each life experience of the older person, both for that person and for their family and community of significant others? It is necessary to name and to mark significant events of ageing, both celebratory and events of closure and loss, so that we may be prepared to move from death denying to take a different stance, a death-acknowledging stance. Whether any individual holds a belief in an afterlife or whether they believe that this is all there is to life, it is still necessary to acknowledge an earthly existence as a temporary one.

In our death-denying society, to acknowledge that death will occur to each of us is in some way to recognise the task that each should take up, to come to a realisation of what one's life has meant, to answer the questions: 'Why was I here?; What is the final purpose of my life?; Have I made a difference by my life?'. By trying to deny that death is waiting for each human being we deny the possibilities of constructing that 'last career', as it was termed by Heinz (1994). Heinz sees the last career as having two parts, the making sense of our own lives as we have lived them, and second, passing on our heritage to the next generation. Thus our lives take on both a retrospective and a prospective meaning as we look towards our death. In an ageing society this last career is becoming available to more and more people, but a problem may be that by denying death we have also lost the skills to make that last career. It is by up taking that challenge that it is possible to learn to take on the characteristics of spiritual maturity. No person will ever reach perfection in spiritual maturity in this life, but we should continue to move towards it until death.

## Application of a model of spirituality in ageing

A model (Figure 2.1) was designed to illustrate the components of spirituality in ageing. This model is drawn from six major themes identified in the study. The model consists of, first, a central core of ultimate meaning for each individual and, second, the individual's response to ultimate meaning. The content of these two themes determines how the other four themes interact. The other four themes are: hope and fear; self-sufficiency and vulnerability; relationship and isolation; and wisdom and the move to final meanings.

Using a developmental approach to spirituality in ageing it is possible to identify tasks for each of these themes. These tasks are to be accomplished in order to move to the wholeness that is the goal of the human being. Absolute wholeness is probably not possible in this life, but the goal is to continue growing in the spiritual dimension until death. The spiritual tasks become more urgent as people move closer to the end of life and begin to realise more clearly a sense of their own mortality.

The outcome of spiritual wholeness is integrity and wisdom, which could be called spiritual maturity. Spiritual wholeness is closely allied to Erikson *et al.*'s (1986) final psychosocial development stage of integrity versus despair, the successful outcome of which is also wisdom. It is contended, however, that the spiritual perspective gives a different view of wisdom from that obtained from the psychosocial perspective alone, a different and vital perspective.

The definition of wisdom used in this study focuses on the spiritual component of wisdom rather than the cognitive component that is emphasised in the psychosocial literature. Wisdom in this study is recognised as an increased tolerance of uncertainty and a deepening search for meaning in life, including an awareness of the paradoxical and contradictory nature of reality. This involves transcendence of uncertainty and a move from external to internal regulation.

It is suggested that in this final spiritual developmental stage spiritual tasks can be identified and knowledge of these can be used pastorally to assist people to move to spiritual wholeness (see Table 14.1). In Table 14.1 all six major themes drawn from the data are listed with their spiritual tasks in later life. It is acknowledged, however, that the data examined in this study is from a number of independently living older adults who, it is assumed, are at varying stages from the end of the life journey. Further study with frail older people, who are closer to the end of the life journey and who have a deeper awareness of the impending end of life may well mean a refocusing of one or more of these tasks, and perhaps even a redesign of the model in the light of further data.

## Table 14.1 Spiritual themes and tasks of ageing

| Themes identified | Task of the individual |
|---|---|
| Ultimate meaning in life | To identify source of ultimate meaning |
| Response to ultimate meaning | To find appropriate ways to respond |
| Self-sufficiency/Vulnerability | To transcend disabilities, loss |
| Wisdom/Final meanings | To search for final meanings |
| Relationship/Isolation | To find intimacy with God and/or others |
| Hope/Fear | To find hope |

### The spiritual tasks of ageing

These tasks (illustrated in Figure 14.1) arise from the four themes that relate to ultimate meaning for each individual. The first task, ultimate meaning in life, has been discussed in Chapter 5, and is addressed here in the task, search for final meaning. The second task, response to ultimate meaning, has been discussed in Chapters 6 and 7. Content of the tasks will vary according to the individual's sense of the Ultimate and their response to this.

Thus, for continued spiritual development, it is necessary for the individual to identify and acknowledge their sense of ultimate meaning in life, and then to be able to respond to this in some way. That is, ultimate meaning and response to this meaning are a starting point for spiritual growth in ageing. The model used here is a generic one that can be adapted to a variety of contents. For example, the model can be applied to an individual who is a Christian, a member of another religion, an agnostic or an individual whose centres of meaning may be a variety of other aspects, such as relationship, music and so forth. Note that there is interaction between each of the spiritual tasks, as indicated in the model.

## Theme 1. Self-sufficiency/vulnerability: the task – to transcend disabilities and loss

Although most of the informants in this study were self-sufficient, they all expressed at least a perception of future vulnerability. Fears expressed related to physical disabilities that would force lifestyle changes on them, perhaps even amounting to the need for nursing home accommodation. The other very real fear of these older people was of dementia. The reality of the informants' fears are well known. Residents of nursing homes testify to these. Yet, also well known is the ability of many older people to transcend difficulties such as loss, pain and suffering. At the same time there are other older people who are weighed down by these same types of difficulty. Is it possible to assist these people to move to self-transcendence? Clements (1990) spoke of the stripping by society of the roles of earlier life. A number of authors have written of the transition from doing to being that occurs in frail old age and is evident in some of the informants of the current study. Tillich (1963) wrote of sanctification in ageing; all these are aspects of the process of transcendence.

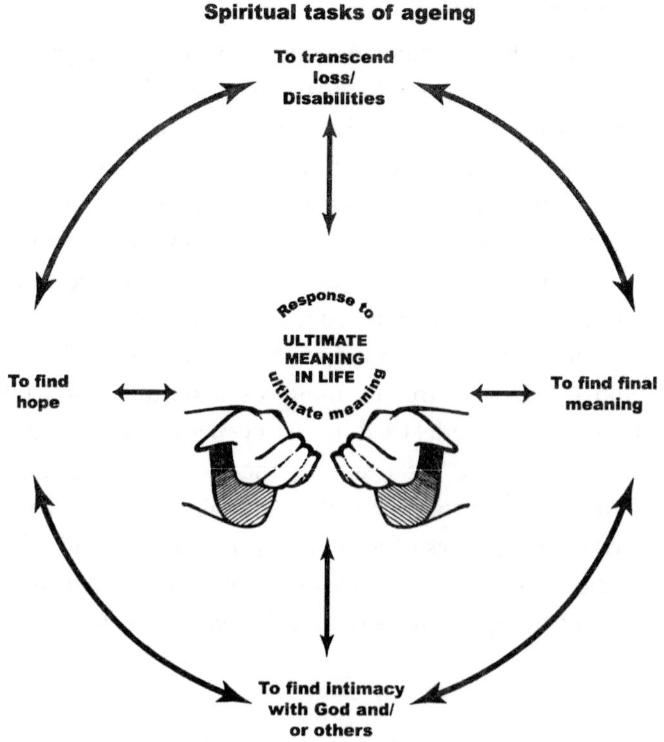

**Spiritual tasks of ageing**

Figure 14.1 The spiritual tasks of ageing

The spiritual task of ageing is to transcend the disabilities and the losses: to move beyond.

### Theme 2. Wisdom/ final meanings: the task – to search for final meanings

Wisdom is acknowledged to be an important part of ageing, and part of this is moving from provisional to final meanings. It is, as Frankl (1984) has written, like the viewing of the many single frames from a movie. It is only at the end of life that the whole movie can be run and all the frames come together as a whole to make sense.

A spiritual task of later years is to go back over one's life and review the single episodes of life in context of the whole. Thus the task is editing, perhaps reframing, past events and their provisional meanings; coming to a sense of final meanings in life.

### Theme 3. Relationship/isolation: the task – to find intimacy with God and/or others

Relationship is an important aspect of being human. The human spirit longs for connection with others. For most, relationship with other people is vital; for some individuals relationship with God is all that is necessary; for others, it is both relationship with God and other people; for still others, the relationship is only with other people.

In ageing some who have shared intimately with another human being have lost that relationship through death. Along with the grief, it may be possible to develop another or other relationships; not replacing the loss, but relationships none the less, that will help fill the void left by death. In these cases new intimacy has to be developed, a difficult process for someone who has to begin again after so many years of being close to one particular person.

Other older people, who have no relationship with God, also have a spiritual need for intimacy, and that need may be nourished in caring relationship with others. Only one older person in this study did not want a close relationship with other people.

The spiritual task in ageing is to grow in intimacy with God and/or others. The spiritual journey, growing in intimacy with God, is likely to be a continuing one, although some older people do have conversion experiences and turn to God for the first time in later life. It is also noted that people who hold an image of a judgemental or punitive God may have difficulties in coming to a relationship of intimacy with God.

*Theme 4. Hope/fear/despair: the task – to find hope*

A number of the informants in this study spoke of fears, particularly related to future perceived vulnerabilities, such as loss of control and possible suffering. For some people loss of loved ones and pain and suffering make it hard for them to maintain a sense of hope. The spiritual task is to find hope, perhaps even in the midst of loss and fear (Frankl 1984). Failure to thrive in older adults may stem from a lack of hope.

## Reminiscence, life review and the spiritual dimension

The in-depth interviews conducted in this study were all done in a framework of reminiscence and, to some extent, life review. Each informant was free to talk about any aspects of his or her life within the broad parameters of spirituality and meaning in life. Questions were framed simply to keep the person on the broad topic. It is noted that the form used in this study was not free reminiscence, nor was it using life review as therapy. In that it was life review, it was focused as a spiritual life review.

*How effective was the method?*

Not one informant showed any evidence of reluctance to discuss the topic. Each informant is obviously an expert on their own life and it was a privilege to be present and listen to the freely shared life stories. The informants were eager to share, and were also often reflective of past happenings in their lives. They appeared willing, for the most part, to admit to past failures and to point to ways in which they would deal with similar issues more effectively now. While all seemed at ease speaking of their past, none of these informants seemed to dwell in the past.

## Reports of using reminiscence in the informants' lives

I did not specifically ask whether a person used reminiscence, but a number commented that they had noticed they were going over past events in their lives. There were definitely a lot of differences between informants regarding the level of reminiscence they engaged in. Some had obviously been working through a lot of things from their past. It is hard to say why there were such differences between the individuals unless, as Coleman (1986) noted, some people are reminiscers and others are not. The informants shared their faith journeys freely and it was easy to see patterns of faith development over a lifespan.

## 'I've never told anyone'

A feature that a number of informants had in common was to share with me at a very deep level, and then to pause and remark: 'I've never told anyone that before'. There was a sense for me as researcher of being very privileged to be a part of their story. This was 'sacred space'. At these points in the interviews it seemed that the person and I really connected, at a deep level. Nothing else existed at that moment. These were cherished moments. Sometimes there seemed to be a sense of relief in the informant that a particular part of the story had been told; at other times there was a realisation that being able to speak of 'it' was to name it, and this brought a sense of freedom to the incident. At still others, it was an 'ah-hah' situation: 'So that's what it meant'. Burnside (Burnside and Schmidt 1994) wrote of this experience of the 'I've never told anyone' phenomenon in some of her sessions of sharing, in her example from a group session.

Coleman (1986) noted that material from reminiscence could be used by health professionals, social workers in his research, to prompt an older person working through some present difficulty to use strategies from their past to deal with the current situation. He noted, importantly, that it can be a way of reminding and focusing hope for the older person. Life review can take the form of a mutual exploration, of the past, between health professional and the older adult, to identify effective coping skills.

## Life review as therapy

### Making final meaning, remaking memories: are reminiscences valid recall of life situations?

In this study all memories appeared to be recalled for a purpose, to remember pleasant experiences, to recall important material from the past, to review past events, particularly of human interactions, and to make sense of these. However, some memories may be too painful for a person to want to face. On a couple of occasions informants remarked that they had a concern relating to something in the past that they felt they 'could never share with anyone'. Such comments were naturally not pursued in the context of this study, as to do so was outside the parameters of the agreement with the individuals for their involvement in the study. As already noted, some informants, on the other hand, shared deeply in the interviews.

### What is the function of life review?

Listening to and being involved in the interviews brought the realisation of the importance of each person's story, that it is vitally important to the individual who owns that story. It is at one level a part of who we are; our life story is our identity, and it is how we would want the world to see us. It is also important as a way in which human beings construct the meanings of life, that is, an individual meaning of the life journey. There is no other life just like your own; no genetic make-up identical to yours, no set of circumstances and experiences just like yours, no set of relationships just like yours.

To arrive at old age and to look back on your life, and recognise the failures, has the potential for disaster. But, life review may be an opportunity to reframe the life lived. Butler (1963, in Neugarten 1968), approaching reminiscence from a psychosocial framework, documented the importance of this. This study has taken a different focus, that of the spiritual. In this context, perhaps, there is need for forgiveness and reconciliation with others, and with God. Some older people carry guilt from episodes in earlier life. Guilt may be a heavy burden to carry. Life review as therapy may hold an important key to overcoming such burdens and allow the person to deal effectively with the guilt and lay it to rest.

Some people may find forgiveness through going to the person they feel they have wronged and asking forgiveness, but for a number of reasons this may not be possible. One very practical reason is that the person they wish to be reconciled with may have died. For another reason, the individual seeking forgiveness may believe what they have done was so bad that the person would not be able to forgive them. At such times the weight of guilt is very heavy. This is particularly so if the person believes that forgiveness can only be worked through themselves, and that they must bear full responsibility for their actions. For Christians, the presence of a loving God can wipe those wrongs away; freedom and forgiveness can really be experienced by the individual seeking forgiveness, even when it is impossible to approach the person who was wronged. For some individuals this can only be effectively achieved through confession and the pronouncement of God's forgiveness.

Some people may have denied the reality of certain events in earlier life. Life review may lead to developing insight, leading to renewed growth and integrity. It must be noted, however, that life review as therapy should not be undertaken by untrained volunteers; this type of work requires skilled pastoral counselling.

## The challenge of vulnerability in ageing

All informants expressed at least a sense of perceived vulnerability as they thought about what the future holds for them. The group of older people in this study were in a way one step back from the process of dying. Although they had a sense of future vulnerability, it seemed that death was still sufficiently distant from them not to have to face its possibility. It will be important to follow this theme in further study with those for whom it is closer and thus more urgent, the frail elderly residents of nursing homes.

### Important issues for independently living older adults

A number of important issues for these independently living older adults were raised in the study: being able to talk about fears of dying; losing control of one's ability to live independently; and fear of developing Alzheimer's disease.

If these issues are perceived as potential areas of difficulty for the group of well older people in this study, then there needs to be a focus on these issues. It is well known that approximately 5 per cent of older adults are in long-term residential care, and that factors related to increasing frailty and dementia are the most likely reasons for their admission to nursing homes.

Initial studies of nursing home residents (MacKinlay 1992) found that these frail elderly people wanted to talk about their fears of dying, of pain and of being unable to care for themselves. It seems that often the culture of nursing homes, in the very provision of a pleasant environment and varied activities for the residents, guards against disclosure of fears and anxieties held by the residents. There is a perception that death should not be talked about in such a 'nice' place. This is despite the fact that for many admitted to such long-term care institutions the move is regarded as a sign of approaching death. The term 'God's waiting room' has been used by some.

Thus the fears of future vulnerability expressed by informants in this study have some basis in reality. What can be done to alleviate their concerns? The most effective way of doing this may be through a two-fold approach of educating well older adults about ageing and the concerns they have through groups and the media. Another way of dealing with these concerns is to conduct further research, this time with the nursing home residents, regarding their spiritual needs, to properly map out the dimension of spirituality in this group of frail older people, then to address their concerns through policy, planning and practice interventions deemed appropriate to rectify identified concerns.

Often being able to express his or her concerns may in itself be sufficient to assist an individual who is experiencing feelings of vulnerability. Once a fear is named, it becomes manageable. Feeling free to speak openly of dying and death as a natural part of the lifespan is an important beginning. But staff must be able to cope with the listening. The concerns of frail older people may raise issues that are unfinished business of grief for staff members. Staff need to have worked through their own griefs and to be able to find support readily to deal with issues as these arise in the process of their work.

## Self-centredness or self-transcendence?

How can an individual be assisted to turn from self-centredness to other-centredness? How can an individual move from focusing on a medical condition that blocks their further spiritual and emotional growth, to transcending the condition?

It has been observed that of the 75 people who took the SHIE questionnaire in this study, many of them had multiple chronic disease states, yet 58.7 per cent said they had good to very good health. Their self-perception was that of health, not disease; their focus seemed often to be on their capacity to function effectively rather than on a medical diagnosis. It seems that physical conditions are less to do with the level of wellness or satisfaction with health status in older adults. This was also a finding in a study of health-related decision making in older people (MacKinlay 1989).

The key to this transition, it is suggested, is the move from doing to being; the move to self-transcendence, which may in itself be a kind of feedback mechanism. Physical disabilities stimulate transcendence, which in turn enables the individual to transcend physical and other difficulties, such as loss in the psychosocial dimension.

### The challenges of living with disabilities and decreasing energy levels

It was considered that most of these independently living older people would not be experiencing factors such as energy loss to any real incapacitating level. It was thus unexpected that a number of these informants spontaneously mentioned their decreasing levels of energy. Still others were evidently unconcerned by energy levels and were able to engage in all the activities they wished.

Informants managed these challenges with varying degrees of success. This is an area where carers can assist, not so much by doing, as this will only take away the individual's sense of independence, but by assisting the person to set priorities in their lives that incorporate their goals and attempt to match their energy levels and what is possible to achieve. This sense of energy lack is often frustrating for older people. One informant shared how she wanted to be much more involved in her community. But she had to keep saying no to invitations as she knew from experience that she would not have enough energy to complete what she wanted to do. Those who had lived with energy depletion for longer seemed often better adjusted to this problem. However, it is difficult to determine just why this is so. It could be that the individual has had time to learn to live with the problem, and perhaps to transcend it. It may also be related to the personality of the individual.

It may be possible to assist planning the day so that the older person can choose what they want to do and perhaps have other energy-consuming tasks performed by others — lawn mowing and house cleaning are two tasks that come to mind. Perhaps the person may want to meet with a friend and is too tired to enjoy the visit by the time they have completed all their tasks. This is related to meeting their spiritual needs as well: low energy levels may mean the person cannot attend a church service, or perhaps even read or pray.

*Individual differences*

The solution that is useful for one older person may well not be at all acceptable to another. In pastoral care, it is vital to work with older people, not to make the decisions *for* them without consultation. Care professionals with the best intentions do not always have the best solution for the older person's problems. The ability to transcend loss and disabilities is a spiritual resource that enables older people to continue to hope and to function in the face of bodily decline and psychosocial loss. A lack of spiritual resources may be a real difficulty for people who continue to rely on their 'doing' ability· and have not developed their 'being' or inner resources as they become older and more frail.

## Transition from doing to being

In the normal lifespan, not cut short for any reason, it can be expected that in the later years, particularly when people live to near the maximum potential of years, then physical decline and physiological changes (Schneider and Rowe 1990) will result in the body being less able to replenish its energy levels. This is well documented already in the field of cardiovascular and respiratory function, where it is known that the body may function well at rest, but becomes less able to handle extra stresses put on it, for example vigorous exercise, in extreme old age.

Of course, there are considerable variations between individuals in the time of onset of physiological decline, and in fact a healthy lifestyle can retard the decline, depending on the inherited potential for longevity. There are also considerable variations between individuals in the development of the psychosocial and spiritual dimensions. Interaction between the physiological, psychosocial and spiritual dimensions becomes more apparent in the later years, and while the physical body runs down, the psychosocial and spiritual dimensions continue to develop, unless blocked in some way.

It is suggested, from informant comments in this study, that the physiological decline may be in some way associated with the psychosocial and spiritual transition from doing to being, and the final spiritual developmental stage of life. The physical decline observed in later years makes it less practical for older people to engage in the same amount of physical work and activity as they used to in the past. Disengagement from former roles becomes more apparent in later life, as family responsibilities of older adults are largely completed, and roles that were important during the middle years have been lost. Some of these changes and losses in the psychosocial dimension trigger a renewed search for meaning that becomes apparent in later life, this spiritual task of ageing, to come to final meanings. There is thus, it seems, a natural process set up of a move from doing as a way of being human, to a growing emphasis on being as a way of *being* human.

Clement's (1990) concept of stripping or shedding of roles that may lead to a revealing of the empty core of the individual has a place here. Indeed, the mystic tradition sets out to deliberately strip the outer facades away to reveal the inner core, or in other words, to die to self. Dying to self is a way of saying that transcendence is occurring. It is this whole complex process of physical decline, psychosocial loss and growing interiority that makes possible the transition from doing to being in ageing.

On reflection, it would seem that there are certain parallels between Tillich's (1963) description of sanctification, of the growing in self-awareness, the move to greater freedom, the increasing search for relatedness, the move towards self-transcendence and the process identified in this study to find final meanings, intimacy with God and/or others, transcend difficulties and losses and to find hope.

The process of moving from doing to being, it is suggested, is most probably a universal one; a process that becomes accentuated and more urgent in later life. While the term 'sanctification' may not really be accessible to the general society, it is possible that the term 'spiritual tasks of ageing' may be more acceptable to the variety of carers who work with elderly people.

### What are the consequences of maintaining a mid-life focus?

It must be asked, then, what are the consequences of endeavouring to maintain oneself in the mid-life mode of function while one is moving into older age? At this stage, it is perhaps uncertain what implications there may be. But it is worth pondering whether trying to maintain oneself at mid life may indeed cut off opportunities for growth and development in the psychosocial and spiritual dimensions of ageing. It is suggested that this may be a fact where ageing is actively denied. It would seem that the last career is a task for all human beings who live long enough to engage in it. The spiritual tasks of ageing, as postulated in this study, would seem to indicate a need to accept the inevitability of the ageing process and to honour ageing rather than to deny it.

### Assisting individuals who are in the process of transition from doing to being

Acceptance of the ageing process is a difficult point to come to for many in the postmodern society. Death and ageing are assigned low values, and many endeavour to retain a mid-life outlook and lifestyle for as long as possible. In fact, ageing itself can at times be regarded as a medical condition that can be 'fixed' (Kirkwood 1999).

One problem that currently seems to confront people who are growing older is a lack of desirable role models – not a lack of models of 'successful' ageing, but a lack of role models of 'effective' ageing. Successful ageing has been largely connected with maintaining the mid-life persona for as long as possible; there are considerable pressures from within society to do so.

It would seem that there exists the potential to develop strong models for effective ageing, and this particularly so among those with a well-developed spirituality. The answer to the denial of ageing does not seem to lie in trying to maintain the youthful body so much as to continue to develop both psychosocially and spiritually into ever more whole human beings. This development should continue until the point of death. There are examples of informants in this study who have a highly developed spirituality, who have journeyed to a point of having spiritual integrity and maturity, who are at peace with themselves and those around them. These people are a joy to be with, and sometimes either in spite of, or because of, their physical disabilities they have achieved a well-developed sense of transcendence.

## Facilitating effective relationships in ageing

The married informants had an average age of 69.7 years, while those whose partners had died had an average age of 73.3 years. This is consistent with increasing likelihood of losing one's spouse the longer one lives. Women are even more likely to be widowed than men are to become widowers, and being both older and more likely, through age, to be more frail, the widowed group in society is more likely to be vulnerable. It was noted, however, in the findings of this study that there did not seem to be a direct link between living alone and being socially or indeed spiritually isolated, which is also consistent with Rubinstein *et al.*'s findings (1992).

One of the spiritual tasks of ageing identified in this study was the need for intimacy in ageing. Ageing is a time of some potentially enormous changes in intimacy. Loss of a spouse was identified as a tremendous loss for those who had experienced it. Intimacy with God may also become more important to some older people. Physical decline may make social and spiritual isolation more likely, although this was not found consistently in this study. One sub-category in the study that seemed to experience particular difficulties of isolation in ageing were the females who had never married. An important variable seemed to be whether the woman had chosen to remain single or not.

## Social and spiritual isolation?

It is important to identify those who are at risk of being socially and spiritually isolated. Living alone is one factor to be examined, and an important one. The reasons the individual has for living alone are probably as important as the fact that they do live alone. Is it by choice? In this study, informants were not asked that question, but their marital status was asked and does have some bearing on the degree of isolation experienced. For example, none of those living with a spouse or partner appeared to be socially isolated. The spiritual journeys, however, varied, even among those who were married.

Entry to widowhood was a profound experience for each of the informants. Their ability to grieve effectively was important, and their support systems were valuable in each case. Some still continued after many years mentally to talk things over with their husbands: 'Now what would he have done, if he was here?' The seven women in this group all had developed good support systems and seemed to enjoy full and active lives.

On the other hand, living alone was much more difficult for one of the divorced women, who was still searching for a stable relationship and was obviously lonely. Two of the women who had never married were also socially isolated, one had well-developed spiritual resources and was not spiritually isolated, but the other never-married woman deeply regretted never having married. She seemed socially isolated and, to some extent, spiritually isolated as well. These two women raised some important questions about the position of never-married women in society. They both expressed the perception of feeling isolated and not accepted as they believed married women, or even widows, would be.

## Isolation within the church of never married women

These two women spoke of the hurt they felt over their lack of acceptance by the church. Both still maintained contact with church, and this is a particularly important point because church was the main place that these women gained social contact. Thus, if their main place of social support was less than supportive of them, that left them very isolated. In spite of the difficulties experienced in this area, one of the two women had deep spiritual resources and managed well. The other did not know why she still went to church.

What can be done by church communities to welcome and affirm single older adults who feel rejected, for the most part unconsciously, by the main place to which they turn for comfort? Often the church seems to reflect the attitudes of the society: that everyone is meant to be part of a family, and to have a partner. The situation of such people needs to be acknowledged and consciously addressed.

## Finding meaning in ageing and pastoral care

Questions raised in the review of literature relate to issues of interventions in the disciplines of nursing, ministry and pastoral care. Such questions include: first, how may the spiritual needs of these people be met, once their image of God is understood?

Then, in certain circumstances, can it be desirable to change one's image of God? for instance, is the image held contributing to a sense of despair for that individual? Or, indeed, does the individual who is in despair or fearful of the future need to learn how to relate more effectively to the God image they already have?

If the individual has no God image, how may these people be assisted to find meaning, through the centres of meaning they hold; how can they be assisted pastorally? It is an essential first step to be able to help the individual identify what their centre(s) of meaning are before being able to assist them to find meaning in life.

After finding what the individual's centre(s) of meaning are, then it is necessary to identify how they respond to the Ultimate in their lives. An important starting point then for all pastoral interventions is to accurately determine where the individual's point of need is *now*. Thus effective spiritual assessment is a necessary prerequisite for effective spiritual care.

### Assessment of spiritual needs in ageing

Health care professionals and pastoral workers have often been reluctant to assess the spiritual needs of people within their care. In fact, until recently, numbers of health care professionals have probably been unsure that spiritual needs are even a part of health care. This is changing rapidly as society begins to acknowledge that the medical paradigm does not have all the knowledge required to deliver holistic care.

The area of assessment of spiritual needs is still in its early stages. In this study two forms of assessment were used, first, a spiritual health inventory for elderly people (SHIE), and then in-depth interviews were used to obtain a wider view of spirituality in ageing and to compare the findings against the closed responses of the SHIE.

The SHIE trialed in this study did not connect the same themes that were ·identified from the in-depth data. Effective assessment of the spiritual needs of frail older adults remains an important issue to be resolved.

### Assisting the individual to explore their God image or whatever they hold as ultimate meaning in life

Among the informants in this study a search for meaning in life was a common focus. Some mentioned that it had become more directed or more urgent as they grew older. Realisation of increasing frailty was one factor that seemed to emphasise the importance of this search. For many, the search seems to be a natural one that needs no outside intervention; however, it does seem to be valuable for many of those who are happy with their search to be able to share this with one or more others. This relates to the human need for intimacy, found to be a spiritual task of ageing.

Still others may experience blocks along the search that retard the process of finding final meanings in life. It is possible that some of these. blockages may be from earlier life experiences that the person finds difficult to deal with.

### Spiritual tasks of ageing: to find hope; to search for final meanings

Hope is essential for the continuance of humanity. Hope stems from meaning and the ability to see that life is worth living. There is already a high level of suicide among older adults, and particularly for older men. While economic, social and health problems may make continued living very difficult for older people, lack of meaning may be a critical feature in the final decision to commit suicide. Using the definition of wisdom in this study, which focuses on the spiritual component rather than the cognitive aspects of wisdom, hope can be seen as an outcome of wisdom. Hope springs out of meaning in life and a spiritual task of ageing is to come to final meanings.

One of the aspects of wisdom defined in this study is that it includes development of transcendence of uncertainty and a move towards internal regulation. The move towards internal regulation also recognises the increasing sense of interiority that seems to become more apparent in older age. It seems that much can be learnt from mysticism in the process of developing effective strategies for the spiritual tasks of ageing. Yet in this study only three informants spoke of using meditation, which could be regarded as being within the broad arena of spirituality that deals with mysticism. This could be for two reasons: first, because meditation is not widely regarded to be within the practice of Christian religion – a common misconception; second, it could be because meditation only appeals to certain personality types. This area may be worth exploring further.

## Response of older adults to the Ultimate: implications for nursing, clergy, pastoral workers

Ashbrook (1996, p.107) wrote that in care-giving relationships we need to 'risk being open to *their* perception of what is and what might be' (my emphasis). It is so important to reach out to the older person, to identify where they are spiritually. Are they in touch with their own inner needs? What kind of a belief system are they working from? It is important to identify that, whether they have a deeply developed sense of the spiritual or not and even when they have no religious beliefs at all. Each person does have a spiritual dimension, and the challenge is for nurses, social workers, clergy or other pastoral carers to be able to reach the older person at their point of need, that is, to connect with them.

Many in the current cohort of older people have had some contact with the Christian faith even if only in childhood. It may be that early contact resulted in unhelpful images of God. Can it be desirable to change one's image of God, for instance, if the image held is contributing to a sense of despair in the individual? In assessing the spiritual needs of older adults, it is important to identify blockages to spiritual growth. In this study one woman had rejected God after a couple of tragic deaths in the family. She has continued to search for a God she could relate to for many years now. She is unable to relate to a God of love; her own image of God blocks any other image. Unless she can accept a new image of God, she is blocked from further spiritual growth.

How may the spiritual needs of older adults be met, once their image of God is understood? The first goal is to assist the individual to get in touch with their own sense of the spiritual, to explore with them their centres of meaning in life, including their image of God. This exploration may sometimes be a part of the meaning-making role of the nurse. At other times, it may become a specialist role of clergy, including chaplains, and spiritual counsellors.

*Assisting an individual to relate more effectively*
*to the God image they already have*

This may involve input suggested by the older person, relating to current and former religious practices, or other behaviours of spiritual significance for that particular person. It may also be necessary to make referrals to chaplains and other clergy for assistance in the pastoral role. In some cases, simply having a pastoral worker who can sit and listen to the older person may be very helpful.

For the particular cohort of older people it may be important to identify their world views. It may also be possible to identify any particular myths held by the group of older people. These may be important factors related to the ability of these people to grow towards spiritual integrity.

*Health professionals and the recognition of their own spiritual needs*

Like other members of society health professionals may be at various points in their own spiritual development and spiritual awareness. Regardless of the belief system of an individual health worker, it is both possible and desirable for that person to be able to identify the spiritual needs of those in his/her care. The findings of research into the spiritual dimension, such as those identified in this study, can only be of value if health professionals are in touch with their own spirituality.

There is a danger that if health professionals are not sensitive to their own spirituality then they may project their own beliefs or lack of them on to patients or residents. In the study that considered assessing and raising the spiritual awareness of nursing staff in nursing homes (MacKinlay forthcoming 2001), a number of the participants were acknowledged agnostics. However, they were open to considering that all people in their care may have spiritual needs and to learning how to assess these prior to making referral to others who could meet these needs.

## Worship and older people

Worship is an important part of the lives of a proportion of the informants in this study; 46 per cent regularly attend church. Others have either stopped attending or rarely have attended in recent years. Other studies have also identified the worship habits of older adults. It has been documented (Harris 1990) and is also seen in this study that non-organisational aspects of religion become more important for older people. In this study disabilities did not seem to be very important in preventing informants from attending church. This will probably be more important in more frail older people. However, prayer, reading Scripture and other religious material, and meditation were all activities engaged in by the group. Prayer seemed to be changing for those who prayed, after the pattern noted by other researchers (Greeley 1982).

## Summary

*In this chapter the themes related to spirituality in ageing identified in this study have been discussed and a model for spiritual tasks of ageing has been outlined. Characteristics of those who appear to be moving towards spiritual maturity have been outlined. The use of reminiscence and life review in this study have been examined and linked to the spiritual tasks of ageing. The challenge of vulnerability, the process of transcendence and the associated move from doing to being in ageing were discussed.*

*Assessment of spiritual needs of older people and the importance of meeting the older person at their point of need have been emphasised. Meeting the spiritual needs of older people is presented as a multidisciplinary responsibility largely involving health professionals, in particular, nurses, social workers, clergy and other pastoral workers.*

# CHAPTER 15

# The spiritual dimension of ageing
## Challenges and preparation for ageing

### The search for the spiritual

While there has been an increased interest in both spirituality and ageing in society in recent decades, knowledge of spirituality in ageing still requires further exploration. This study of the spiritual dimension in older adults living independently has produced a picture of older adults who, on the whole, have a zest for living, who really are finding meaning in their lives and who are functioning effectively in their communities. The search for meaning through the spiritual journey continues for these older individuals. There is evidence of wisdom as a spiritual construct among this group of informants.

One of the most striking features of the older people interviewed in this study is the differences they show in ageing. They have distinct and different personal histories, and bring skills based on these to meet their current needs and the demands made on them from the environment. Although there are broad aspects of experience that are common in a number of the spiritual journeys, the journeys of the informants are still markedly different.

This study of spirituality in independently living older adults has shown the real need not to make assumptions about the spiritual needs of all older people. Whatever the differences between older people, of the 75 who completed the SHIE, 92 per cent said they had a faith. This is important to note in planning chaplaincy and other pastoral services for older people. It is vital that any person attempting to provide spiritual care must first affirm what spiritual needs a particular person may have. It may be that the individual has not previously clearly thought through these needs them-selves, and in this case the carers may need to assist the person to examine their spiritual needs.

In this study, the informants seemed to have in common a search for meaning in life, although not all of this group had in any way come to the point of consciously constructing final life meanings. Many of the meanings they assigned at this stage were still provisional.

As demonstrated in this study the sacraments are certainly important for some, and effective assessment of the individual's spiritual needs related to worship and other ways of responding to the Ultimate is most important.

Growing in knowledge of faith is important for some; the need to learn more of their faith and to be able to talk of this may be a part of the clergy role. As well, the preparation of pastoral workers who may support frail older people in this development is an important part of ministry in ageing.

## Personal belief systems of older people

In this study, informants had a wide range of belief systems. In a multicultural, multifaith society, great diversity can be expected. To some extent, spirituality will differ for each person. Some may hold very similar beliefs, however where they are on their faith journeys will vary tremendously, even within the same religious and denominational group. It is noted that this study, due to the method of recruiting informants, sampled only Anglo-Celtic people for the in-depth interviewing. Members of other major faiths or humanists, or followers of New Age philosophy, will hold different belief systems.

In a multicultural and multifaith society we can make no assumptions as to any individual's belief system, and indeed to any individual's spiritual needs. What should be understood at the outset, however, is that spiritual needs seem to be almost universal. In this study only one informant said she did not think the spiritual dimension existed. It is acknowledged that this self-selected group may not be typical of the wider society, in that only those people willing to talk about their spiritual dimension would have been included in this study. Nevertheless, if we take spirituality as defined in this study, considering ultimate meaning in life for each person and relationship, then spirituality is part of the condition of being human.

## Perceived vulnerability in older adults

For all the positive aspects of ageing experienced by these informants, there seemed to be a heightened sense of perceived vulnerability within this group. This took the form of concerns for the future, fears of losing control of their lives, fears of developing Alzheimer's disease, fears of physical disabilities that may make it impossible to maintain an independent lifestyle, and fears of the process of dying.

An important value of the present society is that of independence, and of being able to do things, that is, being able to contribute to society. People are valued on their ability to achieve. Older adults, who can see the possibility of loss of these abilities, express fears for the future, their future.

It is noted that those in this study who had developed a deep self-awareness and self-transcendence that is a part of wisdom, seemed more able to face the future with a sense of peace and integrity. In Chapter 14 it was suggested that there are four spiritual tasks of ageing: to transcend difficulties and loss in ageing; to search for final meanings; to find intimacy with God and/or others; and to find hope. Further, it is suggested that how effectively any person manages to achieve these tasks is related to their core or ultimate meanings in life, and how they respond to these.

In this chapter, ways that these developmental tasks may be facilitated are explored and recommendations for education in spirituality in ageing and further research directions are made.

## The relationship between psychosocial and spiritual

The spiritual dimension underlies and is closely related to the psychosocial. It is this factor that complicates the process of distinguishing between psychosocial and spiritual needs. Throughout this study it has been necessary to tease apart the components of the stories as told by the informants, and to ask the questions: What is the psychosocial? What is the spiritual?

We may indeed ask: how important is it to distinguish between psycho-social and spiritual needs? It is important to the extent that *spiritual* needs diagnosed as *psychosocial* will not be met by appropriate health and pastoral strategies. As well, clergy may not be asked to intervene if a nurse or social worker does not recognise a specific spiritual need. The focus of the spiritual is different from that of the psychosocial.

It was important in this study to start with the psychosocial developmental stages of ageing, recognising the interaction between the dimensions. But then it was also necessary to go further and identify what really are the aspects of the spiritual that can be addressed by nurses and social workers or by clergy or other health care workers. The spiritual tasks of ageing identified in this study point to strategies that may be used by gerontology professionals in addressing spiritual needs.

## Pastoral care, ministry, nursing, social work: multidisciplinary practice – what are the parameters?

In view of the current structures of aged care, the roles of people who work in aged care and the findings of this study, it appears that there is a place for facilitating spiritual development in ageing people and assisting them in their vulnerability. It is not expected that all care professionals will feel comfortable or be able to provide for all spiritual needs of people in their care. Yet, as identified in this study, there are generic spiritual tasks of ageing. These are illustrated in the model (Figure 14.1): transcending disabilities and losses of ageing; searching for final meanings; finding intimacy with God/and or others; and finding hope. These are tasks that can be facilitated through the multidisciplinary practices within gerontology by nurses, social workers, pastoral counsellors, pastoral carers and clergy. All should at least be able to recognise and respect the spiritual needs of people in their care.

It also seems that no one professional group can have a monopoly in addressing the spiritual needs of older people. If, as it seems reasonable to do, spirituality can be acknowledged as a universal component of being human, then addressing the meaning issues of human life is a universal function. Yet, it would seem appropriate for there to be some specialisation of role in different aspects of facilitating spiritual development in ageing and addressing spiritual distress. There is a definite need to consider developing effective strategies to address the spiritual tasks of ageing.

## How do the particular professional groups function in multidisciplinary practice in working with older adults in spiritual care?

### The clergy role

Clergy have a traditional role in society of meeting the needs of people for ritual and sacrament and of gathering and ministering to the community of faith. But the role is much broader, and includes pastoral counselling and spiritual direction that is important in ageing too. This role also extends to dealing with grief and guilt, both of which featured in data from this study. Guilt may be a critical block to spiritual development. Confession and pronouncement of God's forgiveness may be important for those whose belief system accepts this. Reconciliation is a part of the process of forgiveness, which allows the person to move towards new spiritual growth and wholeness.

The spiritual tasks of ageing, including the way individuals respond to ultimate meaning in their lives, that were identified in this study can be used in ministering to frail older people. Sacraments are certainly important to a proportion of older adults, but there is also a critical move to a greater sense of interiority in older age. The clergy need to minister to the individual at his or her point of need.

### The nursing role

Nurses have traditionally had a close and intimate role with patients. This role is based on trust and has centred on care. This central caring component of nursing is still present, even in the midst of high-technology nursing. The caring role, worked out in close co-operation and communication with patients over extended periods of time, and more often in an institutional setting, is what identifies nursing as being different from the other helping professionals.

It is contended that the spiritual is the caring aspect of nursing. Nursing cannot be holistic without the spiritual. It is now possible for nurses to name that role, and to claim it as their own. An important part of the nursing role in gerontology could be described, in some instances, as meaning making; that is, assisting frail older people to find meaning in life; to walk beside those who are fearful, those who are progressing into dementia and those who are no longer in control of their lives. Addressing the generic spiritual tasks of ageing identified in this study are well within the nursing role, and are in part the tasks described by Henderson (1966, p.16): to do for these people the tasks they would do for themselves, if they were able.

The spiritual tasks of ageing identified in this study would seem to be tasks that can be adopted into the nursing role: to assist older people in their vulnerability, in the transcendence of disabilities and loss; to search for final meanings; to find hope; and even to assist older people finding intimacy with God and/or others. Nurses can provide care by listening, assessing and meeting patient needs.

Group work in life-review therapy is an important aspect of the spiritual role of appropriately educated nurses. While most life-review work has been done in the areas of activity and psychosocial interventions, life review can readily be focused to consider the spiritual dimension. Indeed, reminiscence is a developmental task of ageing.

PUTTING THE SPIRITUAL INTO NURSING PRACTICE

There is only one area of nursing practice that, as far as can be seen, has fully embraced the inclusion of the spiritual dimension into practice, and that is parish nursing (Westberg 1987). This unique type of nursing endeavours to take healing back to the roots of the church and to acknowledge the wholeness of human beings. Parish nursing is a relatively new type of holistic nursing that has developed rapidly in North America in recent decades. Practice of parish nursing is just beginning in Australia. Parish nursing is practised with a background of community health nursing and pastoral care skills. This nurse works as part of the healing and ministry team of one or more parishes and it can work well ecumenically. The parish nurse often liaises closely with hospitals and other health agencies to provide holistic health care that fills a gap in current health services. Although a large proportion of informants in this study expressed some reservations with the church, they still seemed to find parish structures useful and may respond well to parish nursing.

The parish nurses are able to acknowledge the vital dimension of human spirituality as a legitimate component of nursing. There is, after all, an enormous challenge in reaching people at their point of need for reconciliation with God and others and to find meaning in their lives. Although parish nurses provide care for people of all age groups, a large number of their patients will be the older and more vulnerable people of the community.

Many nurses still do not really know the parameters of the spiritual dimension, and therefore do not acknowledge that spirituality is really part of nursing. This raises the question, in the light of findings such as in this study, of the need for further education for nurses in spirituality in nursing.

## Other pastoral workers

The findings of this study would seem to point to the multidisciplinary nature of the spiritual dimension in gerontology. Spiritual tasks in ageing do not fall neatly into one area of care. It is recommended that liaison between the disciplines working with older adults be encouraged to increase understanding of the holistic nature of spiritual needs in older adults and to improve interventions to address spiritual needs of frail older people.

There are roles for others too in the provision of spiritual care: social workers, activity officers, pastoral counsellors and pastoral visitors. The role varies for different types of professional preparation, ranging from therapy in life review for social workers and pastoral counsellors (as well as chaplains and clinical nurse specialists in gerontology) to the non-professional but important functions of being with, listening to and being involved in group work with older people that can be done effectively by pastoral visitors who have attended short courses specifically designed for their needs.

## Education in gerontology and spirituality

Ageing and pastoral care are specialist areas of practice requiring appropriate professional preparation. As members of an ageing society there is a responsibility carefully to examine the needs for relevant education in these areas. What are the needs now? What are the needs projected into the new century, when even greater numbers of older people will form part of the population? This growing number of older people can also be expected to include proportionate numbers of people who have dementia. With misconceptions still present in the society at large, a question recently asked by some people preparing for ministry was, is there a difference between Alzheimer's disease and the senility that older people get? Findings of this study point to the diversity of experiences in spirituality as people age, and the importance of this dimension in their lives.

## Education in ministry in an ageing society

The demographics of society alone would set a high priority on including research-based content of aged care as a core component of all pastoral ministry programmes. As demonstrated in this study, the spiritual dimension of ageing is a real component of the whole picture of ageing, and would thus be an important component of such courses. Gerontology, as a specialty subject, should be available as a graduate studies course, both by graduate diploma or by masters degree. These courses should be readily available for all those who work in aged care, in parishes, in chaplaincy and other pastoral carer roles. These courses should be available both on campus and by distance learning.

Opportunities should also be available for clergy and pastoral carers in aged care to take short courses to develop appropriate skills in this specialist area of practice. Thus it is recommended that gerontology be a recognised component of clergy training, with particular emphasis on the spiritual tasks of ageing. It is also recommended that pastoral care courses include content on ageing and spiritual needs of older adults.

## Education in nursing in an ageing society

Similar comments can be made for nursing. The increasing numbers of older people in the population alone justify the inclusion of gerontology as a core component of the undergraduate nursing programmes. Added to this is the information readily available of the higher hospital bed use by older people in comparison with younger people.

In nursing, however, there is still much to be learnt about how to 'do' spiritual care, and in particular how to address the spiritual needs of older adults. Many nurses are unaware of what spiritual care is, and may need to be convinced of its place in the nursing role and how it can be fitted with all the other things nurses do. It is often said that there is no time to give spiritual care. It is suggested that providing spiritual care is a natural nursing role, it is what lies at the heart of nursing. Often the spiritual needs of frail elderly people can be met while the nurse is attending to other physical needs, for example showering, assisting with meals, doing dressings. An essential aspect of spiritual care in nursing is *being with*, listening and connecting deeply with the elderly person. However, nurses do need to have skills in effective listening and, just as important, they need to be in touch with their own spirituality. Nurses need to be spiritually healthy and self-aware before they can be effective in providing spiritual care.

Spirituality should be taught as part of holistic nursing care in all undergraduate nursing programmes. In particular speciality areas, spiritual care becomes even more important, for example in oncology and palliative care, and in gerontology. The spiritual dimension should be a recognisable component of all such courses. Courses such as Clinical Pastoral Education (CPE) would be valuable for nurses working in aged care and palliative and hospice care. Short courses based on CPE principles may be valuable.

## Further research

As the research base in the field of spirituality in ageing increases it is being seen that this is an important component of holistic care, addressing a universal human need. As this dimension has been so neglected until recently, it is of particular importance that urgent steps are taken to fill the deficits in education and research. The increasing levels of suicide and sense of lack of meaning among the oldest of old people make it crucial to develop this area so that more effective strategies can be developed to assist older people to meet the challenge of ageing and of coming to process the final meanings of life.

There is a critical need to continue to research this area, to provide a sound basis for both teaching and practice in this field. The multi-disciplinary nature of gerontology makes this a unique area for intervention and an area that may assist society as we move into the early years of the twenty-first century and beyond to vision a new way of being old, a way that is valued, that is full and challenging – a way that enables new freedoms for older people and that breaks down ageism at any point of the lifespan. This way of growing older will enable older people to make the transitions from doing to being, but at the same time affirm each one of them in being loved and being human.

This should open up new ways of growing older and being able to live out one's last career in fulfilment of life, to reach one's human potential for wholeness and make links with the coming generations. These are new possibilities that are only now becoming open to so many people. But if the challenge is not taken up, and people do not learn how to develop in wholeness of life, to grow spiritually, then it may be too difficult to come to find life's meanings; and Frankl (1984) and others like him, who could see meaning even through the greatest of human sufferings, will not have endeavoured in vain for this and the coming generations.

## Other cultural and faith groups

This study examined spirituality in older adults living independently in the community. The method of selection of the informants resulted in a sample of two groups, Christian and others who had no religious affiliation. The informants in the in-depth interviews were all of Anglo-Celtic background; it would be valuable to study the spiritual needs of older people from a wider cultural and religious background.

While several of the informants had read widely in other religions, and one had constructed her own religion with some Christian and Buddhist background, it would be valuable to study the spiritual dimension in other older adults who hold different religious affiliations. This may be particularly valuable as the multifaith societies age. There is always the possibility that older people of a faith different from the majority of the society may experience discrimination in the area of practice of their faith, particularly if little is understood of the spiritual needs of the particular group of older individuals.

## The spiritual dimension and frail older adults

This study was proposed as the basis from which further research can develop. In particular this study was viewed as setting the ground work prior to investigation into the spiritual needs of frail older adults. It was important not to begin investigations with that group of frail older adults, although it is noted that an earlier, preliminary study (MacKinlay 1992) began with assessment of the spiritual needs of older people resident in nursing homes. The 1992 study did not use in-depth interviewing and provided only an insight into the lack of knowledge of spiritual needs of frail aged people resident in nursing homes.

It is now planned to use in-depth methodology to return to interview residents of nursing homes to gain a better understanding of their spiritual needs. There are two main areas for investigation, first frail but cognitively competent older adults and, second, but no less important, cognitively impaired older adults.

### Spirituality and frail older adults in long term care

It is these frail older people who do not simply perceive themselves to be vulnerable, but who *know* they are vulnerable, for whom spiritual care is so important. Yet not enough is known of the spiritual dimension in frail older people. With the information gained in the current study it will be much more realistic to proceed with interviewing the frail older group.

The residents of nursing homes have added difficulties that make both communication and assessment of spiritual needs more complex. First, they may not be fully able to articulate their needs for spiritual care. Perhaps because they have not developed their spiritual dimension in earlier life, as some people do not exercise their physical body, so some may not exercise their spiritual dimension. Second, physical disabilities may make communication difficult, for instance stroke and aphasia, depression, sight and/or hearing deficits make communication harder. As well, language difficulties in older frail people for whom English is a second language may make it harder for these frail older people to be understood.

Depleted energy levels may make it hard for frail older people to concentrate for long periods of time; this in itself was a reason why frail older people were not included in this study. It seemed important to gain a better understanding of well older people and spirituality before interviewing frail older people. There is also a better chance that any problems with techniques and questions have been dealt with prior to interviewing the frail group of older people.

Frail older adults are not only more likely to suffer from energy depletion, but also to have multiple pathological conditions. They are more likely to be grieving, to be suffering from multiple losses, to be forming final meanings in life, to be fearing the possibility of pain and suffering in the process of dying. They are also more likely to be developing skills in transcending physiological difficulties, to be wanting to deal with guilt and the need for reconciliation. All these tasks are part of the spiritual domain and frail older people are also likely to be needing some kind of spiritual care and assistance with meeting their spiritual needs. Even prayer may be hard at times for some who have been good 'pray-ers' most of their lives. Above all, it is postulated that these people need affirmation and love.

### Vulnerability and the transition from doing to being

It appears that an important task of spirituality in ageing is negotiating the transition that frail older people need to make from *doing* to *being*. This remains a difficult task, more so for some than others, although the reasons for this are uncertain. From the informants in this study it would appear there may be a link between increasing vulnerability and the transition from doing to being. In the first place, simply because the individual can no longer do certain things and, perhaps, because they need to learn to depend on others for certain of their needs, a transition begins. But not all older people seem to be able to make this transition successfully. The need to *do* has been effectively programmed into the socialisation of most people in society. The attitudes and habits of a lifetime must be unlearnt or rejected.

The Christian ideal of dying to self may be of great value in this process. Fischer's (1985) view of needing to let go in order to move forward gives an idea of the process involved. Clinging to mid-life strategies that may no longer be effective will make the ageing process more difficult. It is often said that older people cannot change, but it seems that to grow older with integrity involves some of the greatest changes of a lifespan.

This process of changing from doing to being is an essential area to study further in frail older people, particularly residents of nursing homes. It is only by investigating this area further that we can hope to identify the kinds of strategies that can be effective in assisting these frail older people to negotiate what might only be termed a 'mine-field' of learning to accomplish the spiritual tasks of ageing. It is recommended that spirituality in frail aged people be a high priority for further research. This research should be conducted by interviewers highly skilled in the interview techniques and who have a high level of understanding of the spiritual needs of older adults.

Specific topics for research are: to map out spirituality in frail older adults; to study the process of transition from doing to being in frail older adults; how pastoral care can assist older people in this process. Another area for study is vulnerability in frail older adults: what are the roles for nurses and clergy in providing spiritual support for vulnerable older adults? Included in this would be fears of the process of dying.

### Spirituality in dementia

A number of the informants in this study spoke of their fears of developing dementia and some talked of people who have dementia as being 'non-people'. Anecdotal evidence already points to the possibility of being able to connect much more effectively on a spiritual level with people who have dementia. There is a real urgency in the present society to investigate this area so as to enable more effective strategies of care to be developed.

An important part of further research will be to use the knowledge already gained of spirituality in independent older people as a basis for studying frail older people and those suffering from dementia. It is recommended that a high priority be given to research to be conducted into the spiritual needs of the latter.

### Assessment of spiritual needs

Effective assessment of spiritual needs is a first important step to being able to give effective spiritual care to frail older adults. Assessment instruments need to be developed for this purpose.

A spiritual health assessment inventory (SHIE) has been trialed with this study. Factor analysis performed on the data from the SHIE was disappointing, and the data from the SHIE did not produce the same concepts as the data from in-depth data in this study. These findings highlight the need for care in the construction of questionnaires to achieve a valid questionnaire. However, it is envisaged that such instruments could be valuable in both nursing and pastoral care practice.

A new questionnaire could be designed based on the themes identified in this study. It would be necessary to test this new assessment instrument with frail older people and to do in-depth interviews with this group as well. This would be crucial as there may be different aspects of spiritual needs identified within this frail older group that were not evident in a group of independently living older adults. It is recommended that a new instrument to assess spiritual needs of older adults be designed based on the themes identified in this study. This instrument would then be trialed in another study, this time with older adults who are residents of hostels and nursing homes. In-depth interviews should be conducted with a large sample of these older people.

### Life review therapy in dementia

Valuable work has already been done using life review therapy (Burnside 1994). Further qualitative research would be valuable in the use of this with people who have early dementia.

### Laughter, humour and spirituality

The in-depth interviews disclosed the use of humour and laughter by a number of the informants in this study. Gender differences were noticed in the use of humour. It appeared that the females in the study were using humour as a way of connecting more deeply, while humour seemed to be used by the male informants more in regard to content. These findings are interesting and further study may be useful in examining whether it is possible to use humour therapeutically in spiritual care.

## Potential obstacles to implementing findings from this study

In practice a number of factors need to be taken into account when planning spiritual care.

### The need to recognise the universal nature of human spirituality

First, the technological basis of the postmodern society tends to devalue the place of concepts that are difficult to quantify. Spirituality can be considered as an example of an area that does not easily fit the scientific model or the medical model of health. Yet the spiritual dimension can clearly be seen to be a component of human being, it could reasonably be said to be a universal component. Of the 24 informants in this study, only one was not sure of the spiritual part of being human. Even those who did not have any religious affiliation acknowledged that there was a spiritual aspect of life. The ways in which the spiritual was worked out by different informants varied a great deal. Nevertheless, it was recognised and acknowledged to be important.

### Ageism that prevents people being open to the possibilities of continued spiritual development in ageing

An attitude of openness to possibilities in ageing is necessary before any changes in the spiritual tasks of ageing can be addressed. This attitudinal change is required right across society: within the community, where opportunities are provided for learning and activities for older adults; in policy and planning, to take account of the holistic approach to care for older people; and not least in new attitudes of openness towards the wonderful resources of these older adults that await exploration.

The church community also needs to recognise the opportunities for developing new ways of 'being church' in an ageing society. Not only do the present and coming cohorts of older people need health care services, including spiritual care, but also these older people are resources in themselves. Thus, the great diversity of older people ought to be recognised, allowing for care and ministry by older people, with older people to older people.

### The reluctance to push a particular belief system in a multicultural society

In one way this is good; tolerance of others' beliefs is valued. Yet, at another level, it is detrimental to the whole society, because we fail to acknowledge our own belief systems. The result can be to develop a culture that has a spiritual vacuum.

This can lead to people searching in all sorts of places for their own spirituality with little support or guidance. Yet there is one important effect of not wanting to discriminate against any belief system: we may fail to acknowledge adequately any spiritual needs.

### A misconception: the spiritual dimension is not really part of health care

Only when the spiritual dimension is included can nursing truly be said to be holistic. The spiritual is that very core of nursing, the caring dimension.

The spiritual dimension is worked out in our connecting at a deep level with other people. This ability to connect deeply with other people is vital for effective nursing care. We may argue a great deal about the content of nursing, but we can never convincingly argue that caring is not part of nursing. And yet, even the socialisation of nurses in the past has often denied the spiritual and religious needs of patients. This is perhaps why it is so hard for nurses to actually include the spiritual dimension in nursing practice. It means first acknowledging that spiritual care really is a component of nursing and, second, it means acknowledging one's own spirituality. Many in our society are out of touch in this area. To recognise the nursing diagnosis of *spiritual distress* is only to see the problem. To acknowledge the nursing diagnosis of *potential for enhanced spiritual well-being* is a major jump for nurses, and particularly for those who are not in touch with their own spirituality.

## Conclusion

This study of spirituality and ageing in a group of independently living older adults has produced an image of richness of experience and development of the spiritual life journey. It has produced a picture of great diversity among this group of informants and it has also pointed to fears of perceived future vulnerabilities that these people experience. A model relating to ultimate meaning, response to ultimate meaning and four spiritual tasks of ageing have been identified and considered in relation to possible pastoral implications.

A number of recommendations for further research and education have been made, based on these findings.

This study has been a privileged experience of sharing the spiritual journeys of these older adults. It has also been a rich learning experience for me; I hope it will be of value to others, both to older people themselves and to all who are working with older people.

# References

Annells, M. (1996) 'Grounded Theory Method: Philosophical Perspectives, Paradigm of Inquiry, and Postmodernism.' *Qualitative Health Research 6*, 3, Aug., 379–93.

Ashbrook, J. B. (1996) *Minding the Soul: Pastoral Counseling as Remembering.* Minneapolis: Fortress Press.

Astley, J. and Francis, L. J. (1992) *Christian Perspectives on Faith Development.* Grand Rapids:William B. Eerdmans Publishing Company.

Au, T. and Cobb, J. B. (1995) 'A Process Theology Perspective.' In M. A. Kimble, S. H. McFadden, J. W. Ellor and J. J. Seeber (eds) *Aging, Spirituality, and Religion: A Handbook.* Minneapolis: Augsburg Fortress Press.

Baltes, P. B. and Baltes, M. M. (eds) (1990) *Successful Aging: Perspectives from the Behavioral Sciences.* New York: Cambridge University Press.

Balthasar, H. U. von (1965) 'The Gospel as Norm or Test of all Spirituality in the Church.' *Concilium 9*, 1, 5 Nov.

Bauckham, R. (1995) *The Theology of Jurgen Moltmann.* Edinburgh: T & T Clark.

Beauvoir de, S. (1970) *Old Age.* Harmondsworth: Penguin Books.

Bellah, R. N. (1969) 'Transcendence in Contemporary Piety.' In H.W. Richardson and D.R. Culter (eds) *Transcendence.* Boston: Beacon Press.

Bellah, R. N., Madsen, R., Sullivan, W. M., Swidler A. and Tipton S. M. (1985) *Habits of the Heart: Individualism and Commitment to American Life.* Berkeley: University of California Press.

Bianchi, E. C. (1992) *Aging as a Spiritual Journey.* New York: Crossroad.

Birren, J. E. and Deutchman, D. E. (1994) 'Guided Autobiography Groups.' In I. Burnside, and M. G. Schmidt (eds) *Working with Older People: Group Process and Techniques.* Boston: Jones and Bartlett Publishers.

Blanchard-Fields, F. and Norris, L. (1995) 'The Development of Wisdom.' In M. A. Kimble, S. H. McFadden, J. W. Ellor and J. J. Seeber (eds) *Aging, Spirituality, and Religion: A Handbook.* Minneapolis: Augsburg Fortress Press.

Boden, C. (1998) *Who Will I Be When I Die?* Pymble: HarperCollins. Religious.

Booth, D. (1993) *Care of the Elderly in the Acute Care Setting: A Different Perspective.* Unpublished Master's project, University of Canberra.

Bornat, J. (ed) (1994) *Reminiscence Reviewed.* Buckingham: Open University Press.

Broughton, J. M. (1986) 'The Political Psychology of Faith Development Theory'. In C. Dykstra and S. Parks (eds) (1986) *Faith Development and Fowler.* Birmingham, Alabama: Religious Education Press.

Burnard, P. (1988) 'Searching for Meaning.' *Nursing Times, 84,* 37, 34–6.

Burnside, I. (1988) *Nursing and the Aged.* New York: McGraw-Hill Book Company.

Burnside, I. and Schmidt, M. G. (1994) *Working with Older People: Group Process and Techniques.* Boston: Jones and Bartlett Publishers.

Butler, R. N. (1963) 'The Life Review: An Interpretation of Reminiscence in the Aged.' In B. L. Neugarten (ed) (1968) *Middle Age and Aging: A Reader in Social Psychology.* Chicago: The University of Chicago Press.

Carroll, L. P. and Dyckman, K. M. (1986) *Chaos or Creation: Spirituality in mid-life.* New York: Paulist Press.

Carson, V. B. (1989) *Spiritual Dimensions of Nursing Practice.* Philadelphia: W. B. Saunders Co.

Carson, V. B. and Arnold, E. N. (1996) *Mental Health Nursing: The Nurse–Patient Journey.* Philadelphia: W. B. Saunders company

Chadwick, H. (1991) *Saint Augustine Confessions.* Oxford: Oxford University Press.

Chandler, M. J. and Holliday, S. (1990) 'Wisdom in a Postapocalyptic Age.' In R. J. Sternberg (ed) *Wisdom: Its Nature, Origins, and Development.* New York: Cambridge University Press.

Clements, W. M. (1990) 'Spiritual Development in the Fourth Quarter of Life.' In J.J. Seeber (ed) *Spiritual Maturity in the Later Years.* New York: The Haworth Press.

Clinebell, H. J. (1966) 'Basic Types of Pastoral Counseling: New Resources for Ministering to the Troubled.' In M. Highfield (1981) *Oncology Nurses' Awareness of their Patients' Spiritual Needs and Problems.* Unpublished Masters' Thesis, University of Arkansas for Medical Sciences.

Clinebell, H. J. (1984) *Basic Types of Pastoral Care and Counseling.* London: SCM Press.

Coleman, P. G. (1986) *Ageing and Reminiscence Processes: Social and Clinical Implications.* Chichester: John Wiley & Sons.

Coleman, P. G. (1994) 'Reminiscence within the Study of Ageing: The Social Significance of Story.' In J. Bornat (ed) *Reminiscence Reviewed.* Buckingham: Open University Press.

Cumming, E. and Henry, W. H. (1961) *Growing Old: The Process of Disengagement.* New York: Basic Books.

de Vaus, D. A. (1995) *Surveys in Social Research.* Sydney: Allen and Unwin.

Dykstra, C. and Parks, S. (eds) (1986) *Faith Development and Fowler.* Birmingham, Alabama: Religious Education Press.

Ellor, J. W. and Bracki, M. A. (1995) 'Assessment, Referral, and Networking.' In M. A. Kimble, S. H. McFadden, J. W. Ellor and J. J. Seeber (eds) *Aging, Spirituality, and Religion: A Handbook.* Minneapolis: Augsburg Fortress Press.

Ellor, J. W., Thibault, J. M., Netting, F. E. and Carey, C. B. (1990) 'Wholistic Theology as a Conceptual Foundation for Services for the Oldest Old.' In J. J Seeber (ed) (1990) *Spiritual Maturity in the Later Years.* New York: The Haworth Press.

Erikson, E. H. (1968) 'The Development of Ritualisation.' In D. R. Cutler (ed) *The World Year Book of Religion: The Religious Situation,* Vol 1. Boston: Beacon Press.

Erikson, E. H., Erikson, J. M. and Kivnick, H. Q. (1986) *Vital Involvement in Old Age.* New York: W. W. Norton & Co.

Fischer, K. (1985) *Winter Grace: Spirituality for the Later Years.* New York: Paulist Press.

Fowler, J. W. (1981) *Stages of Faith: The Psychology of Human Development and the Quest for Meaning.* Harper: San Francisco.

Fowler, J. W., (1986) 'Dialogue Towards a Future.' In C. Dykstra and S. Parks (eds) *Faith Development and Fowler.* Birmingham, Alabama: Religious Education Press.

Fowler, J. W., Nipkow, K. E. and Schweitzer, F. (eds) (1992) *Stages of Faith and Religious Development: Implications for Church, Education, and Society.* London: SCM Press.

Frankl, V. E. (1984) *Man's Search for Meaning.* New York: Washington Square Press.

Gardner, I., Brooke, E., Ozanne, E. and Kendig, H. (1998) *Improving Social Networks: A Research Report.* Canberra: Department of Veteran's Affairs.

Geertz, C. (1968) 'Religion as a Cultural System.' In D. R. Cutler (ed) *The World Year Book of Religion: The Religious Situation,* Vol 1. Boston: Beacon Press.

Geertz, C. (1975) *The Interpretation of Cultures.* London: Hutchinson.

Gilligan, C. (1993) *In a Different Voice.* Cambridge, Massachusetts: Harvard University Press.

Glaser, B. G. and Strauss, A. L. (1967) *The Discovery of Grounded Theory: Strategies for Qualitative Research.* Chicago: Aldine Atherton.

Glaser, B. G. and Strauss, A. L. (1968) *Time for Dying.* Chicago: Aldine Publishing Company.

Goldsmith, M. (1996) *Hearing the Voice of the People with Dementia.* London: Jessica Kingsley Publishers.

Greeley, A. M. (1969) *Religion in the Year 2000.* New York: Sheed and Ward.

Greeley, A. M. (1973) *The Persistence of Religion.* London: SCM Press.

Greeley, A. M. (1982) *Religion: A Secular Theory.* New York: The Free Press.

Greeley, A. M. and Durkin, M. G. (1984) *Angry Catholic Women.* Chicago: The Thomas Moore Press.

Guibert, J. de (1986) *The Jesuits: Their Spiritual Doctrine and Practice: A Historical Study.* St. Louis: Institute of Jesuit Sources. (3rd printing.)

Gustafson, M. (1994) 'Reminiscence, Her Way.' *American Journal of Nursing,* June, 64–5.

Haight, B. K. and Webster, J. D. (eds) (1995) *The Art and Science of Reminiscence: Theory, Research, Methods, and Applications.* Washington DC: Taylor & Francis.

Hair, J. F. Jr., Anderson, R. E., Tatham, R. L. and Black, W. C. (1995) *Multivariate Data Analysis with Readings.* Englewood Cliffs: Prentice-Hall.

Hardy, A. (1979) *The Spiritual Nature of Man.* Oxford: Clarendon Press.

Harris, D. K. (1990) *Sociology of Aging.* New York: Harper and Rowe.

Harris, M. (1986) 'Completion and Faith Development.' In C. Dykstra and S. Parks (eds) *Faith Development and Fowler.* Birmingham, Alabama: Religious Education Press.

Hassan, R. (1995) *Suicide Explained: The Australian Experience.* Melbourne: Melbourne University Press.

Havighurst, R. J., Neugarten, B. L. and Tobin, S. S. (1968) 'Disengagement and Patterns of Aging.' In B. L. Neugarten (ed) *Middle Age and Aging: A Reader in Social Psychology.* Chicago: The University of Chicago Press.

Hay, D. (1982) *Exploring Inner Space: Is God Still Possible in the Twentieth Century?* Harmondsworth: Penguin Books.

Heimbrock, H. (1992) 'Religious Development and the Ritual Dimension.' In Fowler, J. W, Nipkow, K. E. and Schweitzer, F. (eds) (1992) *Stages of Faith and Religious Development: Implications for Church, Education, and Society.* London: SCM Press.

Heinz, D. (1994) 'Finishing the Story: Aging, Spirituality and the Work of Culture.' *Journal of Religious Gerontology 9,* 1, 3–19.

Henderson, V. (1966) *The Nature of Nursing.* New York: Macmillan.

Highfield, M. F. (1981) *Oncology Nurses' Awareness of their Patients' Spiritual Needs and Problems.* Unpublished thesis, University of Arkansas for Medical Sciences.

Highfield, M. F. (1989) *The Spiritual Health of Oncology Patients: A Comparison of Nurse and Patient Perceptions.* Unpublished dissertation, Texas Woman's University.

Highfield, M. F. (1992) 'Spiritual Health of Oncology Patients. Nurse and Patient Perspectives.' *Cancer Nursing 15*, 1, 1–8.

Holmes, U. T. (1985) 'Spirituality for Ministry.' In N. S. T. Thayer *Spirituality and Pastoral Care.* Philadelphia: Fortress Press.

Hughes, P. (1993) *Religion: A View From the Australian Census.* Surrey Hills: Christian Research Association.

Hulicka, I. M. (1992) 'Teaching Aging in Psychology Courses: Comments on Why, What, and How.' In T. B. Sonderegger (ed) *Psychology and Aging.* Nebraska Symposium on Motivation, Lincoln: University of Nebraska Press.

Jorm, A. F. (1987) *Understanding Senile Dementia.* London: Croom Helm.

Kaldor, P. (1987) *Who Goes Where? Who Doesn't Care?* Homebush West: Lancer Books.

Kaldor, P. (1994) *Winds of Change: The Experience of Church in a Changing Australia.* National Church Life Survey. Homebush West: Lancer Books.

Kendig, H. L. (ed) (1986) *Ageing and Families: A Support Networks Perspective.* Sydney: Allen and Unwin.

Kendig, H. L. and McCallum, J. (eds) (1990) *Grey Policy: Australian Policies for an Ageing Society.* North Sydney: Allen and Unwin Australia, Pty. Ltd.

Keith. P. M. (1989) *The Unmarried in Later Life.* New York: Praeger Publishers.

Kimble, M. A, (1990) 'Aging and the Search for Meaning.' In J. J. Seeber, (ed) *Spiritual Maturity in the Later Years.* New York: Haworth Press.

Kimble, M. A., McFadden, S. H., Ellor, J. W. and Seeber, J. J. (eds) (1995) *Aging, Spirituality, and Religion: A Handbook.* Minneapolis: Augsburg Fortress Press.

Kirkwood, T. (1999) *Time of Our Lives.* London: Weidenfeld and Nicolson.

Kitwood, T. (1997) *Dementia Reconsidered.* Buckingham: Open University Press.

Klinger, J. (1999) 'Suicide Among Seniors.' *Australasian Journal on Ageing*, 18, 3, Aug., 114–16.

Koenig, H. G. (1994) *Aging and God: Spiritual Pathways to Mental Health in Midlife and Later Years.* New York: The Haworth Pastoral Press.

Labun, E. (1988) 'Spiritual Care: An Element in Nursing Care Planning.' *Journal of Advanced Nursing*, 13, 314–20.

Lefcourt, H. M. and Martin, R. A. (1986) *Humor and Life Stress: Antidote to Adversity.* New York: Springer-Verlag.

Lewis, H. D. (1965) *Philosophy of Religion.* London: The English Universities Press Ltd.

Lowenthal, M. F. (1968) 'Social Isolation and Mental Health in Old Age.' In B. L. Neugarten (ed) *Middle Age and Aging: A Reader in Social Psychology.* Chicago: The University of Chicago Press.

McCallum, J. (1986) 'Retirement and Widowhood Transitions.' In H. L. Kendig (ed) (1986) *Ageing and Families: A Support Networks Perspective.* Sydney: Allen and Unwin.

McCallum, J. (1990) 'The Future of Age Policy: An Optimistic View.' In: H. L. Kendig, and J. McCallum (eds) *Grey Policy: Australian Policies for an Ageing Society.* North Sydney: Allen and Unwin Australia, Pty. Ltd.

McFadden, S. H. (1990) 'Authentic Humor as an Expression of Spiritual Maturity.' In J. J. Seeber (ed) *Spiritual Maturity in the Later Years.* New York: The Haworth Press.

MacKinlay, E. B. (1989) *Health Related Decision Making and the Elderly: The Acceptance of Influenza Vaccine.* Unpublished Master's thesis, University of Canberra.

MacKinlay, E. B.( 1992) *Spiritual Needs of the Elderly Residents of Nursing Homes.* Unpublished report, submitted in part fulfilment of requirements for BTh at St Mark's National Theological Centre, Canberra.

MacKinlay, E. B. (1993) 'Spirituality and Ageing: Bringing Meaning to Life.' *St Mark's Review.* Spring, *155,* 26–30.

MacKinlay, E. B. (1997) 'Ageing, Spirituality and the Nursing Role.' In S. Ronaldson (ed) (1997) *Spirituality: the Heart of Nursing.* Melbourne: AUSMED Publications.

MacKinlay (forthcoming 2001) In *Journal of Religious Gerontology 12,* 3–4. Haworth Pastoral Press.

*The Macquarie Dictionary* (1981) Macquarie Library Pty. Ltd. St Leonards.

Manis, J. G. and Meltzer, B. N. (eds) (1978) *Symbolic Interactionism: A Reader in Social Psychology.* Boston: Allyn and Bacon Inc.

Maslow, A. H. (1970) *Motivation and Personality.* New York: Harper and Rowe.

Masters, W. H. and Johnson, V. E. (1968) 'Human Sexual Response: The Aging Female and the Aging Male.' In B. L. Neugarten (ed) *Middle Age and Aging: A Reader in Social Psychology.* Chicago: The University of Chicago Press.

Minichiello, V., Aroni, R., Timewell, E. and Alexander, L. (1995) *In-Depth Interviewing: Principles Techniques.* Sydney: Longman.

Moberg, D. O. (1968) 'Religiosity in Old Age.' In B. L. Neugarten (ed) *Middle Age and Aging: A Reader in Social Psychology.* Chicago: The University of Chicago Press.

Moberg, D. O. (1990) 'Spiritual Maturity and Wholeness in the Later Years.' In J. J. Seeber (ed) *Spiritual Maturity in the Later Years.* New York: The Haworth Press.

Moltmann, J. (1992) *The Spirit of Life.* Minneapolis: Fortress Press.

Moody, H. R. (1995) 'Mysticism.' In M. A. Kimble, S. H. McFadden, J. W. Ellor and J. J. Seeber (eds) *Aging, Spirituality, and Religion: A Handbook.* Minneapolis: Augsburg Fortress Press.

Morgan, R. L. (1995) 'Guiding Spiritual Autobiography Groups for Third and Fourth Agers.' *Journal of Religious Gerontology 9,* 2, 1–14.

Neugarten, B. L. (1968) 'Adult Personality: Toward a Psychology of the Life Cycle.' In B. L. Neugarten (ed) *Middle Age and Aging: A Reader in Social Psychology.* Chicago: The University of Chicago Press.

Neugarten, B. L. (ed) (1968) *Middle Age and Aging: A Reader in Social Psychology.* Chicago: The University of Chicago Press.

Newbigin, L. (1989) *The Gospel in Pluralist Society.* Grand Rapids: William Eerdmans Publishing Company.

*New Revised Standard Version Bible* (1989) Nashville: Thomas Nelson Inc.

O'Brien, L. (1994) *Mary MacKillop Unveiled.* North Blackburn: Collins Dove.

Oser, F. K. (1992) 'Towards a Logic of Religious Development: A Reply to my Critics.' In J. W. Fowler, K. E. Nipkow and F. Schweitzer (eds) (1992) *Stages of Faith and Religious Development: Implications for Church, Education, and Society.* London: SCM Press.

Otterness, O. (1995) 'A Neo-Orthodox Perspective.' In M. A. Kimble, S. H. McFadden, J. W. Ellor and J. J.Seeber (eds) *Aging, Spirituality, and Religion: A Handbook.* Minneapolis: Augsburg Fortress Press.

Otto, R. (1952) *The Idea of the Holy.* London: Oxford University Press.

Peck, R. C. (1968) 'Psychological Developments in the Second Half of Life.' In B. L. Neugarten (ed) (1968) *Middle Age and Aging: A Reader in Social Psychology.* Chicago: The University of Chicago Press.

Report of the Social Policy Committee of the Board for Social Responsibility, (1990) *Ageing.* London: Church House Publishing.

Rice, D. (1990) *Shattered Vows: Priests Who Leave.* New York: William Morrow and Company Inc.

Ronaldson, S. (ed) (1997) *Spirituality: the Heart of Nursing.* Melbourne: AUSMED Publications.

Rubinstein, R. L., Kilbride, J. C. and Nagy, S. (1992) *Elders Living Alone: Frailty and the Perception of Choice.* New York: Aldine De Gruyter.

Russell, C. (1981) *The Ageing Experience.* Sydney: Allen & Unwin.

Sax, S. (1990) 'Development of Public Policy for the Aged.' In H. L. Kendig and J. McCallum (eds) *Grey Policy: Australian Policies for an Ageing Society.* North Sydney: Allen and Unwin Australia, Pty. Ltd.

Schaie, K. W. and Willis, S. L. (1991) *Adult Development and Aging.* New York: HarperCollins.

Schneider, E. L. and Rowe, J. W. (eds) (1990) *Handbook of The Biology of Aging.* San Diego: Academic Press, Inc.

Seeber, J. J. (ed) (1990) *Spiritual Maturity in Later Years.* New York: The Haworth Press.

Stott, J. (1992) *The Contemporary Christian.* Leicester: Inter-Varsity Press.

Strauss, A. and Corbin, J. (1990) *Basics of Qualitative Research: Grounded Theory Procedures and Techniques.* Newbury Park: Sage Publications.

Thayer, N. S. T. (1985) *Spirituality and Pastoral Care.* Philadelphia: Fortress Press.

Thibault, J. M. (1995) 'Congregation as a Spiritual Care Community.' In M. A. Kimble, S. H. McFadden, J. W. Ellor and J. J. Seeber (eds) *Aging, Spirituality, and Religion: A Handbook.* Minneapolis: Augsburg Fortress Press.

Tillich, P. (1963) *Systemic Theology.* Vol 3. Chicago: The University of Chicago Press.

Tournier, P. (1972) *Learning to Grow Old.* London: SCM Press.

Tuck, I. Pullen, L. and Lynn, C. (1997) 'Spiritual Interventions Provided by Mental Health Nurses.' *Western Journal of Nursing Research 19,* 3, 351–63.

Vogel, L. J. (1984) *The Religious Education of Older Adults.* Birmingham, Alabama: Religious Education Press.

Vogel, L. J. (1995) 'Spiritual Development in Later Life.' In M. A. Kimble, S. H. McFadden, J. W. Ellor, and J. J. Seeber (eds) *Aging, Spirituality, and Religion: A Handbook.* Minneapolis: Augsburg Fortress Press.

Westberg, G. (1987) *The Parish Nurse.* Park Ridge: National Parish Nurse Resource Center.

# Subject Index

# Name Index

Annells, M. 27
Arnold, E.N. 18
Ashbrook, J.B. 51, 59, 91, 238
Astley, J. 121, 124
Au, T.135

Baltes, P.B. 12
Baltes, M.M. 12
Balthasar, H.U. von 49
Bauckham, R. 57
Beauvoir, S. de 11
Bellah, R.N. 45, 64, 65, 83, 90, 92, 99
Birren, J.E. 71
Blanchard-Fields, F. 153, 156, 157, 174
Boden, C. 150
Booth, D. 175
Bornat, J. 21, 22, 67, 68, 72, 135
Bracki, M.A. 88
Broughton, J.M. 124
Burnside, I. 68, 69, 70, 72, 227, 253
Butler, R.N. 62, 68, 69, 73, 157, 228

Carroll, L.P. 79, 198, 199
Carson, V.B. 18, 48, 52
Chadwick, H. 87
Chandler, M.J. 155
Clements, W.M. 59, 60, 61, 74, 134, 146,
   171, 174, 224, 232
Cobb, J.B. 135
Coleman, P.G. 22, 68, 69, 70, 72, 74, 135,
   170, 227
Corbin, J. 27
Cumming, E. 61, 145

Deutchman, D.E. 71
Durkin, M.G. 94, 96
Dyckman, K.M. 79, 198, 199
Dykstra, C. 124

Ellor, J.W. 70, 88
Erikson, E.H. 12, 22, 53, 55, 56, 59, 68, 70,
   71, 87, 100, 121, 123, 124, 134, 156,
   157, 169, 180, 222

Fischer, K. 48, 60, 251
Fowler, J.W. 37, 45, 46, 47, 48, 51, 65, 115,
   119, 120, 121, 122, 123, 124, 127, 128,
   129, 132, 163, 180
Francis, L.J. 121, 124

Frankl, V.E. 62, 63, 64, 65, 78, 92, 132, 133,
   136, 143, 151, 177, 189, 191, 225, 226,
   249
Freud, S. 191

Gardner, I. 15
Geertz, C. 45, 46, 91, 92, 93, 98
Gilligan, C. 19, 123, 163
Glaser, B.G. 26, 27, 28, 29, 44
Goldsmith, M. 150
Greeley, A.M. 45, 46, 47, 76, 77, 91, 94, 96,
   101, 103, 110, 111, 112, 117, 240
Guibert, J. de 49, 50
Gustafson, M. 21, 67

Haight, B.K. 68
Hair, J.F. Jr 34
Hardy, A. 110, 111, 112, 117, 159
Harris, D.K. 88, 89, 239
Harris, M. 113, 119, 123
Hassan, R. 56, 73, 140
Havighurst, R.J. 61, 146
Hay, D. 93, 103, 111, 117, 118
Heinz, D. 184, 221
Henderson, V. 245
Henry, W.H. 61, 145
Highfield, M.F. 18, 20, 31, 32, 52, 53
Holliday, S. 155
Hughes, P. 89, 90
Hulicka, I.M. 136

Johnson, V.E. 204
Jorm, A.F. 139

Kaldor, P. 89, 94
Keith, P.M. 201
Kendig, H.L. 15, 207
Kilbride, J.C. 200
Kimble, M.A. 52, 70, 72, 73, 74, 92, 177
Kirkwood, T. 233
Kitwood, T. 150
Klinger, J. 56
Koenig, H.G. 52, 119, 122

Labun, E. 50
Lefcourt, H.M. 191, 192, 196
Lewis, H.D. 45
Lowenthal, M.F. 201

McCallum, J. 15, 32, 200
McFadden, S.H. 192–3, 196
MacKinlay, E.B. 16, 18, 19, 23, 30, 31, 52,
   53, 54, 61, 67, 162, 176, 185, 229, 230,
   250
Manis, J.G. 92
Martin, R.A. 191, 192, 196